Rumer Godden

ANNE CHISHOLM is a writer, reviewer and interviewer who has worked in journalism and publishing in England, America and Australia. This is her fifth book. Her biography of Nancy Cunard won the Silver PEN award in 1979 and *Beaverbrook*, co-written with her husband Michael Davie, was shortlisted for the James Tait Black Prize in 1993.

Also by Anne Chisholm

Philosophers of the Earth

Nancy Cunard

Faces of Hiroshima

Beaverbrook
(with Michael Davie)

ANNE CHISHOLM

Rumer Godden

A Storyteller's Life

PAN BOOKS

First published 1998 by Macmillan

This edition published 1999 by Pan Books
an imprint of Macmillan Publishers Ltd
25 Eccleston Place, London SW1W 9NF
Basingstoke and Oxford
Associated companies throughout the world
www.macmillan.co.uk

ISBN 0 333 36747 1

1 3 5 7 9 8 6 4 2

A CIP catalogue record for this book is available from
the British Library.

Typeset by SetSystems Ltd, Saffron Walden, Essex
Printed and bound in Great Britain by
Mackays of Chatham plc, Chatham, Kent

In memory of my I.C.S. grandfather

J. E. Goudge, O.B.E. 1869–1957

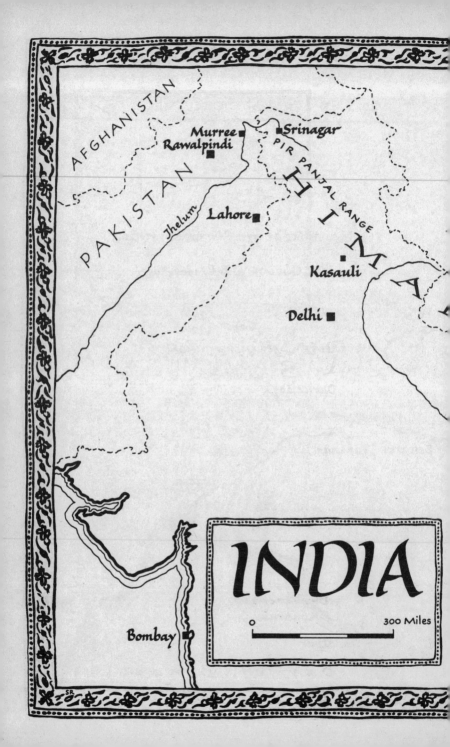

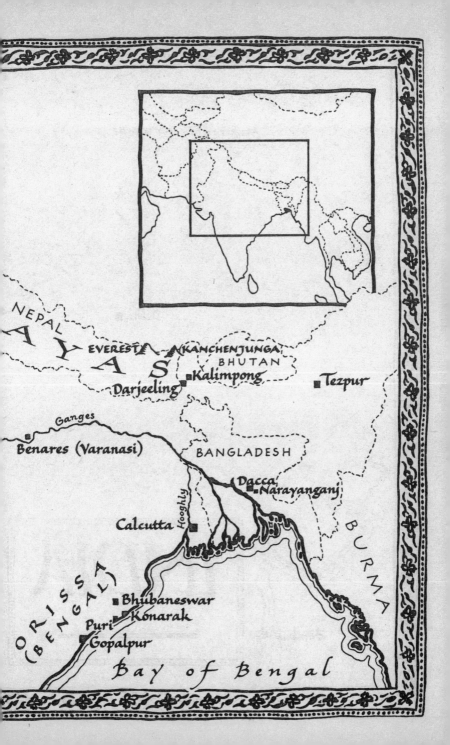

NEPAL

EVEREST KANCHENJUNGA
BHUTAN
Darjeeling Kalimpong
Tezpur

Ganges
Benares (Varanasi) BANGLADESH

Dacca
Narayangang

Calcutta
Hooghly

BURMA

ORISSA
(BENGALA)
Bhubaneswar
Konarak
Puri
Gopalpur

Bay of Bengal

Contents

List of Illustrations xi

One – Childhood and Growing Up: 1907–19
1

Two – Schooldays and After: 1920–29
27

Three – Calcutta Dust: 1929–34
44

Four – Marriage, Motherhood, Writing: 1934–8
68

Five – Black Narcissus: 1938–40
86

Six – Thus Far and No Further: 1940–42
102

Seven – Kashmir: 1942–4
125

Eight – Drama at Dove House: 1944
161

Nine – Return to England: 1944–8
183

Ten – Filming The River: *1948–50*
207

Eleven – Houses and Writing: 1950–61
234

Twelve – Stanbrook and Brede: *1961–9*
256

Thirteen – Moving On: 1970–93
271

Fourteen – Back to India: 1994
292

Afterword: 1995–8 308

Note on Sources 313

Acknowledgements 315

List of Rumer Godden's Books 317

Index 321

List of Illustrations

SECTION ONE

Arthur Godden
Katherine Godden
Rumer on her mother's knee, and Jon
Rumer and Jon in Assam
The house at Narayanganj
The Godden sisters as young women: Jon, Rumer, Nancy, Rose
Laurence Foster, *c.* 1934
Paula and Jane Foster
Ears, Laurence Foster's bearer
Jane with Ears's children in Calcutta
The Himalayan snows from Darjeeling
The house at Jinglam
Dove House, Bren, Kashmir 1943
Rumer at work, Dove House
Laurence during the war
Jane and Paula in the mountains, Kashmir 1944
Jobara, the pony man, Sonamarg 1944

SECTION TWO

Rumer with Jane and Paula, Buckinghamshire 1949
On the set of *Black Narcissus*, with David Farrar, Deborah Kerr
    and Jean Simmons, 1946

Filming *The River* with Jean Renoir and Rumer's nephew, Richard
    Foster, 1950
On the set of *The Greengage Summer*, 1960, with Susannah York,
    Jane Asher, Elizabeth Deare and Richard Williams
With her second husband, James Haynes-Dixon, 1960s
Dame Felicitas Corrigan, 1987
In Scotland, 1980s
With Rose and great-grandaughter Victoria, 1989
Filming with the BBC, Narayanganj, 1994
With Mrs Monisha Chaudhuri, Calcutta 1994
Rumer Godden at ninety

Rumer Godden

CHAPTER ONE

Childhood and Growing Up

1907–19

O NCE UPON A TIME, by a river in India, there lived a little
English girl called Margaret Rumer Godden. She had three
sisters, one older called Jon, two younger called Nancy and Rose.
Until Rumer grew up everyone called her Peggie. She always knew
that she wanted to be a writer, and although it was not easy for
her she became, in the end, a well-known and successful one. She
wrote many books set in many different places, but all her life
her thoughts and her writing would take her back to India, to
the places and the people there that had made her what she was,
the country where, in her heart, she always felt that she
belonged. 'Children in India are greatly loved and indulged,
and we never felt that we were foreigners, not India's own,' she
wrote, twenty years after she left India to live the second half of
her life in England. 'We felt at home, safely held in her large warm
embrace, content as we never were to be content in our own
country.'

A happy childhood is always a paradise lost. The English
children of the Indian Empire knew a special paradise, and most of
them never forgot it and always missed it. Over and over again in
the memories of people who grew up in India the same longings
and vivid recollections recur: they remember the warmth, the sun,
the colours, the light, the space, the sounds; above all, perhaps, the
smell of India. Rumer Godden was born on a winter's night in
Eastbourne on 10 December 1907 but most of her childhood was
spent in Bengal. She described it like this:

It was the honey smell of the fuzz-buzz flowers, of thorn trees in the sun, and the smell of open drains and urine, of coconut oil on shining black human hair, of mustard cooking oil and the blue smoke from cowdung used as fuel; it was a smell redolent of the sun, more alive and vivid than anything in the West . . .

She wrote directly about her childhood in three books: first in 1946 in her short novel *The River*, twenty years later in *Two Under the Indian Sun*, written jointly with her sister Jon, and then in 1987 in her autobiography. The emotional and imaginative truth about those years, until 1920 when she was sent back to school in England, is distilled in *The River*, the story of how a twelve-year-old English girl living by a river in Bengal learns about life, death and love, and what it means to grow up. The facts of her own family life, however, are clearest in the book she wrote with Jon, always her sternest critic and someone for whom truthfulness was paramount. Within the family, Rumer came under fire all her life for making things up, for her tendency to embroider and dramatize the facts. She was, and remained, unrepentant. She was always a story-teller, someone for whom events took on a dramatic shape almost as they happened to her or as she heard about them from someone else. By the time she came to write her autobiography, she was almost eighty; what she remembered about her early years and what she had already written or imagined was densely woven together. 'To me and my kind life itself is a story and we have to tell it in stories; that is the way it falls.'

*

MARGARET RUMER GODDEN spent her childhood in India because her father chose to work there. Arthur Leigh Godden was a tall, good-looking man, well-educated but not an intellectual. Like many others he decided to live and work in India because at that time, in the late nineteenth century, high-Victorian heyday of the Empire, India offered spirited, strong-willed young men, from solid but not especially grand or rich families, the chance to use their energies constructively and enjoy the privileges and pleasures of a ruling élite. Many middle-class English families have an imperial, often an Indian involvement in their past; in some, especially those with Army or government connections, the link spanned several generations. The Goddens were originally farmers and corn-merchants from Kent, and Arthur Godden's family links with India were not especially strong: on his mother's side, an early nineteenth-century military forebear spent most of his life there after fighting at Waterloo. According to family lore, though, Arthur ran away to India at eighteen because he could not bear the thought of becoming a stockbroker like his father. After trying land management, he enlisted in the Calcutta Light Horse in 1901 and fought in the Boer War; but by 1903 when he met Rumer's mother, Katherine Norah Hingley, he was working as an agent for one of the big shipping companies based in Calcutta, running steamers up and down the great rivers of the Ganges delta in Bengal.

The Hingley family's roots and prosperity were in the Midlands and dated from the industrial revolution. Katherine's father, Samuel, was the son of a successful ironmaster, but did not himself make money; his children had to fend for themselves. His widow, Harriet, whose unusual second name, Rumer, was to pass to her second granddaughter, went to live in Eastbourne with her son Alfred and her youngest daughter Mary. Her eldest daughter, Ethel, had already married a clever young man who had joined the Indian Civil Service (ICS) and was living in India, where Katherine went to join her. It must have occurred to Katherine and to her widowed mother, that she, like other girls known as the fishing fleet, might find a husband in India: she was very pretty, small and round with clear blue eyes, a cloud of dark hair and a sweet, undemanding nature. She was presented to the Viceroy in Calcutta – until 1911 the capital city of the Indian Empire – during the Christmas season, wearing a pink tulle dress embroidered with daisies. She probably met Arthur Godden, down from his posting in Assam, at one of the many parties held during the cold-weather months between October and March.

Godden was attractive to women: his daughters were brought up on a story of how his good looks impressed even Mary Curzon, wife of the most imposing Viceroy of them all. After a long and arduous tour of the remote regions of Bengal, Lady Curzon apparently said that she had found it all rather dreary, but that there had been one memorably handsome young man, a steamer agent, whom she described as 'an Adonis'. When Arthur met Miss Hingley, he was engaged to another girl, but broke it off; he and Katherine were married in England in 1905 when Arthur was home on leave. Soon afterwards they returned to India together. A favourite family tale relates how on their Indian honeymoon Arthur one day took his new bride on a duck shoot, which required him to get up before dawn and wait in the reeds. When Katherine later came to find him, wearing a white dress, he said she would frighten the birds and persuaded her to wait on a nearby island in midstream. Several hours later, he was on his way home when his shikari (huntsman) reminded him that they had forgotten the memsahib.

Like many family stories, this one conveys a message. Arthur Godden was a confident and independent-minded man who liked to have his own way, and sporting pursuits were his passion in life. His wife had little choice but to adapt herself to his interests and build their family life around them, which she seems to have done with remarkably good grace. She loved to read, and enjoyed music and the theatre and pretty clothes, but none of this mattered much to her husband. 'Looking back I believe that, unconsciously, he relegated women to a different category,' wrote Rumer. 'It really surprised him if they had passions of their own.'

Family, and the traditions of the family, were always important to Rumer. She was especially proud of her most intellectual forebear, her great-grandfather on her father's side, Thomas Hewitt

Key, a Cambridge-educated mathematician and philologist of great distinction, who in 1826 was made professor of mathematics and astronomy at the newly founded University of Virginia by President Thomas Jefferson himself, and who on his return to England became headmaster of University College School and one of the founders of the London Library. However, apart from her sister Jon, Rumer's immediate family was not bookish, and Rumer liked to think that her interest in words and writing derived from the professor. She also greatly valued one or two family possessions, especially a delicate Cosway study of a family group including a small red-haired girl, her great-grandmother. There were also two prized pictures by Benjamin West, one showing her great-great-grandfather, Richard Ironmonger Troward, dressed as an archer with cocked hat and tasselled boots. He was a lawyer, who became extremely rich, and had an historic Indian association: he prepared the prosecution case against Warren Hastings. The mahogany secretaire said to have been used for this purpose is still in the family.

Rumer grew up to revere such associations for two reasons: they linked her family with an artistic and intellectual milieu, albeit of several generations back, and they placed the Goddens on the map. Anglo-Indian* society was openly and strongly hierarchical, status-conscious and snobbish; in the hierarchy, the Goddens did not rank at the top. Perhaps in response to the caste-ridden society they ruled, by the late nineteenth century the British in India had established three main castes of their own: the ICS administrators, known as the Heaven-born; the Army; and the businessmen or merchant class, broadly known as the box-wallahs. (In later life, like many of her contemporaries, Rumer would express dislike of the term Raj, which was never used or heard among them at the time; nor, she said, had she ever heard of 'box-wallahs' or 'the fishing fleet'.) This last group, in which Arthur Godden's profession placed him, was by far the largest and by some way the least

---

* This book follows the practice of Rumer's time, and refers to the English who lived and worked in India as Anglo-Indians and people of mixed race as Eurasians.

prestigious, although trade was the reason why the British were in India in the first place. Within his caste, though, Godden had several advantages. He was English, he was a gentleman, he was a sportsman, and he was not involved in actually selling anything; the business class contained its own subdivisions, and to be in trade was definitely the lowest. Also he was not particularly interested in making money, and he had no desire to live in a city, attend an office every day and play company politics. He chose to live in the comparative wilderness, socially and geographically, so that he could run his own life and be free to ride, shoot and fish as much as possible. As a result, his wife and daughters were spared much of the ritual snobbery and competitiveness of Anglo-Indian life. They were able to make and enjoy their own small world, and it revolved around Arthur, his work and interests, the household, the nursery and each other.

The Goddens' first married home was on a houseboat in Assam, where in 1906 their eldest daughter, christened Winsome Ruth but always known as Jon, was born. Rumer was taken back to Assam in 1908 when she was a few months old. Their sister Nancy was also born in India, in 1910 when Rumer was two. One of the most vivid and earliest of Rumer's childhood memories centred around Nancy's birth. Not everything about an Anglo-Indian childhood was idyllic: one nightmare common to most families was the fear of rabies. Pets, especially dogs, were exceptionally important to Anglo-Indians, but much-loved domestic animals were frequently bitten by rabid jackals or native dogs, and the consequences were unpleasant. Katherine Godden had asked her husband not to keep dogs for fear of the danger to their small children, but he acquired three spaniels for shooting, assuring her that they would not be kept in the house. Somehow the dogs contracted rabies and both Rumer and her father were bitten. The vital treatment that could stop rabies developing was a course of painful injections into the stomach; in those days, it was to be had only at the Pasteur Institute at Kasauli in the Himalayan foothills north of Delhi, a long and exhausting journey from Assam. Katherine, who was seven months' pregnant, took Jon to stay with friends on a tea estate while her husband and Rumer were away. There, her host's pet Pomeranian also caught rabies and bit Jon's lip. Katherine had no choice but to take her on a sweltering train – it was July, when the heat was at its worst – across India to be treated. Heavily pregnant and frantic with worry, Katherine gave birth to Nancy in Kasauli soon after she arrived. The labour was difficult, the baby small, and in Rumer's view, her mother never quite forgave her father for this episode. The family continued to keep dogs.

When Jon was six and Rumer five, they had to go through another, much worse ordeal, familiar to the children of the Empire: their parents obeyed the custom of the time and sent them back to England to embark on their education. It was assumed that unless children were sent 'home', their characters and, almost more important, their accents would be ruined by Indian influences. The experience was agonizing for both parents and children, but at least the parents knew, or thought they did, what they were doing and why. For the children, as countless stories told by them in later years attest, the separation from everyone they knew and loved, the loss of warmth, colour and sunlight, and the sudden immersion in a cold, grey, buttoned-up society where they were told they belonged but sensed they were strangers, was always misery and felt like betrayal. That was certainly how it seemed to Jon and Rumer Godden when, in 1913, they found themselves living with their paternal grandmother and five maiden aunts in a large terraced house in Maida Vale.

'In India children are largely left to grow,' wrote Jon and Rumer, half a century later. 'We had not really been "brought up" before. It was a painful process for us and for the aunts.' They disliked the sour smell of the aunts' clothes, the dull food and the pervasive, baffling rituals of High Anglican piety. The house was always quiet and always gloomy. 'Never, in all that tall dark house, was there a gleam of laughter or enterprise or fun and slowly,

slowly our lives began to loosen from their roots . . . That is perhaps the secret agony of children separated from their family – the secret agony that slowly, inexorably they must forget.'

The First World War gave them back their happy Indian childhood. After August 1914, the Goddens decided that they could not bear to leave their daughters on the other side of the world, perhaps in danger, for an indefinite time. They decided to bring them back to India while they still could, with their aunt Mary, Katherine's youngest and unmarried sister, to escort them and be their governess. When Rumer and Jon grew up, they appreciated the irony that it was because of the huge, hideous European convulsion, by which millions of lives were blighted, that they, two small girls, were restored to a happiness they thought they had lost. At the time, though, all they cared about was that they were released from Maida Vale. Aunt Mary, smart and pretty in comparison to the worthy Godden aunts, took them on board a P. and O. liner that left Tilbury in November 1914. Their parents met them in Calcutta and took them the rest of the way by rail and steamer. This time they were not going to Assam, for Arthur had acquired a new and better posting while they had been in England. Their home now was in Narayanganj, a small but well-placed town in East Bengal, twelve miles from Dacca (now Dhaka) on the banks of the river Lakya, a tributary of the Brahmaputra in the vast delta of the Ganges. It was in a large house near the river in Narayanganj that Rumer grew up.

> I suppose ours was a monstrous house [she wrote when she was old]. A great, rectangular, pale grey stucco house standing on a high plinth that was hidden by plumbago and a hedge of poinsettias. Stone-arched, green-shuttered verandahs ran the full length of the two floors. The roof was flat, with a high parapet that was cut into loopholes. Double steps, banked with pots of budding chrysanthemums, led up from the drive. White-dressed white-turbaned servants went in and out. In

front of the house was an enormous cork tree covered in white blossom every spring: the flower-bed round its base held amaryllis lilies. Every morning at sunrise and every evening at sunset a flag was run up or down the flagstaff on our roof; it was the company flag but we thought it was Fa's.

The Goddens' house was certainly one of the largest and grandest in Narayanganj, a town that had grown up around the processing and transportation of the jute that was the backbone of the Bengal economy. The noise of the steam-operated jute works along the river – puff, wait, puff – was the background noise of the sisters' childhood. As the jute trade expanded in the late nineteenth century, the young men, often Scottish, sent out to run the works needed decent houses to live in, both as bachelors and when, eventually, their companies allowed them to marry; most companies prohibited marriage for a number of years. These houses were substantial, built to last, with few concessions to the climate or local architectural traditions. Although they had shady pillared verandahs, they were usually built of red brick and stucco outside and dark wood within, in imitation of the solid Scottish provincial style back home. Inside they were dark, with heavy wooden staircases, fireplaces for the damp winter months, propeller ceiling fans against the searing summer heat, and walls frequently adorned with stuffed animal heads, like a highland hunting lodge. Dacca, reached either by a country road along the river or by boat, was already a large and important city, the administrative centre for the area, with a cathedral, a university, hospitals, law courts, and the all-important club around which the life of the European community revolved. By comparison Narayanganj was insignificant, but there Arthur Godden, as the manager of the Brahmaputra River Steam Navigation Company, running a fleet of passenger and freight ships up and down the complex system of waterways that flowed from the foothills of the Himalayas down to Calcutta, was a commanding figure and a man of substance. 'In

Narayanganj,' as Jon and Rumer put it, 'there were no higher circles than ours.'

Like many expatriate imperial families, the Goddens' standard of living was higher in India than it could ever have been in England. They were part of the ruling class, and rulers have to maintain their prestige and set standards. The children took it all for granted. How were they to know that the large, grand house did not belong to their father but was rented by the company? It emerged long after the Goddens had left Narayanganj and the British had left India that the house was the property of their head servant, Azad Ali, the imposing Muslim butler. At the time, this had been a well-kept secret.

The house had large rooms, high and cool with dark red, polished-stone floors and white-painted walls. The nursery was enormous, opening off the verandah next to the dining room; the two smaller children – Rose Mary, the last of the four sisters, had been born in Eastbourne in 1913 – and their nurse slept there, while Rumer and Jon shared a room upstairs with Aunt Mary. The kitchen and servants' quarters were, as was usual, in a separate building behind the house. As well as the big main staircase, with its row of potted palms, there were white-painted stairs at the side of the house and a rickety servants' staircase outside that the children were not meant to use but did. A narrow flight of steps like a ladder led from the top landing up to one of the children's favourite spots, the roof. They loved to clamber up there, to fly kites or just to look down over the town, the river, the jute works, the bazaar, the gatehouse and – their special domain – the garden.

Gardens and flowers held a special significance for the British in India. A lovely garden was more than a refuge from the ugliness and squalor outside: it could be made into a reminder of home, ordered and controlled, filled with reassuring British plants as well as the spectacular exotic natives. Indian gardeners, the malis, were skilled and respected, often of a higher caste than the other servants, and the memsahibs depended on them to keep the house full of flowers. Usually a huge basket of the best blooms would arrive in the early morning, picked with the dew still on them, to be arranged before breakfast. They were always perfect, fresh, copious; for Rumer the scent of sweet peas would always evoke a Bengali winter. Like all the familiar, delicate plants, they came into bloom in the cold-weather months between October and March; the summers were too hot. The garden was linked to the house by rows of large pots of flowering plants, changed according to the season, ranged in ranks up the steps on to the verandah; a photograph shows Rumer and her sisters in their frilly dresses and solar topees, just able to see over the potted chrysanthemums.

In front of the house was the enormous cork tree, its green feathery branches reaching almost to the roof. Brilliant red and orange canna lilies surrounded its trunk. There was a hedge of scarlet poinsettia, and pale blue plumbago ran wild; the shrubbery was full of purple and magenta bougainvillaea and bright hibiscus with its long gilded stamens. Chickens scratched in the vegetable garden; and behind a screen of morning glory was the tennis court. The children spent much of their time in the garden: they played in it endlessly, and when it was not too hot lessons were held under the trees. 'There should still be children's voices in that garden.' Sometimes they would spot Indian urchins peering in at them under the big wooden gates at the end of their drive, but the gatekeeper, who lived in the tiny lodge, would chase them away.

Indian children might not have been allowed in, but it would be a mistake to think that the Godden children grew up isolated from Indian life. The house was right in the town; the bazaar, with its constant activity, colour and noise, was just outside their gate, they shared the large water tank on the edge of their property with the local people and they watched the ebb and flow of Bengali life from their rooftop vantage point. In an Indian household, or in an English household set in India, solitude and privacy are rare; the Goddens were constantly observed, and the children were quick to respond by becoming sharp-eyed observers themselves. Above all, they were intimately linked with India through their easy, companionable, sometimes deeply affectionate relationships with the family's servants.

The whole idea of servants, especially in the imperial context, has become self-conscious and uneasy, but it was very different then. In India, as in England, middle-class people, let alone the aristocracy, took service for granted; on neither side was it regarded as demeaning. In India in 1915, to be a trusted servant in a British household was to be privileged, envied and secure; no doubt there was sometimes arrogance on one side and resentment on the other, but in the memoirs and autobiographies of the old India hands there is no mistaking the genuineness of the respect and liking felt by many for the people who helped them run their daily lives. Families and servants lived closely together; rules and routines were carefully observed but within them a kind of intimacy grew. And for British children, especially in a relatively easy-going household like the Goddens', the servants were their first and best friends.

Rumer noticed, remembered and celebrated many times in her Indian writings the house and garden at Narayanganj and the cast of characters on her childhood stage. After a short and unsuccessful experiment with an English nanny, the children were looked after for a year by a flamboyant Eurasian, Nana, who told them tall stories about her mysterious origins and the cruel nuns in the orphanage where she had grown up. She also told them that their parents were snobs for requiring her to wear the usual nanny's uniform, and taught them music-hall songs – 'Swanee River', 'K-K-K-Katie' – which they sang until their father could bear it no longer. They adored the dramatic Nana, with her near-mahogany-coloured skin and knee-length blue-black hair, despite her fierce temper and appalling sulks, but at the end of a year she disappeared. Soon Rumer and Jon would have realized that although Eurasian nurses were sought after – they were educated, Christian, and could speak English – they were looked down on by both races, perhaps even more by the Indians than by the British; and the girls would certainly have learned that the lilting, sing-song Eurasian accent, punctuated by frequent Mmms and exclamations of 'My God', was considered as undesirable as it was contagious.

Nana was succeeded by Hannah, a middle-aged ayah from Madras. Christian Madrassi ayahs had the reputation in British circles of making the most reliable and sensible nannies, and Hannah, with her dark skin and her grey hair in a bun, was untemperamental, dignified and deeply religious, bringing a measure of order and calm to the nursery. Jon, especially, was not an easy child, given to dark moods and fits of fury, and Rumer herself had a strong wilful streak, but Hannah could manage them.

Outside the nursery, the household servants were all men. There was the magnificent Azad Ali, a towering figure in immaculate white tunic and pleated turban, who stood behind Arthur Godden's chair at meals, poured tea and drinks, carried trays into the garden and delivered letters on a silver salver. His staff were also Muslims: Mustapha, the handsome young khitmagar, waited at table, and Abdul, who the children disliked because he was ugly and told tales, was the nursery bearer. Their father's personal bearer (man-servant or valet), Jetta, was a Lepcha, a Buddhist from Sikkim; mountain people, it was said, made the most loyal servants. Guru, the gatekeeper who kept watch on all comings and goings and also ran errands to the bazaar, was a particular favourite with the children: he was a Hindu, as were the gardeners, who were high-caste Brahmins. Nitai, the sweeper, who cleaned the family's bathrooms and lavatories, was an Untouchable. Then there were the syces, Arthur's smart, uniformed grooms, and the cook, and the cook's boy; altogether some fifteen people to wait on a family of six. No wonder that the children acquired what Jon and Rumer later called 'a princess quality', an unconscious assumption that they were special and that other people should do what they wanted. Indians of all classes tend to indulge small children; apart from waiting on them and catering to their every need, the Goddens' servants, even the imposing Azad Ali, would join in the missibabas' games. Guru chose their kites in the bazaar – 'as brilliant as huge butterflies and almost as light' – and showed them how to brace themselves, legs apart, how to hold the bamboo rollers and send the kites soaring and wheeling into the sky. Once he let them dye his white clothes bright orange with petals from the garden supplied by the malis, who would also give them flowers to make into wreaths and vegetables for a mock bazaar. Such games were not always popular with their parents.

Occasionally, of course, the alliance between servants and children broke down and the great gulf between English and Indian culture was exposed. Once, Rumer picked up a small clay drinking vessel she found outside the gardener's hut; when Govind, the head gardener, saw it in her hand he took it from her angrily and smashed it on the ground. It was unclean from her touch. More gravely, she once thought it would be fun to tease Govind by saying the sacred Hindu name for God. 'Ram, Ram Ram,' she chanted. He was so angry she felt ashamed, and later her father summoned her to his study, made her apologize to Govind and told her she must always respect all religions. This was a lesson she never forgot. The Goddens were Church of England, but as there was no church in Narayanganj they seldom attended a service. Hannah, however, got up at dawn on Sundays to reach the Catholic Church in Dacca in time for Mass.

For all the fun and games, the Godden children grew up well aware that, in their household as in all India, the British ruled the roost. This lesson was brought home to them every day, when the older girls would help their mother in her ritual inspection of the kitchen and the store-cupboard. It was taken for granted that otherwise the rules of hygiene would be broken and the stores pilfered. As Jon and Rumer observed, to say of an Englishwoman that 'she trusts her servants' would have been tantamount to saying 'she is lazy' or 'no good'. Thus Rumer's affection and respect for the Indians she knew as a child was combined with a sense of innate superiority and the feeling that they were not quite to be trusted.

All the Godden sisters grew up reckoning that theirs had been a wonderfully happy childhood. 'Halcyon' was Rumer's favourite word for it; her sister Nancy said simply, 'No one ever had a childhood like ours.' Nevertheless, for Rumer herself, there were some hard lessons to learn. If in her writings there is a recurrent figure, it is that of a child, usually a girl, who grows up slightly at odds with her surroundings, emotionally vulnerable, with more originality than charm. The sisters fell naturally into two groups; Rumer and Jon, so close in age, grew up sharing their thoughts and emotions, while Nancy and Rose, although not such soulmates as their older sisters, were natural allies. Jon, the eldest, was the dominant sister, a gifted and original child, who showed an early talent for painting and drawing, and who seems to have been able to weave spells over all her sisters, to their alarm as well as delight. Rumer never felt she would ever be as remarkable as Jon. She was lovely to look at; and Nancy and Rose were also strikingly pretty. Rumer was the least attractive of the four, and she knew it. Her face was longer and more angular than theirs, and she had a prominent, aquiline nose. One day her father made the classic mistake: he looked down the table at his second daughter and said, half to himself, 'Where did that child get that face?' Rumer knew what he meant and was deeply wounded. She always acknowledged that she was born with a jealous streak: 'I had green eyes, and not for nothing . . .' It was hard for her always to come second to Jon, although she adored and admired her, and also hard to have two delightful little sisters coming up behind. Nancy, with her round face and slightly slanting eyes, was acknowledged to be Fa's favourite – maybe, according to Rumer, because of his guilt over the rabies drama at the time of her birth. Rose was the youngest, which made her special too. Rumer was somewhere indeterminate in the family structure and she felt it.

She never found her relationship with her father easy: they loved each other, she would say, but perhaps did not greatly like each other. Of her relations with her mother, called by her children

Mam or Mop, she never said or wrote much in detail, but the picture emerges of a naturally good mother who surrounded her daughters with affection and made them all feel valued. What Rumer particularly noted was the way her father always seemed to get what he wanted, even if it was at the expense of the women around him. Something in her instinctively disliked this female subservience.

Aunt Mary, who had never been to school herself, taught Jon and Rumer for the five Narayanganj years. Their father was supposed to teach them geography and handwriting – his own was much admired – but in the end what they learned from him was to fish, to shoot, and to sail. They also learned to ride, and shared two ponies. Again, Rumer was the odd one out: although she loved horses she was not, like the others, a natural rider and after a bad fall she lost her nerve. Their mother was a great reader and she encouraged Jon and Rumer to read the writers she enjoyed so that their taste and knowledge was precocious, if patchy. They read Shakespeare with her, and much poetry, which they were taught to recite aloud and never forgot: Tennyson, Keats, Longfellow, Browning, Christina Rossetti. But it was from Aunt Mary that they received their basic education in arithmetic, spelling, grammar, history and religion.

Because they had comparatively few toys or children's books, and because there was little entertainment locally for children, they amused themselves, and they started early to write their own poems and stories. 'We were all always writing as children,' was Nancy's response to the suggestion that there was perhaps something unusual in Rumer's determination to be a writer; their father was heard to say that it was a good thing they had plenty of waste-paper baskets. At five, Rumer started trying to write hymns; by eight, she had embarked on an autobiography, revealing a strong inventive streak, featuring Peggie, a rich child with no brothers or sisters who lived in Yorkshire but nevertheless met 'a tigger and a loin' in her garden. But it was Jon who impressed the grown-ups with an epic poem about the angels guarding the retreat from Mons, and a story about a family of carrots that she illustrated herself. Nevertheless Rumer persevered: she would take herself away to write in a corner under the stairs leading to the roof. She used homemade notebooks of cheap folded paper, and when she found a large hollow in the big cork tree in front of the house, she hid her writings in it. Her first published piece of writing, to her later considerable embarrassment, was an article in which she purported to be a mother offering advice on how to keep children cool in hot weather, written under a pseudonym when she was about twelve and published in the *Statesman*, a Calcutta newspaper.

Both she and Jon made up games and stories with ease. Jon's imagination had a dark streak: she invented a game called Iurki, which involved ghostly shrieks and feeling nasty things in the dark. It terrified her sisters, and apparently any child asked to tea with the Goddens would beg to be allowed to stay at home. She and Rumer also made up a serial tale, never written down, called 'Big Girls', in which they were the wealthy parents – Jon the father, Rumer the mother – of a family of glamorous girls who had wonderful clothes and exciting love affairs; this saga was fed by the illustrated society magazines like the *Tatler* and the *Sketch*, which they saw at the Narayanganj club. They also borrowed romantic novels from the club library, and devoured them all the more eagerly because Aunt Mary tried to censor them. Many of the ideas for 'Big Girls' derived, they recalled, from the works of a husband-and-wife team called A. N. and C. N. Williamson, which featured seductive women with fur coats and long cigarette-holders, and smooth men with fast cars.

When Rumer and Jon looked back to their childhood, what they recalled most vividly and appreciated most strongly was the freedom they were given to experience the power and natural beauty of the Indian landscape and people. They loved the river at Narayanganj, with its wide banks under an enormous sky, where their father and his crews seemed to rule the waves; their favourite afternoons were spent on his launch, the *Sonachora*, when they were sent off by themselves with the crew. They watched the busy river traffic, the slow country boats with their triangular sails, the big jute barges, the crowded ferries, the black crescent-shaped fishing boats; they saw herds of buffalo wallowing in the shallows, porpoises rolling in midstream, herons and egrets on the sandbanks and brown-skinned boys swimming and splashing on the banks. Once, the whole family spent an unforgettable week taking the slow route back from Calcutta – where they occasionally went to see the dentist or to go shopping – through the Sundarbans, the wild jungle islands of the Ganges delta, where crocodiles basked on the sands and tigers were known to lurk in the undergrowth. Since the coming of the railways in the late nineteenth century, such long river journeys, once the preferred way to travel up-country from Calcutta, had been superseded by shorter trips connecting with the trains; thus the Goddens had the ship to themselves. The children explored it while the grown-ups lay under the awning in easy chairs. Jon and Rumer shared a cabin, with three shuttered windows opening on to the deck. The family had their meals in the big saloon, attended by waiters in immaculate white; all the table linen, china and silver carried the company's crest. All day they watched the passing boats and fishermen, and the countless birds: 'ospreys, fishing eagles, ibis, storks, bee-eaters, kingfishers – streaks of burning colour flashing across the water'. At night, they could hardly bear to go to bed.

> When evening came, the birds, with a great twittering and calling went to their roosts in the tree tops and the jungle seemed to retreat and sink away into the dusk. There was only the river and the steamer sailing into the night and, assailed by a curious melancholy, we leaned on the rail and watched the sunset and listened perhaps to a lascar who, perched on the anchors below us, his long black hair blown back by the breeze, poured out his soul in a song until dark came and the searchlight was switched on . . . We, Jon and Rumer, refused to

go in; we liked to stand above the bows, high on the deck by the flagstaff, scarves tied over our hair, moths hitting our faces, and watch the beam of pale light swing across the water, picking up a distant channel mark, creeping along the mud of the bank, lighting a screen of leaves. We hoped that the light would catch a pair of blazing eyes, that a tiger would suddenly emerge before us ... 'Come in now, missibabas,' Hannah beseeched us. 'Time for bath and supper,' but we would not move until Fa himself came to fetch us.

There were other wonderful journeys. It was the custom, in every English family who could afford it, for wives and children to escape the great heat of the summer months in the plains by moving up to the hills between late March and early October. 'I have always thanked God I did not have sensible parents,' wrote Rumer. 'Sensible parents would have chosen a hill station near us, rented a house, and sent us every year to the same school.' Instead, the Goddens went to many different hill stations, from Mussoorie, north of Delhi, to Coonoor far to the south of Calcutta in the Nilgiri hills, to Shillong in Assam, and – the preferred resort for those living in Bengal – to Darjeeling. 'If we grew up with some idea of India, some idea of her immensity and complexity, we owe it to Mam and Fa's lack of sense.' In Darjeeling, especially, they were given a taste of the more conventional pleasures of the British community: there were concerts and film shows, children's parties and dancing classes. The girls took part in charity matinées to raise money for the Red Cross or to entertain the troops; Rumer especially recalled a butterfly dance with Jon, both of them wearing yellow muslin wings with black spots, and the pangs she felt when Nancy was chosen to be Columbine to Jon's Harlequin instead of her: 'I expect it's because of your nose,' said Jon.

In 1917 they spent the summer months in Kashmir. Their father accompanied them for the whole trip; usually he was able to join them only for a brief holiday, but that year he was entitled to a long leave which, because of the war, had to be spent in India.

This was the first experience for the sisters of a place that came later to mean much to them, most of all to Rumer. Kashmir, with its lakes and valleys, its fruit trees and trout streams and fresh mountain air, was loved and celebrated by British India as the most beautiful and romantic destination of all, not just a British holiday resort but the earthly paradise of the Moghul kings, the pearl of Hind.

Kashmir was not part of British India, but one of more than five hundred independent princely states. In 1846 the British had acquired the state from its Sikh rulers after defeating them in battle, but Kashmir was quickly sold on for a large sum to the Hindu rajah of the neighbouring territory – even though the majority of Kashmiris were Muslims. Kashmir's Hindu rulers soon decided to prohibit the purchase of land in their desirable state, so British visitors took to houseboats on the lakes and rivers instead. In Srinagar, the capital, old wooden houses hung over the waterways, and the Goddens rented two houseboats among the willows on the Dal lake. They explored the lake and the Moghul pleasure gardens at Nishat and Shalimar, and they went on long treks to camp and fish in the mountains.

Camping trips in British India were well ordered and comfortable: teams of ponies and bearers carried all the gear and supplies, and by the time the family reached base after a day's travelling or an expedition, the servants would have erected the large tents of white canvas lined with yellow, each with beds and chairs and a small bathroom at the back, and hot water, smelling of woodsmoke, would be heating in kerosene cans for their baths. The cook prepared a meal, and a big campfire burned all night. All day, while Fa fished or went hunting and their mother and Aunt Mary read or rested at the camp, the children could explore, watch birds, pick flowers and catch frogs. When Fa shot a bear, they watched the shikari skinning it with his curved knife. They much preferred the freedom of the camp to the more decorous life of the resort town of Gulmarg, where the British retreated to play tennis and bridge and hold cocktail parties when Srinagar became too hot. The mountains of Kashmir, with their snowy peaks and pine-covered slopes, their fields of flowers and soaring eagles, seduce and inspire everyone who sees them; for Rumer especially, after that summer Kashmir stood for beauty, wilderness, and escape from the conventional and the mundane.

The Godden children's world was privileged, but it was not possible to shield them from the ugly realities of life in India. Rumer and her sisters grew up well aware of the poverty, disease and cruelty all around them; they knew that in India death can come as suddenly as dusk. When they rode or walked through the bazaar they did not, like the grown-ups, avert their eyes from the beggars, the cripples, the lepers, the children covered with sores. They knew, because Nana told them, that sometimes babies were deliberately deformed to make them more pitiful. They knew that life was short and hard for many of the people outside their gates; they also knew that there was little to be done about it, and learned a certain fatalism about the many risks and dangers surrounding them. 'Indians were always having accidents,' wrote Jon and Rumer briskly. 'There were such swarms of them . . .' Illness was a constant threat and not only to the Indians: for all the boiling and disinfecting that went on, the children had their share of stomach upsets, dysentery, malaria and fevers. But they also had the protection of their mother's medicine cupboard and the attentions of a Welsh doctor. 'The Indians died like flies of all these things because they had no resistance.'

Above all, they became familiar with the presence and aftermath of death. 'We knew, without being told, that in India death was as casual as life, part of every day.' They were fascinated by the rituals that took place on the riverbanks; people were brought there to die, or their bodies were carried down on stretchers, faces exposed, to be burned. 'We knew the smell of burning flesh . . .' Only babies and small children were not burned: they were placed on a little raft, surrounded with flowers, and pushed out into the stream for the river to take away.

Some of the fears and anxieties aroused by their exposure to these powerful and frightening realities were displaced, partly into games and stories, but also and more openly on to their pets. In India, the British love of animals, like their love of gardens, was focused and intensified by exile. With their dogs especially they could relax and be playful, giving and receiving affection without restraint. With each other, and still more with the Indians, the British as rulers had to watch their step and keep up appearances. Like their father, the Godden children were passionate about animals, and the casual cruelties inflicted by the less sentimentally inclined Indians upset them. The sufferings endured by innocent creatures, human or animal, marked Rumer's imagination permanently: she was drawn ever after to cruelty and drama, half attracted, half terrified. Two episodes in her childhood involving pets remained with her for life.

One was all her own fault. The children each owned a rabbit, white and silky with pink-lined ears. Rumer called hers Connie. One day when Nancy's rabbit, Betsy, produced four delicious babies, Rumer could not bear it. She took two of Betsy's young and presented them to Connie, as seemed only fair. Connie immediately tore the baby rabbits into bloody shreds. No one was in the least sorry for poor Rumer; she had been punished for taking Nancy's rabbits. If this taught her a lesson about animal nature, or the unfairness of life, the fate of her father's pet fox terrier, Sally, taught her a harder lesson still about adult ruthlessness and responsibility. When Sally's leg was broken, the vet was called to set it; the children were sure she would recover. That night, it was Jon who woke to hear the little dog crying in pain; Rumer was woken by the revolver shot with which Fa put her out of her misery. Jon and Rumer told their father they would never trust him again. 'Sally's was only a small death but it broke our unquestioning faith in Mam and Fa.' Rumer's fiction is haunted by Sally's ghost. One novel in particular, *Breakfast with the Nikolides*, revolves around the treacherous destruction by a parent of a dog.

As the older girls approached adolescence, it was inevitable that disturbing intimations of the power of sex should also reach them. They learned the facts of life as most children then did, from observation of their animals and from their mother's careful explanations. Gradually, the invented exploits of the 'Big Girls' faded from their minds as they began to notice the romantic entanglements of the young men and women around them. But it was from something that happened within their household, in the world of their friends the servants, which ran parallel to their own, that they discovered something of the dark and destructive powers of sexual passion. Guru the gatekeeper began to appear distracted and even to neglect his duties; certainly he was no longer interested in their games. One day they noticed a girl living in his hut, cooking and cleaning for him, like a wife, although they knew he already had a wife in his village. From the other servants they gathered that the beautiful girl was Nitai the sweeper's daughter – the sweeper himself was away – and that Nitai was harsh with the girl, who was often heard weeping in their hut. At first they were glad for her and for Guru, but something made them uneasy: the sly Abdul hinted that when Nitai returned there would be trouble, and Hannah tried without success to keep them away from the lodge. Their parents seemed oblivious to what was going on, and Jon and Rumer, who usually told their mother everything, instinctively felt it was better not to talk about this. They would creep up to Guru's hut and watch the beautiful girl combing and oiling her long black hair.

After a month or two the girl had a child. Now the secret was out, and something terrible happened. Nitai came back, found his daughter and the baby in Guru's hut and beat her so savagely that she died. The police were called, Guru disappeared, and the baby was handed over to her grandmother, Nitai's wife. It was Abdul who told them, smacking his lips, that the baby was Nitai's, and that he had killed his daughter out of jealousy. 'We did not understand then the full meaning of what Abdul had said,' wrote Jon and Rumer eventually. 'We only knew that we hated the way he said it and by an unspoken act we did not speak of it . . .' They never saw Guru again, and the new gatekeeper did not share their games. The baby grew into a lovely little girl. 'She was a laughing, gay child, unstained, untouched by her dark history or her mother's violent death, but ever after this Jon and Rumer had an awareness, two breathing-in little antennae that caught every wind, each new violence.'

For Rumer, the early Narayanganj years remained a magic time, bounded as they were before and afterwards by journeys 'home'; but changes arrived even inside the charmed circle and broke the spell. A new self-consciousness arose in both herself and Jon, a disturbing awareness of people outside the family. The young men around Narayanganj and Dacca, junior Scots or English employees of the jute mills or minor government officials, were often lonely and homesick and the Goddens, with their big house and tennis court and nursery full of attractive children, were kind and hospitable hosts. At first they were indistinguishable to Rumer, friends of her parents, part of the landscape, but gradually she began to notice some more than others. One who stood out, John Ordish, had been badly wounded in the war and lost a leg; he seemed to enjoy being with the children more than adult social life. At first Jon and Rumer found him worrying: his difficulties with his artificial leg and the effort he put into trying to lead a normal life bothered them. Their mother told them not to be so selfish, and gradually they got used to him. Then there were the Hely-Hutchinsons. Mr Hely-Hutchinson was the head of the biggest and grandest of the jute companies, and a wealthy and important man in Narayanganj; he came from a family with aristocratic connections, and he and his wife conveyed an aura of being out of place in a Bengal backwater. Rumer developed an enormous crush on him, to general amusement; but Jon, to her family's slight surprise, became a great favourite of Mrs Hely-Hutchinson, who was reputed to have studied painting in Paris. She appreciated Jon's artistic talent and would ask her over for the day so that they could paint together. Rumer was excluded, and she minded: her sister was moving away from her into the adult world, which she felt ill-equipped to share.

The remote charms of Mr Hely-Hutchinson were eclipsed for Rumer by the eruption into their lives of a new young police inspector. He was an energetic Scotsman with black hair and blue eyes who charmed all of them except Fa. He offered to teach the girls to swim, but their father would not allow it; then he vanished. Once again, it was Abdul who told them what had happened. After the Hogmanay Ball at the club the young inspector, very drunk, had fallen from the police launch into the river and drowned. There were other rumours: apparently he had been flirting for some time with the club belle, a young married woman, and had 'words' with her husband that evening . . . Could he have drowned himself for love? Whether he had or not, a pattern was emerging that stayed with Rumer: adult emotions were dangerous, love and sex could have dark consequences. One day she saw something that came to symbolize for her the discovery of cruelty and sexual disgust. In the bazaar, a pedlar had two monkeys on strings, dressed like small humans; he was encouraging them to mate for the amusement of the onlookers. Rumer used the monkey man several time in her fiction, notably in *The Peacock Spring*, to evoke the ugliness of which humanity is capable.

The story with which she and Jon chose to end their account of their childhood concerned another young man who unwittingly caused trouble between them. During their last winter in Naray-anganj – they had known for some time that once the war was over, they would have to return to school in England – 'Mr Silcock' came on the scene. Rumer could not help noticing that he treated

Jon differently from the way he treated her, and she could not bear it: she was left playing with the little ones while Jon joined in grown-up tennis parties. One evening on the club verandah she saw Jon blushing as he helped her into her coat, lifting her glossy hair over her collar. Later that night she and Jon quarrelled. 'You bother people too much, Peggy. You shouldn't tag on,' said Jon. They ended up fighting in a heap on the floor, until their mother came to separate them and tell them they were too old for such behaviour.

Not long afterwards, they were on their way back to England. This was not the end of their life in Narayanganj, but it was the end of their childhood: when they returned to India it was as young women, not as little girls. For Rumer especially, the power of those years in Narayanganj never diminished. She would draw over and over again on what she had seen and heard and learned, and she turned her own experiences, especially the pangs of loss she felt when childhood drew towards its natural end, into one of her main themes as a writer. At the beginning of *The River* she wrote:

> Perhaps the place and the life were alien, circumscribed, dull to the grown-ups who lived there; for the children it was their world of home. They lived in the Big House in a big garden on the river with the tall flowering cork tree by their front steps. It was their world, complete. Up to this winter it had been completely happy.

CHAPTER TWO

Schooldays and After

1920–29

IN MARCH 1920, the Godden family travelled back to England together. All Rumer's memories of their arrival are bleak, grey and cold: she and Jon were full of foreboding. 'We were cold to our bones – not only with the cold; we had already had a taste of England.' Rumer was twelve and a half, Jon almost fourteen; they were less bewildered than their younger selves had been at the transition from one world to another, but all the same they were confused and miserable. Like many contemporaries who shared the experience, they rejected, deep inside themselves, the notion that this dreary place was their real home. The Goddens were luckier than many: within a few months their father had to return to his job in India, but their mother stayed with them and their younger sisters for the years that Jon and Rumer were at school. They settled in Eastbourne, where there was already a family base. Uncle Alfred, their mother's brother, was a solicitor there and Aunt Mary soon went to keep house for him. They were never handed over, as so many Anglo-Indian children were, to distant relatives or strangers; they were not neglected or treated coldly or made to feel a burden – unlike the writer Raleigh Trevelyan who overheard one relation say to another, 'It's your turn to have Raleigh for Christmas.' – let alone maltreated like the little boy in Kipling's grim story, 'Baa Baa Black Sheep', the ultimate indictment of the exile of the children of Anglo-India.

Nevertheless, it was hard, especially at first. Instead of their own railway compartment, or Fa's launch, there were second-class rail tickets and buses; instead of their huge house and lovely garden there was a series of cramped, unattractive rented establishments. The Goddens could only afford minimal help with cooking and cleaning; the retinue of servants was a thing of the past. Rumer took strongly against respectable middle-class Eastbourne, in which they were simply one ordinary ex-Indian family among many: Eastbourne was popular with expatriates. Rumer disliked the ordinary; she disliked the quiet suburban streets and the quiet suburban people. She missed the vitality, drama and extraordinariness of life in Narayanganj.

Most of all, she disliked school. She and Jon went to five schools in two years. The first, a strict High Anglican convent boarding school, was the worst, and her account of it, both in her autobiography and in a short story, 'The Little Fishes', is suffused with indignation: at her parents, for thinking, no doubt, that a boarding school might make adaptation to their new surroundings and the acquiring of new friends easier, and at the nuns, for their rigid, unsympathetic, unimaginative approach to the two new girls from India. The golden years of their reprieve had made them, perhaps, just what parents and teachers feared children left too long in India would become: spoiled – in other words, girls with minds of their own, unused to rules and restrictions, precocious in some ways, ignorant and innocent in others, with heads full of exotic memories and longings and a trace of the chi-chi in their voices. The freedom, physical and imaginative, of their childhood had not made them tractable. Rumer was not good schoolgirl material: she hated games, she questioned the rules, she found the religious routine pointless, she could hardly eat the food and was constantly getting bad marks for untidiness (she and Jon were, after all, looking after themselves for the first time in their lives).

Hardly surprisingly, they were not popular either with the nuns or with the other children. If Rumer made any friends at her first four schools, they were neither lasting nor memorable; what she never forgot was the cold unkindness of the convent headmistress, and that none of the other girls chose either her or Jon as their partner in the crocodile when they went for a walk. They were not allowed to walk together: Jon would end up with a Chinese girl who hardly spoke English, and Rumer with a child who was slightly mentally handicapped. Jon had a worse time than Rumer did, being defiant and stubborn by nature; Rumer was more devious, and took to cheating at her homework and lying her way out of trouble. She also discovered that she could attract attention and win a kind of popularity by telling her schoolmates tall stories about India. 'It was like writing aloud.' But one of the nuns overheard her one day assuring her audience that a tale of her father, three snakes and a tiger was true; she was punished for telling lies and made to wear her class badge upside down so that everyone would know she was a liar. Jon wore hers upside down too, to demonstrate solidarity. The humiliation was intense, and the feeling of being unpopular and a misfit marked her deeply. The penalty, always, of living in one place while feeling in your heart that you belong in another is to be a perpetual outsider. Afterwards Rumer could never be quite sure that she belonged anywhere, and she was never happy in a group.

Again, she and Jon were comparatively lucky. It seemed an age but it was less than a school year before their misery and endless ailments worried their mother so much that she decided that they should live at home and go to a day school; things began, slowly, to look up. But to Rumer's store of the characters who would one day people her stories, especially those she wrote for children, was added Sister Gertrude, not so much because she was a nun but because she was a bully.

Eastbourne offered its own compensations. There was the theatre, where they saw romantic middle-brow musicals, like *The Maid of the Mountains*, and the Winter Garden, where the concerts they attended were of a higher calibre: Rumer recalled hearing Kubelik, Heifetz and Rubinstein there. Uncle Alfred took them for outings in his car, up into the downs or along the river where he kept a canoe. For the first time she realized that the English landscape could be beautiful. Then, for her sixteenth birthday, her mother gave her five pounds with which to buy herself a Persian kitten. Rumer went to the pet shop, where she saw a Pekinese puppy, dark with cream nose and paws. Enchanted, she bought him, though the five pounds was only a down payment, and called him Piers. He was the first of the Pekinese who were to accompany and delight her through life, whose affection and loyalty never failed her, whose response to her, and still more hers to them, was uncomplicated love. Relationships with people, she was beginning to discover, were complex and troubling. A bond with an animal, though it often ended in tears, was a great deal simpler.

Rumer was still writing: she kept a journal, since destroyed, half fact and half fiction, and she wrote poems. One day she saw an advertisement in a newspaper offering to publish poetry; she sent in her poems and soon received a flattering letter asking for fifteen pounds. Knowing nothing of the vanity press, she thought this was perhaps how publishing worked: she borrowed the money from her mother, telling her it was for something important and promising somehow to pay it back. Their mother found it hard to refuse her daughters anything, and anyway Rumer was convinced that once they were printed her poems would make her rich and famous. She sent off the money; fifty copies of sixteen of her poems duly arrived, in a cheap-looking pamphlet. To her mortification, no one seemed much impressed, and her father, though amused, was also displeased by her boldness. 'Females, according to Fa, should not have initiative.' Later, she realized that the poems were very bad; she also, eventually, decided that her family's lack of interest in or encouragement of her writing was a stroke of luck. Jon, who had won a gold medal for a watercolour in the annual summer competition in Kashmir and been praised by the judge, who had predicted a great future for her, was under constant pressure from her proud parents; they sent her to art classes and waited for her to begin a dazzling artistic career. Rumer was left to make her own way.

The fifth and final school to which Mrs Godden, doubtless by this time slightly desperate, sent Rumer in 1923 was Moira House, in Eastbourne. It was ahead of its time in that it dispensed with uniforms, allowed the girls to share in the running of the school and encouraged innovative, flexible teaching. For the first time, Rumer and Jon were separated, as Jon went on to art school. Nancy started at Moira House at the same time as Rumer; Rose was to follow in due course. Rumer went into the senior school, and in her second week encountered the vice-principal, Mona Swann, one of those gifted teachers who make a real difference to their pupils' lives. Miss Swann, who was at Moira House for many years and became headmistress in her turn, was something of a legend to many of her pupils; it was she who first saw in Rumer the making of a writer, took her seriously and set out to help her.

Years later Mona Swann wrote her own account of what she called the Godden saga. Rumer, she recalled, 'had already been a misfit at several schools. She would, I realised with some trepidation, be in my form.' Miss Swann taught English, choral speech and drama; she set her new class an essay about the seasons.

> When I looked through my usual crop of undistinguished efforts I found one that was far from commonplace. Rumer had created a Red Indian's alert-sensed record of his varying seasonal experience. When I asked her how the idea had come to her, 'I had to write it that way, it just came,' she said. Further reading of Rumer's work confirmed my first assessment that she was unusually gifted.

How, Miss Swann asked herself, could she help her pupil develop and discipline her natural talent without stifling her creativity and imagination? She invited Rumer to work with her privately on her writing. Rumer was ecstatic. 'Now, I thought, now there will be someone who will really appreciate my stories! In the two years I worked with Mona I did not write a single story.'

Miss Swann put her through a thorough, strict, old-fashioned course in the writing of English. She set her to work doing précis, analysing structure, grammar and punctuation. All she was allowed to write were exercises without adjectives or adverbs or personal pronouns, or in one of the existing poetic forms. 'Anything I could devise to increase linguistic control and to curb verbal wastefulness,' as Miss Swann recalled. She was impressed with her pupil's willingness to work hard and to listen. 'Voluntarily Rumer rewrote draft after draft and was ever ready to discuss and learn from the most ruthless criticism.'

Mona Swann understood character as well as prose. Her description of Rumer at sixteen is shrewd. She saw her as a curious mixture: in her awareness of and sympathy for 'deprived humanity' she was mature for her age, and in the 'rather patriarchal devotion' she showed towards her sisters. But three characteristics, to Miss Swann, were less mature and made her relationships with other people difficult: 'intolerance of ordinariness in people or situations; a veneer of imperialism from her childhood upbringing in India and, also, submission to a novelist's urge to endow everyday facts with fictive interest, consequently fascinating listeners by her colourful reporting of them while exasperating and alienating realists'. All her writing life, Rumer was to combine a deep certainty about her need to write and the inspiration that seldom failed her, with an equally deep need for reassurance from people she could trust. She did not want flattery from them, she wanted the truth, even if it was painful; she called such people her touchstones. Mona Swann was the first. Rumer trusted Mona, and turned to her for advice for many years after her schooldays were over. Miss Swann's interest in her made all the difference to Rumer's attitude to school, but she still found it hard to make friends. Two former pupils at Moira House, who remembered her and her younger sisters, told me that the Goddens were not much liked: they gave themselves airs and talked endlessly about their exotic life in India. It was even whispered that they might be part Indian themselves.

In the summer of 1924, Mrs Godden took her four daughters on a journey to France. She had decided that it would do them good, Jon and Rumer in particular, to see the First World War battlefields. Rumer acknowledged that both she and Jon were difficult adolescents, critical, discontented and often a great trial to their mother; their chequered school careers had not helped, nor the absence of their father, nor the lingering feelings of displacement and loss and the drabness of Eastbourne. Mop wanted to make them think of something other than themselves. 'Perhaps when you see the rows and rows of crosses for those young men who gave their lives for you, it might make you stop and think of your selfishness.'

They never reached the battlefields: their mother became unwell on the journey, and by the time they reached the small hotel in Château Thierry, on the Marne, where they had arranged to stay, she was seriously ill. What followed was Rumer's greengage summer, and it became one of her most effective stories of innocence lost. As she explained: 'It is difficult, with the novel I was to write about those two months in Château Thierry and the film that followed it, to know what I remember as happening, what is transposed in the novel, and what is overlaid by the film; each seems to shimmer through the others.' The bones of the story are clear: Mrs Godden was confined to bed in the Hôtel des Violettes, and the girls were befriended by an English couple. The *patronne* had a lover; both he and the Englishman were taken with Jon, who was about to be eighteen and ravishingly pretty. Rumer, at sixteen and a half, was half envious, half disgusted: she watched as Jon began to realize and to test her power over men. It was champagne country; the grapes ripened, the sun shone, the Englishman drove the girls around in his fast car. On her eighteenth birthday, Jon was given a special dinner and a bottle of champagne; the *patronne* became jealous and made an embarrassing scene. One day, the police arrived; the kind Englishman and his wife had disappeared. It emerged that he was a crook, and the Goddens were cross-questioned about their friendship with him. Katherine Godden was by now recovered; they went back to Eastbourne, and Rumer returned to school.

Around this episode, dramatized and extended to include a murder, Rumer wrote an evocation of the beauty of rural France, especially compared with Eastbourne. Her picture of the hotel – its faded grandeur, four-poster beds and dining room with blue satin wallpaper, the formal garden with its flower-beds, the orchards with ripe fruit dropping from the trees, the slow-moving river, the vineyards, the old town – has the intensity and nostalgia special to early discovery of a foreign country. The two sisters, Cecil and Joss, are versions of herself and Jon; the pain felt by Cecil as she sees her sister's beauty, her own passion for the seductive Englishman unnoticed, his hand lifting Joss's hair from her collar, recall what had happened on the club verandah in Narayanganj. The story is suffused with the green and gold radiance of summer memories, and the painful tenderness of growing up. The fruit they could not resist was real enough, but Rumer makes it a symbol of another kind of ripening.

> The greengages had a pale blue look, especially in the shade, but in the sun the flesh showed amber through the clear green skin; if it were cracked the juice was doubly warm and sweet. Coming from the streets and small front gardens of Southstone, we had not been let loose in an orchard before; it was no wonder we ate too much.

In the summer of 1925, Rumer left school. Her parents had decided that, with Jon now nineteen and Rumer coming up to eighteen, it was time for them to return with their mother to Narayanganj where, except for short, awkward periods of leave, Arthur Godden had remained without his family for five years. Nancy and Rose were left in Eastbourne to finish their education.

The idea of university or training for a profession does not seem to have occurred to either the girls or their parents: 'In our family we did not have women professionals,' wrote Rumer. There was no question either of a formal coming-out in London, but in India their parents knew that the girls would have a good time during the Bengal cold-weather season: there were plenty of lonely young men in the jute firms, tea gardens and merchant houses of Calcutta. Rumer, though, was suddenly not sure that she wanted to go back, after all. At Moira House she had, finally, formed a close friendship with another girl, who in her autobiography she called Shelagh. They fell in love, she wrote; it is the only time she uses the phrase about herself. Shelagh was tall, dark, with a short straight nose 'which I did not envy but adored', and she was 'cool, almost laconic, the opposite of my five foot two impassioned self'. Their love was innocent, but deep: when Shelagh's mother proposed that instead of leaving for India Rumer go with them to Tours to learn French, Rumer was torn between her sister and her friend. At first she thought she would go to Tours, then she changed her mind: 'It was not Jon or Shelagh that decided me, it was India.'

By the time she left Eastbourne with Jon and her mother to catch the boat to Calcutta, their trunks full of new clothes and romantic possibilities in the air, it was not for Shelagh that Rumer recalled shedding tears but for Piers, her Pekinese. She continued to believe that one day she would be a writer; but on leaving school Mona Swann had strongly advised her not to publish anything before she was twenty-five.

When Rumer came to consider the next stage of her life, the eighteen months she spent in Narayanganj between 1925 and 1927 appeared to have been a time of false starts and discontent. It was not a time on which she looked back with much satisfaction, or that fed directly, as did her childhood or the summer in France, into her writing. Like most eighteen-year-olds, she had not yet become the person she wanted to be; it was hard to fit the fragments she chose to recall into the story she later made of her life. But one thing is clear: on her return the magic and power of Narayanganj, that re-emerged so clearly and powerfully later in her memory and her writing, was absent. She saw it all, the house, the garden, the river, with new eyes; like everyone who goes back to the place where they grew up, she found it smaller and shabbier. For the first time she realized how remote Narayanganj was, how provincial. When she climbed up to the roof and looked down, she felt trapped. 'From the parapet, Narayanganj looks an ugly squalid little town; how had it once seemed enchanted? The river that had been its whole meaning now has only one meaning for me – it leads to the outside world. Here, there is nothing for me, nothing.'

Moreover, now that she was no longer a child, Rumer was not protected by childish ignorance of the nature of the society around her. After the war, change was in the air: in 1919 the Government of India Act was designed to speed up the Indianization, as it was called, of the civil service and the Army. In the same year, the killing of several hundred unarmed Indian demonstrators by British troops under General Dyer at Amritsar provoked a furious reaction. Gandhi had returned from South Africa in 1916 and was beginning his campaign against British rule: 'Dear me,' remarked Lord Chelmsford, the Viceroy of the time, 'what a damn nuisance these saintly fanatics are.' No one expected rapid change, but the conventions and prejudices of the British community in India were not as unselfconscious as they had been, especially for people within Calcutta's radius where in the wake of the Amritsar killings, Rabindranath Tagore, the celebrated poet embraced by the West, returned the Nobel Prize he had been awarded in 1913. Neither Rumer nor anyone else in her immediate family was politically minded, and the pros and cons of moves towards dominion status, self-government, the merits of swaraj or Gandhi's non-violent campaigns were little discussed among them. Arthur Godden was conservative by inclination, although his daughters remembered him saying that he had always known independence would and should come to India, eventually. But Rumer at eighteen was self-conscious and sensitive, she was reading widely, she wanted above all to write herself and she sensed that she was part of a way of life in India that most writers and intellectuals deplored. By the time she came to reflect upon this period of her life, she was writing with hindsight, having long known that it was prudent to express misgivings about the privileges and assumptions of the Empire. At the time, any unease she felt seems to have been fleeting.

To everyone's astonishment, including her own, by Christmas 1925, within a few weeks of her arrival in Calcutta, Rumer was engaged. The romance did not last long and her account of it is wry, almost dismissive: it was not an episode of which she was proud. Her admirer, a man in his early thirties called Ian Finlayson, seemed old to Rumer at barely eighteen; she remembered him as one of the young men who used to come to tea in Narayanganj, and who had been thought a possible suitor for her aunt Mary. He was among a group of her parents' friends who met the ship in Calcutta; soon after, he told her he had been waiting for her to grow up. He asked her father's permission, and then proposed to her on a launch on a river far upstream during a Christmas duck shoot. He took her acceptance for granted, and kissed her. Looking back, she wrote that she knew it was wrong but that she let it all happen. Her parents seemed pleased, especially her father, and for once she was the centre of attention. She wore a big sapphire engagement ring, there was a whirl of parties in Narayanganj and Calcutta; her fiancé sent her flowers every day and provided her with a car and driver. But one day she realized she felt trapped, and broke it off. Everyone was cross with her, except Jon, who had never really approved. Her mother wondered if she would like to go back to England, but Rumer decided to stay. She felt guilty, and a bit foolish; nevertheless the episode must surely have boosted her confidence in her capacity to attract men, even when Jon was around. Those who knew Rumer as a young woman remember that she was never short of admirers; she may not have been as conventionally pretty as her sisters, but there was something compelling about her. One of the lonely young men who came to Sunday lunch at Narayanganj was Anthony Bent, who remembered that Peggie Godden, as he knew her, appealed to him most, because she was the most interesting of the girls to talk to.

In fact, she had rather a good time for the next two years, even if she later disapproved of herself for enjoying it. India, for girls like Jon and Rumer in the late 1920s, could be great fun, as long as they did not question the conventions; little was expected of them but to look decorative and to enjoy themselves. It was certainly more glamorous and exciting than Eastbourne. They went to Assam for the winter race weeks, when the tea gardens held a round of tennis parties, polo, race meetings and dances; they spent the summers in the hills at Shillong, and went on camping trips with their father to shoot and fish on the borders of Bhutan. They listened at night to the jackals and hyenas howl as they lay under the stars by the campfire. Sometimes they heard a tiger. They rode on elephants through the jungle, watching wild peacocks and red spotted deer. Unlike Jon, Rumer did not enjoy shooting or fishing but she loved the beauty and wildness, and remembered it. She also loved their first winter visit to Delhi, where they stayed in the new city, recently laid out, with the architect John Blomfield who had worked with Lutyens; they explored the narrow streets of the old city and the Red Fort, with its delicate mosaic fountains, and walked in the Lodi Gardens under the jacaranda and flame trees. At one lunch party, Rumer remembered, she wore a pale pink dress and matching hat. 'As we sat under the trees, eating curry puffs, game pie, cherry cake, peaches and ice-cream, small brown monkeys peered down at us from the branches. Suddenly one of them let fall a stream of shit on my precious hat.' Apparently this meant she would have good luck for life.

At home in Narayanganj, Rumer sank again into discontent. She wrote her diary, read the magazines in the club, especially the book reviews (she and Jon both kept commonplace books full of cuttings all their lives), went to parties in Dacca – a younger friend who lived there as a child recalls that Rumer used to rest in the afternoons, lying limp in a darkened room under a propeller fan, before changing for an evening out – and felt that life was slipping away from her. Meanwhile, Jon had fallen in love with a young man living in a chummery (a shared house for bachelors) called Nigel Baughan. He worked for Imperial Tobacco and the terms of his contract precluded marriage, but they became engaged and radiated happiness. Jon seemed absorbed in her love affair and to have forgotten her desire to be a painter, while Rumer was more and more painfully aware that a career as a writer would be hard to build from Bengal. She read and admired Katherine Mansfield, Virginia Woolf, D. H. Lawrence, and Constance Garnett's translations of Chekhov. Around this time, she also read E. M. Forster's *A Passage to India*, first published in 1924, which, she later declared, changed her life.

Most English people who lived and worked in India regarded the way Forster portrayed the Anglo-Indian community as a travesty. They pointed out, with some justification, how short a time he had spent in the country, and how little of that time he had spent with the British who were running it. Many wrote to him in protest, but he had never intended to write a balanced portrait of either community: 'Isn't fair-mindedness dreary?' he wrote to a friend. 'A rare achievement, and a valuable one, you will tell me, but how sterile in one's own soul. I fall in love with Orientals, with Anglo-Indians – no: that is roughly my internal condition, and all the time I had to repress the consequences, or fail to hold the scales.' He expressed a more considered reaction to a retired Indian civil servant: '. . . I believe that I have seen certain important truths that have been hidden from you despite your thirty years on the spot.'

As soon as she read it, *A Passage to India* with its depiction of British arrogance and insensitivity towards Indians, their culture and their aspirations, made a huge impression on Rumer. She sensed that it was a milestone in the way that the British in India were perceived; and she disliked the painful realization that she, her family and friends were among Forster's targets, no matter how different they all felt themselves to be. To Forster and his circle, to critics and publishers, anyone from the heart of Anglo-India, like herself, must be suspect, if not an object of derision. 'Were we, the English in India, really like the Turtons, the McBrydes and the Callendars, those righteous, insensitive characters? Was this how people saw us, those people in London whom we had set up almost as gods?' No wonder Rumer decided to identify herself with Mrs Moore, the elderly woman who allows herself to be open to the mystery and power of India, rather than with Adela Quested, the blundering girl whose emotional inadequacy leads to disaster. But at the same time a seed of encouragement may have been planted in her by the success of Forster's novel and the interest it aroused in the Anglo-Indian scene. The everyday life of the British in India, as opposed to romantic melodrama and adventure stories, had not been seen since Kipling as promising material for fiction.

It was during this generally uneasy time that Rumer began to be aware of her ignorance of the cultural riches of India, of Indian religion and philosophy, art and literature. As children, the Goddens had all picked up a smattering of information, mainly from the servants, about the principal festivals of the Hindu year: Holi, the spring festival when love and fertility were celebrated with drinking and feasting and people threw coloured dyes over each other in the streets, and Diwali, the lovely October festival of lights. They knew from the Muslims in the household about Mecca, about Ramadan, when fasting was obligatory, and Id, the great feast when it was over. They also knew some of the stories every Indian child knows, about Krishna and the Gopis, and Rama and Sita, the perfect lovers. But, as in all expatriate communities, the first concern of the British living in India was to keep their own culture alive. Even the young intellectuals of the ICS often spent their leisure time reading classical or European literature, not studying Indian texts. They learned the languages to help them with their work, but in the main they regarded Indian culture as impenetrable at best, barbaric and crude at worst, certainly not something for women and children to discover.

In the Godden household it was simply accepted, as it was in most Anglo-Indian homes, that English and Indian families did not mix. There was the problem of purdah for Muslim women, and of Hindu strictures on contact with foreigners, and of language: Arthur Godden spoke Bengali, Hindi and some Assamese, but his wife and children learned only pidgin Hindi, enough to communicate with shopkeepers and servants. His daughters always recalled with pride that Fa was on excellent terms with his staff and employees, but also that their wives and children would never mix with his except on one or two special occasions each year, such as Diwali or Christmas. As for culture, Fa was not much of a reader of English literature let alone Indian, so that the great works of Indian culture, the Upanishads, the *Bhagavadgita*, the *Mahabharata* were mysteries to them all. On their rare visits to Calcutta, the great metropolis two hundred miles to the south, the Goddens were absorbed in shopping, social life and catching up with the news and fashions from England. Rumer did not, as a child or young woman, ever visit the superb collections of Indian sculpture and bronzes in the India Museum opened in 1875. As for the Bengal renaissance in art and writing, symbolized by the great Tagore, that was only for Bohemian intellectuals, who were regarded with suspicion whether in Calcutta or London. Arthur Godden's knowledge of India and Indians was limited: it comprised the natural history of the rivers and hills, the animals and birds he observed and hunted, and the customs and character of the people with whom he worked. To all these he showed respect and affection, but anything more abstract or challenging was not for him. It would not have occurred to his wife to question such attitudes, which she no doubt shared, and their daughters absorbed the unwritten rules as children do.

Though Arthur Godden sometimes found Rumer's moods difficult and her aspirations peculiar (she described herself as 'the family enigma'), when she expressed a desire to learn Hindi properly, he tried to help: he found an Indian clerk from his office who came regularly to the house to give her lessons. The experiment did not last long. But her father may have understood some things about her better than she realized: she badly needed an occupation, and was delighted when he asked her if she would like to work with him on one of his projects. He was trying to develop an improved jute seed, which would enable Bengali farmers to increase their crop and exploit their small plots of land more effectively. The authorities gave him a base in an agricultural college outside Dacca, and for six months or so in late 1926 and early 1927, Rumer went regularly to work at the college, keeping records and monitoring experiments, sometimes with her father, sometimes on her own. She discovered that she liked the discipline and 'the precious anonymity' of work, and for the first time mixed with intelligent young Indians on more or less equal terms. She did not exactly make friends with them but she liked them, and observed them closely. Later, several of her books included Indian students, handsome, emotionally volatile young men, often in a state of some intellectual and political confusion, whose contacts with English families, especially with English girls, tended to lead to suspicion and misunderstanding.

In the spring of 1927, Rumer returned to England. She spent the summer with her family, partly in Eastbourne and partly on the wild and romantic Scottish island of Mull, where her father, on his last long leave, had rented a shoot. In the early autumn, she left for London. She had decided to use a small legacy from a godfather to train as a dancing teacher.

Her decision now seems curious. She said to herself that she never quite understood what made her take it. She knew she needed to work and that it would help her parents if she could earn her own living: her father's retirement was not far off. She had always enjoyed the dancing classes and amateur performances in which she had taken part as a child, and she knew that there was scope in India for properly trained teachers. Music and ballet appealed to her sense of drama and her imagination. Even so, it was an odd choice, as her family were not slow to point out, especially as she had been prone to back trouble since falling off a swing when she was seven, but Rumer was determined. Those around her were beginning to realize how tenacious she could be.

To her mother's distress she decided to find a school in London rather than in Eastbourne; and her time at the Vandyke School in the Finchley Road taught her to discover and love the city. She worked hard and found that despite her physical limitations – she was starting late and her old injury restricted her movements – she enjoyed the discipline and her growing sense of independence, of learning a skill and applying it. She had a natural aptitude for working with children, and a natural authority with them. Ballroom dancing suited her particularly well: she loved the fashionable tea dances in big London hotels she attended as part of her training. Her confidence grew: in her second year she rented a studio in Mayfair and taught débutantes to curtsy. When she had completed the course, and qualified as a dance teacher, the school asked her to join the staff; but although she was proud to have been asked, her mind was made up. She would go back to India and open her own school of dancing in Calcutta.

CHAPTER THREE

Calcutta Dust

1929–34

IN OCTOBER 1929, Rumer, with her mother and Nancy, made the four-week journey back to Calcutta from Liverpool on the SS *City of Canterbury*. Jon and Rose stayed behind: Rose was to be 'finished' in Paris, and Jon had decided to go with her and study painting. The family was concerned about Jon: she had been unwell and depressed, although her spirits had lifted after a summer spent in Dorset near her fiancé's home. Nigel Baughan had been on leave in England for several weeks and the romance had intensified, but he had returned alone to India: he was not allowed to marry for another couple of years. Rumer, though, was in good spirits, and made a strong impression on another young man off to seek his fortune in Calcutta.

Owain Jenkins was a bouncy, confident Balliol graduate with good connections, but not much money, who had decided to join Balmer Lawrie, one of Calcutta's oldest and grandest managing agencies. His elder brother in the ICS in the Punjab had told him it would not be sensible for him to follow in the family footsteps – their father had also been in India, on the Viceroy's staff – as India would become independent before he reached the top. Jenkins liked the idea of getting rich, and he was attracted by India's famous sporting opportunities: 'India was a country in which even a penniless young man could shoot and ride. Trade had preceded British rule and would presumably survive it.' One of his aunts had moved in grand Calcutta circles in Curzon's day: 'She told me that many of the business people (though not in the warrant of precedence) were quite presentable and on the Government House List.' Jenkins embarked on the *City of Canterbury* with two shotguns, a bag of golf clubs and high hopes.

Most of his fellow passengers, he soon observed, were 'the small fry of the Imperial community. More important people used the faster route to Bombay and then overland.' He shared a cabin with two men going out to tea gardens, and he soon spotted Mrs Godden 'and her two attractive daughters'. Nancy, at nineteen, seemed a pretty, horsy girl, but Rumer, at twenty-one, struck him as 'sophisticated and amusing', and they spent a good deal of time together. In his memoirs, after they had been friends for more than fifty years, he wrote – to her slight annoyance – that 'she already showed a talent for imaginative narration that puzzled our duller fellow passengers: "That older Godden girl is a terrible liar . . ."' He went on to remind her, teasingly, that he had cherished a hopeless passion for her but that she had preferred the ship's doctor.

Rumer had decided not to tackle Calcutta straight away but to launch her career as a professional dancing teacher in Darjeeling. The hill station was a smaller, friendlier and more familiar community in which after several visits with her family she felt at home, and she reckoned that once she had made a start there, Calcutta would be less daunting.

In the late 1920s Darjeeling was flourishing. In the 1830s, when the East India Company had picked it as the perfect spot for a summer resort, it was four days travel from Calcutta; now, better roads and comfortable trains made the journey from the plains less arduous, and the schools, clinics, hotels and boarding-houses of the expanding town were all doing well. The narrow streets climbing the hillside above the railway station, where the miniature train from Siliguri arrived in the middle of the bustling bazaar, were lined with shops and small villas, built in wood with steeply pitched roofs, decorative fretwork and balconies; this small-scale, gingerbread architecture made the town seem cosy and endearing, while

the great natural beauty of its tumbling tree-covered slopes, huge
rhododendrons and ferns and many streams and, above all, the
views of the snow-covered Himalayan peaks was bracing and
inspiring. It is still, in the age of air travel and air-conditioning, a
wonderful sensation for the traveller arriving from Calcutta to take
the first breaths of clear, cool Darjeeling air after the stagnant
atmosphere of the plains. In the 1920s most people still got around
on horseback, and the Chowrasta, the town square near the top of
the ridge, was crowded with ponies and bearers for hire. The
inhabitants of Darjeeling were hill people, Gurkhas, Lepchas and
Nepalis; they had high cheekbones and slanting eyes, and struck
English visitors as reassuringly sturdy and cheerful, with their pink
cheeks and beaming smiles. They wore embroidered woollen
jackets, the women with colourful long skirts, striped brocade
aprons, and heavy coral and turquoise jewellery. Treks into Sikkim
or Tibet were easy to arrange, to fish or shoot or just to picnic and
admire the landscape. The great mountain range to the north,
especially the majestic Kinchinjunga, gave Darjeeling a dignity that
not even Simla could outdo. And while Simla remained an imperial
enclave, revolving in a stately ritual around the comings and goings
of viceroys, generals and high-ranking officials from Delhi, Darjeeling had become steadily more relaxed and friendly in the years
since the war. The Governor of Bengal still moved up from
Calcutta for the hot weather, the Planters Club was still off limits
to women and Indians, but increasing numbers of Indians,
especially Bengalis, were spending holidays there. Gradually, away
from the restrictions and conventions of Calcutta, ordinary friendships were established between Anglo-Indian professional families
and their Indian equivalents. Such friendships began while watching polo or at the tennis courts or the skating rink, and continued
over cakes at one of the tea-shops and gradually moved, through
children's parties or games of bridge, into each other's homes. In
this way one Indian family became part of Rumer's life.

First to make friends were Rumer's mother and Mrs Agnes

Majumdar, who was married to a barrister with three children in their late teens: a daughter, Tara, and two sons, Jai and Karun. The Majumdars were part of a remarkable clan of highly educated and accomplished Bengalis, with strong English connections. Agnes was the youngest child and fourth daughter of a well-known family called Bonnerjee; her father, Womesh Chandra, had caused a sensation in Calcutta in the 1860s by abandoning the strict Brahmin traditions of his family to go to England to study law. He was called to the bar, and then returned to practise in Calcutta where he went even further, as Agnes put it in a family memoir, by 'bringing his wife out of purdah to live in English style'. A founder member of the Congress Party, established in 1885, he believed that India should gradually and peacefully become self-governing; but he was part of the generation and class of Indians for whom Western culture and political and educational institutions seemed to embody all that was enlightened. He proceeded to arrange the best of English educations for all his children, daughters as well as sons, at a time when few middle-class English girls could expect as much. The girls all had English as well as Indian names: Nalini Heloise, known as Nelly, Susila Anita, known as Susie, Pramila Florence, known as Milly, and Agnes Janaki. For twenty years the Bonnerjees moved between Calcutta and Croydon, where they had a large house with a billiard room and a tennis court. Their sons went to Rugby and Oxford, while the girls went first to Croydon High School and then to Cambridge. In 1890 Nelly became the second Indian girl to go to Girton; both she and her sister Susie became doctors, while Milly read classics at Newnham, and Agnes English literature. The children spoke English before they spoke Bengali, both they and their parents had many English friends, Mrs Bonnerjee became a Christian, and they habitually wore Western clothes. Nevertheless Mr Bonnerjee was taken aback when first his eldest son, also a lawyer, and then Nelly married into English families. However, in 1907 Milly married a well-connected young man called Amiya Chaudhuri, whom she met as a student in

London, and in 1909 Agnes married another English-educated Bengali, Prio Majumdar.

By the time the Goddens met them, the Majumdar and Chaudhuri families, their Bonnerjee cousins and friends, had been spending holidays in Darjeeling for twenty years. They were handsome, high-spirited and clever, and their background made them not only pro-British but perhaps more British than the British; they were undoubtedly the cream of Calcutta and Darjeeling society, pillars of the legal and political establishment. Both socially and intellectually they were more than the Godden family's equals; and they were not short of money. In 1919 the Chaudhuris had decided to buy a house in Darjeeling, and chose one of the newest and best. Just off the Chowrasta in the heart of the town was a house with modern sanitation and central heating, unusual then in Darjeeling, built by an American dentist with a practice in Calcutta. It had huge windows and glorious views, and was called the Wigwam. When it was suggested that the name be changed, Mr Chaudhuri said that as the dictionary defined a wigwam as an Indian dwelling the name might as well stay. The Chaudhuris continued to be based in Calcutta, in an enormous house in one of the best residential areas, Ballygunge, which was then still green and rural. Many of the clan lived nearby. Several of Milly Chaudhuri's best friends were Englishwomen: one was Evelyn Denham White, whose husband was their doctor, a woman of great character and strong principle who rode round Calcutta on her bicycle. The sisters and their children all congregated in Darjeeling for festivals and holidays, and in 1920 the Majumdars decided to move to Darjeeling to live. They bought another large house looking down on the town centre called Point Clear.

Rumer was pleased that her mother had made friends with such an attractive and interesting group; she admired both Milly and Agnes and made friends with Agnes Majumdar's daughter, Tara. Nancy Godden, who was and remained horse-mad, loved to sit in the stables at Point Clear: the boys especially were excellent riders.

She developed a teenage crush on Jai, who was exceptionally handsome; for a while it seemed as though it might have developed further, to both families' slight anxiety. Although marriages between Indians and English were acceptable, provided both parties were socially and educationally superior, reservations persisted in the communities about such alliances. The children of mixed-race marriages at any level never had an easy time. The many thousands of Eurasians in Calcutta – who usually had European fathers and Indian mothers – often with modest positions in the railways or the police, were looked down on by Indians as much as by the British.

Rumer's Darjeeling dancing classes for children were held in the ballroom of the Gymkhana Club, the large, rambling red-brick building set among deodar trees high up beyond the Windamere Hotel at the apex of the town on Observatory Hill. The club, with its skating rink, tennis courts, library, card room, billiard room (the extension presented in 1918 by the Maharajah of Cooch Behar) and assorted bars and lounges for drinks, tea and snacks was where all the holidaymakers of Darjeeling – provided they were members or invited by a member – went to amuse themselves, English and Indian alike. In the old days it was immaculate, beautifully kept, fully staffed and always busy; now quiet, battered and with an air of neglect, it is still used for parties and weddings and the occasional game of snooker. The famous ice-rink is now only for roller-skating, but an ex-military man darts out of the secretary's office to help enquirers, and a large wooden notice-board with brass lettering still directs guests to various amenities, most of them now non-existent. An enormous elk skull, with imposing antlers, perches over the main staircase; the dusty ballroom is huge, with a vaulted wooden roof and a gallery running around the top.

One of Rumer's Darjeeling pupils, Tigger Ramsay Brown, who knew her from Narayanganj, has vivid memories of the dancing classes and of the power of Rumer's personality. 'She was a wonderful teacher,' she remembered, sixty-five years later. 'She had a natural power of command; you really didn't misbehave in her presence.' Tigger, aged ten or eleven, once did behave badly and her punishment was to be excluded from the next class: 'I minded terribly. She came into the ladies' dressing room where we were changing out of our white net dancing dresses and she was serious and stern, and I later wept a lot and remember feeling I would never get over it.' Rumer was a perfectionist, endlessly inventive with stories and themes for the classes and arranging every detail of the children's costumes. Tigger particularly remembered the finale of a show for parents, and how Rumer provided long silk scarves in rainbow colours and had the children run fast around the edge of the hall in single file, the scarves streaming out behind them. Then there was the biggest event of all, the annual performance at the club attended by the Governor, his wife, and all the parents and their friends, when Rumer stood in front of the orchestra below the specially erected stage, directing the children and keeping an eye on everything.

By the cold-weather season of 1930, Rumer was ready to brave Calcutta. In a way, she had no choice: her parents were about to leave Narayanganj and move back to Tezpur, in Assam, where Arthur Godden had begun his career three decades before. He could have moved into Calcutta to spend his last spell in comparative comfort before retirement took him back to England – his wife and daughters might have liked a taste of Calcutta life – but he preferred, as always, the wilderness to the metropolis and his wife, as always, did not try to stop him. So Rumer went to Calcutta alone, and embarked on four years of independent life in the city.

In 1930 Calcutta was the commercial capital of the Indian Empire, although in 1912 the government had moved to Delhi; the British community who lived and worked there felt it belonged to them. Not much had changed for them since Curzon had said firmly, 'Calcutta is in reality a European city set down upon Asiatic soil.' It was a competitive and greedy society where, if you kept the rules, you could live well, make money and enjoy yourself. When people who recall pre-war Calcutta are asked what it was like, nine times out of ten their eyes light up and they say, 'It was such fun.' They were a long way from home, the climate was appalling for at least half the year and they were surrounded by what Kipling called the City of Dreadful Night; but in the 1930s if you were British it was possible, most of the time, to avoid unpleasantness. The knowledge that the dark side of Calcutta was nearby gave your rituals and pleasures an extra edge of excitement. Today, it is barely possible to discern the glamorous, confident heart of late-imperial Calcutta in the chaotic, battered city that has come to epitomize the late-twentieth-century urban nightmare. Calcutta, once redolent of a certain raffish glamour, is now synonymous with poverty, disease, squalor, and man's inhumanity to man. Nevertheless, even today when the light over the Maidan, the great park at the city's centre, fades in the early evening from apricot to pearl, and the flower-sellers and fruit-vendors along the wide pavements of Chowringhee pack up their wares for the night, and people are hurrying home along the pavements, and the lights go on in the back of countless small shops ready for the evening trade, and in the courtyard of the Grand Hotel or on the club verandahs the waiters are taking orders for cold beers or gin-lime sodas, it is possible to feel some of Calcutta's power to seduce.

In the 1930s, the great white neo-classical façades of the City of Palaces were still pristine, buddleia and washing-lines had not yet spoilt the pediments and broken the skyline, the avenues of central Calcutta were lined with flowering trees, the traffic was light, the lawns and flower-beds around the Victoria Memorial were immaculately green and tended, and imposing cavalry officers still exercised their superb horses on the Maidan at dawn. It must have been easy to ignore the slums around the corner, and the social and political tensions not far beneath the impeccable, seemingly unchanging surface. The Calcutta in which Rumer began her independent adult life had a population of about 1.25 million, of which all but about forty thousand were Indian. There were some wealthy

Indians, both Bengalis and the enterprising Marwaris from Rajasthan, for not only the British had made fortunes in Bengal: the Bengali middle class was prosperous and educated, and a lively, contentious intellectual élite gathered around the university. Calcutta's schools, hospitals, and research institutes were unrivalled in India. The Eurasian community was around twenty thousand or so strong; the rest were British, and occupied the apex of the social pyramid. Apart from a small group of government officials and civil servants, and a battalion of soldiers stationed at Fort William, most of the British, as Owain Jenkins noticed, were in business.

> The box-wallahs – that is, merchants, manufacturers and shopkeepers – must have totalled some fifteen thousand. It was a strange community, one of sojourners – in effect a white indentured labour force – aged between twenty and fifty, preponderantly male, unmarried and self-sufficient in the provision of its amusements.

It was also a community, he soon observed, where certain rules had to be obeyed. 'The ruling social principle was that there were two sorts of people: those who were "acceptable" and those who were not. The distinction goes back to the beginnings of Calcutta. In St John's Church, the original cathedral, you will find two doors: one leads the acceptable citizens to an upper gallery, the other takes their inferiors to the floor of the church. Calcutta's Europeans were always snobs. They did not regard each other as equal and saw no reason to believe that God took a different view.'

The key to social success in Calcutta, Jenkins realized, was to wear the right clothes, live at the right address and join the right clubs. It was not difficult for him, with his desirable connections, to fit in, but he was well aware, looking back, of the limitations of the society he had joined. He quickly became known as Oscar, after a somewhat deaf drinking companion insisted that that was his name. 'The prevalence of nicknames in Calcutta was part of the juvenile atmosphere of the place. Until late in life we remained younger and sillier than our contemporaries who had stayed at home.' It was dangerously easy to spend more than you could afford: credit was readily obtainable and most transactions were settled by a scribbled signature on a chit; the bills came in later. Jenkins bought a car – it was not done to use public transport – and joined the most appropriate club for an acceptable young man. The largest and most pompous, the Bengal Club, was for burra-sahibs – senior businessmen – only; the United Services Club was for officers in the forces. So 'I joined the Saturday Club – that acid test of acceptability – where one could play squash or tennis, swim, dance and play billiards. This was a cock-and-hen affair, much influenced by the women and originally designed by scheming mammas to keep the eligible bachelors out of the clutches of pretty Eurasian girls and away from the attractions of the red-lamp district. I would leave the office at nightfall and drive to the club to be met by Abdul with two sets of clothes in a satchel. I would change, play squash, bathe, change again into a dinner jacket and join my friends in the bar, sitting in a group of half a dozen round a little table. Each would stand a round – six small pegs apiece – then home, dinner and bed. We were, on the whole, a rather stupid lot of men . . .' Naturally, Indians could not join these clubs, and only women of the right sort were welcome as guests.

If making money was one of the main preoccupations and *raisons-d'être* of the English community in Calcutta, the other was sport, especially racing and golf. For energetic young men cooped up in offices all day, the saving grace of their routine, and the time-honoured way to work off the effects of drink and to keep reasonably fit in Calcutta's demanding climate, was to start and end the day, and spend most of the weekend, engaging in strenuous physical exercise. Those who were gifted at polo, cricket or golf were local heroes. Jenkins was a keen golfer, and was soon playing regularly at the Royal Calcutta Golf Club, the oldest golf club in India, dating from 1829 and looking, with its mock-Tudor clubhouse, very like its Surrey equivalents. He also frequented the Tollygunge, British Calcutta's favourite country club, founded in 1895 to 'promote all manner of sports', and housed in a handsome white late-eighteenth-century mansion built for an indigo planter, a few miles south of the city in huge and beautiful grounds with its fine golf-course and race-track. 'Tolly' was the place to go for brunch on Sundays after riding or an early round of golf. Women were greatly outnumbered by men and, with one or two exceptions, were spectators rather than participants in Calcutta's sporting life. However, they felt at ease by the swimming-pool or on the shady lawns of the Tollygunge Club, waiting for the men to join them for several large gins, a prawn curry lunch or a traditional tea with cucumber sandwiches.

As well as its strong sporting tradition, British Calcutta had always had a passion for theatrical entertainments, balls and dances. Here, women could shine: they might be superfluous to much of Calcutta's work or play but not on the stage or the dance-floor. Subscription dances began in Calcutta in the 1790s: as a contemporary account noted, 'Strange to say, young unmarried ladies are as scarce as old ones, and naturally more in demand; consequently a lady's dancing days last as long as she remains in India.' The Governor gave a large public dinner and ball on New Year's Day and the monarch's birthday, and military victories were celebrated by fêtes, fireworks, pageants and dancing. Theatres appeared in Calcutta from the 1780s; Shakespeare and other classics were put on, along with large numbers of comedies with titles like *Trick upon Trick, or The Venture in the Suds*, or patriotic extravaganzas like *John Bull, or An Englishman's Fireside in Five Acts*. The actors were often local amateurs, with professionals sometimes brought in from London. By the end of the nineteenth century three theatres had been established in Calcutta, including the Theatre Royal alongside the Grand Hotel on Chowringhee. Amateur dramatics remained immensely popular, although touring companies occasionally visited for a short season. Artistic standards varied; the idea was to have a good time. As Jan Morris points out: 'This was by and large a Philistine society and did not often pine for symphony concerts, exhibitions of contemporary art, or Ibsen.' And in Calcutta, even more than in London, the professional theatre had been long considered rather louche, especially for women.

Something of the elusive flavour of everyday life, the preoccupations and amusements of the British in Rumer's Calcutta can be gleaned from the crumbling files of the city's leading English-language newspaper, then and now, the *Statesman* ('with which the *Friend of India* is incorporated'), founded in 1875. In the early 1930s, its front page was still filled with advertisements, like *The Times* in London: sailing and arrival times of cargo ships and liners were listed and P. and O. were offering short trips to London and back for fifty pounds. There were columns of cars wanted or for sale or hire, sewing machines, tutors, chiropodists, pedigree elk-hounds and houses in the hills, as well as governesses, 'fair young stenographers', and 'Anglo-Indian girl as mother's help, 15 rupees and all found'. In the personal columns, cooking demonstrations, bridal gowns and children's party dresses were on offer; a lost dog: 'White chest, wearing collar, answers to Misty'. Inside, a regular column called *Dog World*, signed 'Luvmi', offered advice on 'Preparing for the Show Season'. Alongside an item alleging that a sixteen-year-old boy had been recruited to a group aiming to murder the British was the news that a pony had escaped from a circus and cantered down Park Street. There was a full page of British sporting news and copious coverage of local events: the Governor had dined as the guest of the Calcutta Cricket Club to meet the touring MCC team at the Saturday Club. A distinguished former resident had died and left instructions for his ashes to be scattered in the Bay of Bengal; London was reported to be shrouded in fog, which had caused several deaths in road accidents. Her Excellency the Governor's wife had attended a performance by Hagenbeck's Circus, which ended with the playing of 'God Save the King' and the presentation of a large bouquet. Several weddings were reported, at St Paul's, Knightsbridge, in London, as well as at St John's, Calcutta. One local bride, making no concessions to climate, wore long white gloves and a fox fur collar although it was 80° Fahrenheit and humid that day. The Viceregal Garden Party was attended by three thousand people 'including many distinguished Indian guests'; the report was illustrated by a picture of two maharajahs in top hats.

There were plenty of entertainments to choose from: *A Cuckoo in the Nest*, by Ben Travers, was on at the Royal, and a muscial called *My Weakness*, starring Lilian Harvey ('famous English star – loveliness personified') was showing at the Palace. The best restaurant in Calcutta was represented by a drawing of a stylish young couple in evening dress saying to each other, 'Let's go to Firpos!' There were dances and cabarets galore, in the Great Eastern and the Grand Hotel and in various nightclubs. The cinemas were showing a Charlie Chaplin and *I Was a Spy*, but *Henry VIII*, with Charles Laughton and Elsa Lanchester, had been banned in Bengal as too suggestive, despite the presence in the cast of Merle Oberon, 'A Calcutta girl who is making a name for herself.' Two questions stood out, the first, 'Is the Bible Fit for Children to Read?' by Julian Huxley, and the second in an advertisement for face cream, 'Is the Indian Sun ruining your complexion?'

One advertisement in particular seemed, in a mournful, silly way, to evoke better than anything else the aspirations and anxieties of a young expatriate couple. A sleek man and a neatly dressed woman in high heels and a trim dress gaze at each other over a wishbone. She says to him, 'I'll tell you my wish. I wish for a really nice English home, with refined society, an artistic suite of rooms, beautifully cooked English fare, good service, nice grounds and no more worries. And it must be well within our means.' He replies: 'Then your wish is granted, dear, because all you ask for is right here in Calcutta' – at a large new apartment block, the Ritz, in Harrington Street.

In later years Rumer always insisted that she never liked Calcutta: she found it heartless, snobbish and corrupt. Certainly neither her upbringing nor her nature made it easy for her to adapt to Calcutta ways. She was not frivolous enough: the world of books and music, which she had begun to discover in London, had little significance in Calcutta society; to be popular in Calcutta, a young woman was well advised not to take such things too seriously. It was not that Rumer could not play the Calcutta social game: she could, and did, but she was never at ease there. She, more than any of her sisters, retained the sense of being different that they had all absorbed in childhood, which was not helpful when she became part of a society that valued conformity and liked people to know their place. Rumer instinctively disliked being expected to behave in a certain way; it was not that she was a rebel, but she had her own ideas and did not find it easy to adapt to other people's. Also, having lived independently and anonymously in London, she was not prepared for how much harder it was to do so in Calcutta, where the British community all knew each other's business. And it seems to have come as something of a shock to discover that by starting a dancing school and living on her own she risked social disapproval. Her father had tried to point this out to her, and he was also sceptical about her financial prospects. It was to take some time for her school to become profitable; until then, for all his misgivings, Arthur Godden subsidized her. She always remembered his wry remark: 'It is more expensive for Rumer to earn her living than to keep her at home.'

The struggle to find her feet financially was simple compared to the more complex and insidious problem of her social standing. A less thin-skinned person might not have noticed or cared that the stuffier element in Calcutta disapproved of what she was doing; the trouble was that, in some ways, Rumer needed to be accepted. She may have been beginning to dislike and question the standards of the people around her, but she was not unconventional enough to disregard them. She wrote later in her autobiography that

In Calcutta's then almost closed society, 'nice girls' did not work or try to earn their living. There were women doctors, school inspectors, matrons of hospitals, missionaries, but they did not rank as 'society', whose girls should stay at home, perhaps do some charity work or amateur acting or painting, strictly unpaid; anything else was taboo, a taboo into which I blithely stepped . . .

Being professional and setting up in business was bad enough; but dancing teachers in particular were considered barely respectable, largely because many of the schools were run or staffed by Eurasian girls. However, Rumer's pride and tenacity made her all the more determined to succeed. At first she could not afford premises of her own; she went out to teach groups who asked for her, or rented rooms. But she also had a stroke of luck: she became a lodger in a large flat in Lower Circular Road with a young married couple, Jay and Jimmie Simon, who knew exactly what she was up against and were in a position to give her much-needed moral support.

In the early 1930s the leading dancing school in Calcutta, and the only one considered respectable, was the Aenid Ballon School, run by a young and attractive Armenian woman. There was a noticeable Armenian community in Calcutta, many of whom were prosperous businessmen, and although the more snobbish element looked down on them, they were not Eurasian. Even so, when an Englishman, Frank Hunt, working for one of the British companies, wanted to marry Aenid Ballon he was asked to resign; he did so, and then joined his wife in running the school, where Rumer remembered them giving 'superb' exhibitions of ballroom dancing. In due course Frank Hunt's sister, a dancer known as June de Vigne but whose real name was Jimmie Hunt, came out from England to join them. She and Rumer had met in Darjeeling when Rumer was first teaching there, and they had become friends. In 1930 Jimmie married Gilbert Simon, known as Jay, who was working in Calcutta for the leading firm Mackinnon Mackenzie.

He was not, however, asked to resign; his father was the leading Liberal lawyer and politician Sir John Simon, well known in India as the head of the commission set up in 1927 to consider progress towards dominion status.

Perhaps because she had not been born or brought up in India, perhaps because of her naturally ebullient, unconventional nature, and also perhaps because her marriage put her in a strong position to ignore criticism, Jimmie Simon regarded the snobberies and bigotry of Calcutta's social arbiters as absurd. Sixty years on, she described with relish how attitudes towards her changed after she married, and ascribed Rumer's difficulties to the fact that, unlike Jimmie, she had an Anglo-Indian background. 'Everyone knew who she was and she was expected to behave properly, whereas I arrived as a ballet teacher to stay with my brother. I was there as a working girl, so of course I couldn't go to the club. When I married and became respectable, and went to lunch at Government House, that was different. I'd already been to Government House, in fact, through the back door to give dancing lessons.' When they first met, Jimmie found Rumer 'great fun, gay and outgoing; she wasn't pretty, exactly, but she was very sweet and charming'; and Rumer responded to Jimmie's gaiety and impulsiveness, her 'bubbling joy in things and people', her positive, generous attitude to life. 'Jimmie did what she wanted in complete innocence of taboos and shibboleths. To her, people were people, white, brown, yellow or black, rich or poor, learned or simple, it did not matter, and she had an enormous circle of friends whom she cheerfully mixed together – her only criterion being that they should be people she liked.'

With the Simons, for the first time, Rumer met Indians of her own age as friends, in an atmosphere where there were no hidden prejudices and no forbidden topics, including the strong desire of most of them to hasten the day when the British would leave India to run itself. Among the Simons' circle were the Bonnerjees, cousins of the Majumdar and Chaudhuri families whom Rumer had met in Darjeeling. The two older Bonnerjee girls, Sheila and Minnie, were exceptionally pretty and lively-minded and their brothers, Bharat and Protab, were keenly interested in politics and how best to speed up progress towards Indian independence. Rumer took it all in, and found herself instinctively sympathetic towards their impatience with British rule; but was not herself much interested in politics nor, it seemed to Jimmie, inclined to involve herself in anything subversive. 'I was a follower of Gandhi and tried to learn as much as possible about his movement; I knew the Bonnerjee boys used to go to secret meetings they didn't want their parents to know about. They used to take refuge with us sometimes; I would leave a window open for them at night. I don't think Rumer really wanted to know about any of that. She was more conventional than I was.' Like most people from her background, Rumer was wary of open support for Indian nationalism in the 1930s. Despite Gandhi's stand against violence, there had always been a dangerously violent streak in Bengali political activists, and in the late 1920s and early 1930s a series of incidents in which British officials were attacked or murdered frightened and infuriated the whole British community. The Goddens had been friendly with one ICS official, Percival Griffiths, when he was in Dacca; he took on the job of Collector of Midnapore in East Bengal after three predecessors had been assassinated. Owain Jenkins joined a self-defence group called the Royalists after a magistrate was murdered in court in Calcutta. One incident made a lasting impression on Rumer: a young woman student fired a shot at the Governor of Bengal at a university meeting. She missed, and was put in prison. These ominous events could not be ignored, but Calcutta's social and business life was not greatly affected by them.

Professionally, Rumer and Jimmie worked together well. Jimmie was impressed with Rumer's skill at teaching small children, and when she decided she wanted to stop teaching full time, she asked Rumer to take on some of her pupils. Rumer also helped Jimmie to train older girls for musicals and cabarets; she took part herself once or twice in shows. Even on stage, racial and social divisions caused trouble: sometimes an English girl would refuse to partner an Indian, and there was often trouble when Eurasians and English girls were in the same troupe, especially when the Eurasian were the more attractive and talented. Jimmie liked to recall how a particularly dazzling girl called Queenie Thomas tried to conceal her background. 'She used to whitewash herself from the waist up, but it was no good: the other girls wouldn't have her in their class.' Queenie Thomas went on to Hollywood and became the star Merle Oberon, who for most of her life kept her Eurasian background very quiet.

Through her work, Rumer found herself getting to know Eurasian families, and the complexities and pitfalls of their position moved and intrigued her. She began to store up her observations and collect their stories. Her first regular pianist was an elderly Eurasian, a Miss Agnes de Souza, who lived in one room at the YWCA and was thrilled to be called out of impoverished retirement to play for classes. Rumer recalled 'the face powder caught in her wrinkles and ... her eyes made bigger by the stained flesh around them, stains of worry and indigestion from poor food ...' She was not a very good pianist, but she was cheap and loved the work; unfortunately her melodramatic playing, her inability to keep time and her habit of singing along to the music infuriated Rumer, whose standards were uncompromising. She never forgot the painful scene when she had to tell Miss de Souza that their arrangement was over. She could be ruthless when she had to be, and after two years or so her teaching was going well enough for her to be able to find proper premises, with a flat of her own, an assistant and better pianists.

The Peggie Godden School of Dance was set up on the ground floor of a large old house in Calcutta's best residential area on the way to Alipore. It was divided into flats upstairs, but the grand porticoed entrance led into a big hall; Rumer had barres put along the walls and benches for the children to sit on. The hard stone floor was not ideal, but her young pupils danced either in bare feet or soft ballet slippers. (Eventually she arranged to use the ballroom at the Grand Hotel or at one of the clubs, which had proper sprung wooden floors.) There was a shady verandah where mothers or ayahs could wait: she furnished it with wicker chairs, striped cotton rugs and pots of flowers. Her flat had a bedroom, sitting room and bathroom, a cook-bearer, an ayah and a sweeper shared with the other flats. She felt she was doing something daring by setting up house alone: certain people, she knew, were saying that now she was in business she should not be allowed in the Saturday Club, and others whom she had thought were her friends had started not to want to know her. On the whole, although she felt indignant, she was too busy to care. She took on an assistant who had worked with Aenid Ballon, Phyllis Bourillon, who was part French and part Indian, and her two best pianists were also of mixed race. One, Muriel, came from a typical Calcutta Eurasian family, with many children (such families were often Roman Catholics) and a formidable matriarch of a mother. The other, Monisha Sen, was a tall, gentle young woman of exceptional beauty and a rather different background: her mother was English, from a distinguished military family, while her father was a well-connected British-educated Bengali who had studied in London with the Bonnerjees and the Chaudhuris.

Monisha, who was five years younger than Rumer, worked for her when the school was at the height of its success. Later they became friends, but to begin with she was in awe of her small, determined employer: 'She was petrifying. She had a very strong character, and she was always in control of her class, although she often had a bad back. She was able somehow to demonstrate what the class should do without doing it herself. She was very particular about music; she knew exactly what she wanted and how it should be played.' Rumer realized that things were not easy for Monisha: her father had business problems and Monisha lived modestly. She was an excellent musician, often asked to play in public, and her creamy skin, grey eyes and perfect features brought her many admirers. But for all her superior social connections, the fact that she was half Indian caused trouble. Once she was invited to play in a concert at the Saturday Club; the organizers asked her if she would agree to be listed in the programme under her mother's name. 'After all, you could pass for English,' she was informed. Monisha declined. Either she would play as Monisha Sen or not at all. And it was not just British attitudes with which she had to contend: in 1937 when she married into the Chaudhuri clan, despite the long liberal tradition of the family and the several mixed marriages it already contained, some of her in-laws were not best pleased.

Before long, Rumer's school, which had started as classes for British children, had expanded to include Indians, inevitably from the more privileged families, and some Eurasians too. It was then suggested to her, by Phyllis Bourillon, that she should also run a class for older Eurasian girls wanting to train for musicals and cabarets in the theatres, hotels and nightclubs. Rumer could see no reason to refuse: she liked the girls, and she felt sorry for them. 'Many of them had the beauty of so many cross-bred girls, were sweet, loyal and touching in their eagerness to dance and make a little money. Why not? I thought. Even then, there were plenty of respectable and esteemed examples of this kind of chorus dancing; on a famous scale, the Rockettes in New York, the Bluebell Girls in Paris, but this was Calcutta.' She was soon made aware that, for part of the British community, this time she had gone too far. She received an offensive anonymous letter; she had telephone calls, 'Indian and others', suggesting that she supply girls for the evening. Gossip hinted that there could be only one explanation for what she was doing: she must have Indian blood herself. This kind of thing only stiffened Rumer's spine; she never lacked courage, but it was unpleasant.

However, life in Calcutta, for all Rumer's reservations, had its agreeable side: she was not spending all her time working and worrying. When she looked back she felt she had been wrong, perhaps, to put so much energy into her dancing school rather than her writing, and that she should have stuck to teaching children, for which she knew she had a gift. She also realized, later, how frivolous and shallow the Calcutta social round had been. Nevertheless, at the time, she had fun and broke one or two hearts. For all her conviction that she was not as pretty as her sisters, Rumer's neat figure, green eyes, high cheekbones, thick dark hair and, above all perhaps, her spirited nature, made her attractive to men. She loved pretty clothes, and in Calcutta it was not hard to have them made up cheaply. She also loved dancing. The foxtrot and the tango were the rage in Calcutta and Rumer was a perfect partner; she always remembered the thrill of a well-danced foxtrot, to a good tune like 'Stormy Weather': 'You glided . . . with not a chink of light between you and your partner . . .' It helped, of course, that single men greatly outnumbered English girls, and that Rumer was living independently, without a sharp-eyed mother or suspicious father nearby. She could do what she liked, and she did.

One of her admirers was Stuart Connolly, a young tea planter in Assam. He had first met the Goddens in Tezpur in the early 1930s, and later, in Calcutta, sought out Rumer; he soon heard the gossip about her school, and he made a point of taking her regularly to the Saturday Club and trying to show her that she had his full support. 'Calcutta was a terribly snobbish place; running a dancing school certainly wasn't the done thing. Peggie came dangerously near to being considered Eurasian herself, you know.' Stuart lived in a chummery with several friends; they used to have parties and dance on the roof in the cold weather. One of his friends had fallen in love with a Eurasian girl, which was not a sensible thing for a young man to do when his contract specifically forbade marriage. These rules, like the exclusion of Indians from the leading clubs, were beginning to seem absurd; Stuart, like Owain Jenkins, was an early member of a new club, the 300, started in the mid 1930s by

Indians and Europeans who wanted to be able to meet and enjoy themselves freely. It was run by an exotic Russian, Boris Lissanevich. 'The chef, the pianist, the violinist, the cuisine, too, were Russian,' recalled Jenkins. 'The changes from the Saturday Club, with its atmosphere of a well-lit gymnasium, could not have been more complete.'

Stuart himself was more than a little in love with Rumer, but she seemed hardly to notice. He took her once to a Christmas dance on board a destroyer moored off Outram Ghat; he remembered that he lost sight of her soon after they arrived and when the time came to go home he couldn't find her. 'I suppose she had gone off with some officer . . . I stayed on and on, waiting . . .'

Owain Jenkins remained a good friend; by this time he was living the life of a country gentleman in a large house on the edge of Calcutta at Dum Dum, with several horses and a pack of hounds, spending as much time as he could riding in steeplechases and in the Calcutta paperchase, a demanding cross-country race. When Nancy joined Rumer in Calcutta to help with the school, Jenkins admired her riding skills so much that he lent her a horse, on which she won several races. He, too, took a robust attitude to the criticism of the Peggie Godden School of Dance, which he described as 'a socially questionable activity (it being widely held that young persons who taught dancing were no better than they should be) which they [Rumer and Nancy] had no difficulty living down'.

Another of Rumer's contemporaries recalled that she went out sixty-seven nights running in Calcutta, which Rumer said was not only true but 'not uncommon . . . it was all comparatively harmless, no more than dinners in chummeries, dancing, moonlight picnics, sitting out in cars . . . Nevertheless, I soon had a reputation for being fast.' A local saying held that once a bag of Calcutta dust was placed beneath the bed of even a virtuous woman she would be virtuous no longer.

Before long, Rumer began a serious love affair with one of the more persistent of her young English admirers. He was Laurence Sinclair Foster. Three years older than Rumer, he worked for Place Siddons, a firm of stockbrokers, and he was one of British Calcutta's sporting heroes. His father was a doctor in Assam, but the Foster family was based in Worcestershire, where they had provided so many of the county's leading cricketers that it was nicknamed Fostershire. Laurence was sent home to school, at Malvern; he was not academic and his father was not rich, so rather than going on to university he came back to Calcutta to start work. Cricket, tennis and, above all, golf were his passions. He won the Royal Calcutta Golf Club centenary cup for three years running, and in 1933 the Assam Championship; by the time Rumer knew him, he was well known and well liked in Calcutta as an excellent golfer and as an amiable and amusing young man. He was small and fair-haired, not conventionally handsome but with considerable charm: 'His hazel eyes seemed always happy, as if there were no worries in the world,' Rumer recalled. To some of her friends, including Jimmie Simon, it seemed clear at the time that for all Laurence's amiability he and Rumer had little in common: he did not pretend to have much interest in books or music, he saw little point in questioning the social or political status quo in India, and his friends were mostly sports-minded businessmen like himself. Nevertheless, according to Jimmie, Rumer was infatuated with him, determined that they should be married and they became engaged. During the engagement when Rumer had to leave Calcutta for a time, Laurence became involved with someone else. 'He was terribly keen on this other girl,' Jimmie believed, 'but Rumer came back expecting to marry him; and he couldn't say he wouldn't marry her by then.' Then came another more urgent reason for them to get married: Rumer found that she was pregnant. Abortions were not impossible to arrange in Calcutta, and they discussed the possibility, but Rumer could not bear the thought. As she recalled, Laurence's attitude was not exactly romantic: 'You'll have to marry me,' he said, 'and pretend you like it.'

On 9 March 1934, Rumer was married in St Paul's Cathedral, Calcutta. The bridegroom was described in the *Statesman* as 'the well-known local sportsman' and the bride as 'Miss Margaret Rumer (Peggie) Godden, one of Calcutta's premier dancing exponents'. Rumer was given away by her father; she wore 'a gown of cream charmeuse with a train of the same material and a pale gold tulle veil. She carried a bouquet of freesias and narcissus.' Her sisters Nancy and Rose were bridesmaids, wearing lettuce green organdie with Tudor head-dresses in green and silver. The reception was held at the United Services Club, 'the sporting community, among whom Mr Foster is very popular, mustering strong'. Later, Rumer changed into a matching dress and coat in blue and white crêpe-de-Chine, and the bride and groom left for their honeymoon at Puri, on the Bay of Bengal.

CHAPTER FOUR

Marriage, Motherhood, Writing
1934–8

THE COAST OF BENGAL, now Orissa, is both beautiful and tranquil: a good place for a honeymoon. Wide beaches of cream-coloured sand stretch between groves of shady tamarisk trees and the sea; at dawn, and again in the evening, fleets of fishing boats set out from the villages dotted along the shore, and their timeless silhouettes, with triangular sails and high prows, skim the waves and break the otherwise uninterrupted view to the horizon. Puri began as a fishing village, but having been for thirty years Calcutta's Brighton, its favourite resort, by the 1930s had grown into a small seaside town, with one serious hotel, the Eastern Railway, many smaller hotels and boarding houses, and a number of villas or beach-houses run by Calcutta companies for their staff and guests. Some twenty miles away stood the Sun Temple of Konarak, a hundred feet high, built in the thirteenth century on the edge of the sea. The temple was conceived as a huge representation in stone of the sun god's chariot: seven giant horses stand before the main building, which has twelve enormous chariot wheels carved into the plinth. Konarak is one of the great monuments of eastern India, a rare surviving example of the medieval Orissan style, with links to the Tantric cults first suppressed by orthodox Hindus and then destroyed by Muslim invaders. The temple is decorated with interlocking erotic sculpture and friezes, all celebrating vitality and sexual pleasure with an unselfconscious cheerfulness that British missionaries and Victorian administrators found hard to stomach. In the nineteenth century it was crumbling and neglected, its main hall filled with sand; until comparatively recently Konarak would not have been on most visitors' itinerary. While archaeologists, art historians and scholars would have made a special journey to see it, the Anglo-Indians on holiday with their families in Puri preferred to ignore it. Today, coach-loads of tourists, Indian and European, surge around the temple all day; the broad road leading to its gates is lined with souvenir stalls, food and drink vendors and small boys selling dirty postcards. Eager guides offer to show middle-aged European women the most interesting antic: Man with man? they offer helpfully. Woman with dog? In the 1930s, no respectable English-woman would have exposed herself to such an onslaught.

Nothing is harder to recapture than the good parts of a failed marriage, or the romantic, hopeful aspects of a honeymoon proved inauspicious by what came next. In all her later references to her marriage in general and her honeymoon in particular, Rumer would stress the incompatibility she came to see as the fatal flaw in her relationship with Laurence. This she ascribed in part to her own nature being less easy-going and sociable than his, partly to his being a 'cheerful Philistine' who thought *Omar Khayyam* was a curry and fell asleep in concerts. As for Indian art and culture, she always depicted Laurence as someone for whom the Konarak temple carvings would have been not only uninteresting but obscene, so that although she would have liked to see them herself she knew it would be a mistake to go there with him. It would have been surprising, though, if either of them had been greatly interested in Hindu temple sculpture at that time. All the evidence is that, like most of her generation in India, Rumer was more concerned then to keep up with what interested her in England than with delving into the rich Indian past. Later, she regretted it; but the fact remains that in 1934 the Fosters did not visit the Konarak temple.

Rumer's honeymoon gave her the atmosphere, over fifty years later, for a novel. *Coromandel Sea Change* concerns a newly married

English couple in a beach hotel on the Bay of Bengal; the story revolves around the young wife's growing realization that she has made a mistake, that in marrying her conventional, disapproving English husband with his innate sense of superiority to India and the Indians she is denying everything creative, romantic and spiritual in her nature. She is open to the beauty and the culture that surround them; he is not. This was undoubtedly how Rumer came to see herself in relation to Laurence. At the time, no doubt, like many couples who marry because they think they have no choice, the young Fosters had mixed feelings when they found themselves alone together with their lives stretching ahead. Later Rumer found it hard to acknowledge that there had ever been any hope for them. Then, religion meant little to her; later, it came to mean a great deal. In her autobiography she called her honeymoon a travesty, implying that because she was already pregnant it was meaningless; her account of the wedding ceremony has a strong undercurrent of shame that she could ever have taken a sacrament so lightly. Rumer is hard on Laurence, and on her younger self for falling in love with him; but people who remember them together in the early days recall him as a sunny, likeable, well-intentioned character. They evidently amused and were strongly attracted to each other; once a child was on the way, it must have seemed natural that they should get married. According to Rumer, her family, especially her father, had reservations about Laurence and none of them, even Jon, knew at the time why she married him; but the capture of a charming, popular young man with many friends must have increased her confidence. After all, in Calcutta terms, it was rather a good marriage.

Back from Puri in the spring of 1934 Rumer found much that was agreeable about setting up home. She and her sisters had high standards about how a house should be furnished and run; this came partly from their mother's example and the memory of the big house at Narayanganj, and was partly, too, the legacy of having grown up in British India, where appearances, routine, and doing things properly mattered as a way of keeping English standards alive, and not allowing disorder, physical or moral, to gain ground. They were far from rich, and living as they preferred was not cheap; but Laurence had a good job with Place Siddons, and Rumer was still running the dancing school. Through one of her pupils, an elderly Parsee called Mr Mehta who had come to her for ballroom-dancing lessons, they found somewhere to live that pleased Rumer far more than a neat apartment in a modern block like the Ritz on Harrington Street. Mr Mehta offered them the bottom half of an old house in Alipore, with a large garden. For a time, all went well. 'I liked being married, having someone to think of and plan for, someone coming home in the evenings with whom to talk over the day, have a drink and dinner, someone to go out with. For a while I tasted again how beguilingly pleasant life in Calcutta could be – as long as you stayed on the surface.' They were invited out to dinner and to dance, and they entertained in their turn. Rumer liked running the house, especially as she now had her own servants; in particular she liked Laurence's devoted bearer Ears, a Lepcha from the hill tribes of Sikkim. Sometimes a new wife found her husband's manservant a trial, but Ears and Rumer appreciated each other, and he became fiercely loyal to her, too.

As Rumer remembered it, the first sign of trouble with Laurence over money came when Mr Mehta stopped coming for his dancing lessons and was unavailable on the telephone. She was worried that perhaps Laurence, whose manner with their benefactor seemed to her offhand, might have offended him. Then she discovered that the rent had not been paid. Rumer felt ashamed: her confidence in Laurence was shaken. They had 'a real scene which neither of us forgot. Goddens have poisonous tongues . . . We know exactly how to wound and how to say it and, though Laurence shrugged it off – "lots of people don't pay their rent" – it made him afraid of me . . .' The trouble was that, by all accounts, Laurence was hope-less with money. Like many of the young men in Calcutta he was used to living on credit, which was not so easy now that he had a wife and a proper home to run; also, his golf was immensely important to him and he had no intention of cutting it back. Tension grew between him and Rumer, and their friends began to notice.

Rumer's recollections of her first summer of married life in Calcutta are bleak. Not prone to self-pity – she was always anxious, tending to fear the worst and, perhaps, to overdramatize, but not to feel sorry for herself – she remembered 'the lonely unhappiness' of the last months of her pregnancy when she tried to make baby clothes in the stifling heat. The baby, a boy named David, was born in August, prematurely; he died four days later. 'I can still see that tiny grave in Calcutta's new cemetery.' Sixty years on, Rumer was kept awake at night in fear that a film crew making a documentary about her might ask her to revisit the grave. No one recorded how Laurence felt about the death of his first-born son, but the loss of the baby was a terrible reminder of the dangerous link between love and death. The whole family had been marked by the tragedy that had befallen Jon in 1930 when her fiancé, Nigel Baughan, back in India, died suddenly of septicaemia. Only when he was dying did he reveal that he and Jon had married in secret during his last leave. It was a blow from which Rumer and her whole family felt she never completely recovered.

Laurence assured Rumer that they would have another child, and within the year, she was pregnant again. This time she went back to England with Laurence, who was due some leave, and on 29 November 1935, at the Foster parents' house in Esher, their daughter Jane was born. She was delivered by Laurence's father, who had retired early from Assam after an illness and had set up a practice there. 'He had especially bought a new anaesthetic machine, which did not work, and I was fully conscious as the baby arrived. "Is it all right? Is it?" "Listen," said the nurse, and I heard a sound, at first fitful like the chattering of sparrows in a chimney . . .'

There was another milestone for Rumer in 1935: her first book was published. She had never stopped trying to write but recently the school and her marriage had taken up most of her time and energy. Nevertheless in the early 1930s she finished a book set in a tea garden beneath the Himalayas, and sent it off to a London literary agent, Curtis Brown, whose name she had learned in Dacca from another young woman with literary aspirations. The month before she married, she heard from them. Addressing her as Mr Godden, they wrote to say that although they felt the book, entitled *Gok*, needed work they would do their best to find a publisher. They did not manage to do so, and her next attempt, a book based on her childhood in Narayanganj, was no more successful. However, Rumer was nothing if not determined and the third book she submitted was bought at once and published by Peter Davies.

She always discounted *Chinese Puzzle* as if it were a false start. She called it 'a piece of whimsy *chinoiserie*'. In the late 1920s she and Jon had together produced an illustrated poem for a London magazine along similar lines; it is a tale of a Pekinese, Ting-Ling, inhabited by the spirit of a Chinese gentleman, Wong Li, who had lived in ancient China a thousand years before. For all Rumer's distaste, Peter Davies thought it 'an exquisite little book'. It was not a commercial success, but it was well reviewed, notably by G. B. Stern, the novelist, who herself had made a success with books about dogs. *Chinese Puzzle* is written with confidence and control and has a certain delicacy and wit. Moreover, the book stands as testimony to one of the passions of Rumer's life, reawakened by the present of a Pekinese puppy given to her by Jon while she was awaiting Jane's birth.

She had finished the book in Dr Foster's surgery while he was out on his rounds or during the evenings; Laurence was often away playing golf and, although the Fosters were kind, Rumer found Esher uncongenial. Her writing was an escape. She called the little dog Chini, which means sugar in Hindi, and he was, like Ting-Ling in her book, 'Black Face, Full Feathered, Cream with

Flowerings of Gold'. She wrote with him asleep in his basket at her feet. Ever since, she has preferred to write with at least one Pekinese nearby.

In December Laurence had to return to work in Calcutta; he went back alone. Long separations were commonplace at the time for couples living in India with children; air travel was prohibitively expensive, the voyage was demanding and Calcutta was still, despite modern medicine, not a healthy place for babies. It was almost a year before Rumer and Jane were back there; and although Rumer disliked the suburban dullness of Esher she could at least leave the baby in the care of her doting grandparents while she made the most of the exhibitions and ballet in London, and began to make friends with people in the arts and publishing world. Rumer was inclined to be shy, and she worried about not having the right clothes, but nevertheless she had encouraging meetings with her agents and began to feel that perhaps, after all, she might have a future as a writer. Spencer Curtis Brown took her seriously enough to introduce her to his father, the founder of the firm, but she found him rather alarming; Peter Davies, who with his brother Nico had been J. M. Barrie's protégés, she found easier, and he wrote her a perceptive letter that she kept all her life. He told her not to worry about public demand: 'Just write whatever the spirit moves you to write and forget every other consideration. I think you are one of those writers who will appeal to a section of the reading public no matter what approach you make to them.'

From the start of her writing career, Rumer needed to feel personally involved with the people professionally concerned with her work. Living in Calcutta, the London literary world was foreign territory to her; she felt at a permanent disadvantage. Also, with one exception, none of the people with whom she was emotionally linked understood what writing meant to her. The exception, of course, was Jon, on whose support she relied and whose judgement she valued and feared. Recently Jon's mind had been elsewhere: she was only now slowly recovering from her husband's death and was being courted by one of his friends, another young businessman based in Calcutta, Roland Oakley.

In the spring of 1936 Rumer's parents came back to live in England. Those who knew them realized that it would not be easy for them to settle down in the country they had left thirty years before: the plight of the retired couple back from India, unused to the climate, missing their servants, cramming their houses with unsuitable Indian objects, elephants' feet and brass, boring anyone who would listen with stories of the old days, was one of the jokes of the period – which did not make it any easier to deal with. One thing was clear: Arthur Godden could not live in a town, so they decided to look for a house in the West Country, where wild landscape, fishing and shooting could be found. They rented a house near Totnes in Devon as a base. It was from there, in October 1936, that Rumer and Jane, with Jon, set off back to Calcutta. Just as they were leaving, Chini disappeared. Rumer never forgot how stricken and guilty she felt. It is striking how often the plight of an animal, usually one of her dogs, punctuates her telling of her story; these episodes tend to coincide with a drama or a milestone in her own life. Usually the emotion aroused by the animal is expressed without restraint, while the amount of emotion she allots to herself or those around her is limited. Thus her departure for India with her baby, her own feelings, the implications of her removal from the literary scene to domesticity in Calcutta were remembered coolly; the mysterious disappearance of her little dog, ostensibly, hurt the most.

In Calcutta, there was Laurence, there was the dancing school, which Nancy had been running in her sister's absence, there was the social round, the golf and the club. Rumer Godden, the writer, was put to one side while Peggie Foster organized her domestic life. She and Laurence moved to a house in Minto Park, and Ears sent to Sikkim for his aunt to help look after Jane. Old Ayah was a strong, calm presence and both Rumer and Jane came to trust her. Laurence adored his baby daughter, so they 'seemed', as Rumer revealingly put it, a happy family, 'and to make it complete Sol and Wing came to us'. The two Pekinese, father and son, needed a home and Rumer agreed to take them. Laurence was not enthusiastic at first, but he soon became devoted especially to Wing, the older dog, no beauty but full of character. 'Laurence and I had this in common: our love of animals.'

In October, Jon married Roland Oakley in St Paul's Cathedral, Calcutta. A month later came Rose's wedding, also in the cathedral, to a rich and much older man, Clive Smith, always known simply as C.D. Laurence was a witness on both occasions, and Rose was married from the Fosters' house. Looking back, Rumer always considered that none of the grand Calcutta weddings in the family had been auspicious. The family knew that Rose had almost decided not to marry C. D., after all; the marriage was not happy and did not last long. Rumer liked Roland Oakley: he was attractive and humorous, a good dancer and interested in painting and books. However, she sensed that although Jon accepted his devotion she did not love him as she had loved Nigel.

After Christmas Rumer and Laurence went back to Puri for a holiday; one of his photograph albums contains, along with a great many pictures of himself and his friends playing golf, several pages of Puri beach scenes, young men and tousled girls in shorts, lying on the sand, walking in the waves. They look handsome and happy and very physical, squinting into the sun; the only picture of Rumer, though, is not a beach snap, and shows her looking cool and thoughtful.

The Peggie Godden School of Dance was flourishing: Nancy had run it with great success in her sister's absence. Not only was Nancy very pretty and a brilliant horsewoman, but sociable and funny, and she enjoyed Calcutta hugely. She met her future husband, a man confusingly named Dick (short for Ridgeby) Foster but unrelated to Laurence, when he came to her for ballroom-dancing lessons; in 1937 she went back to England to be married,

although she and Dick would soon return to India so that all four
sisters were married to Calcutta businessmen. Rumer had no choice
but to take on the school again. To Monisha Sen, now on the
point of marrying Hem Chaudhuri, it was plain that for all
Rumer's efficiency she was not happy either to be holding dancing
classes or in her marriage. Her mood struck Monisha as 'austere',
especially in contrast with Nancy, whom she described as 'bubbly'
– not a word ever appropriate to Rumer – and Laurence, though
he tried to please, seemed somehow unimpressive. 'He was a little
short fair man with rather a nice face, but he wasn't nearly good
enough for Rumer.' To a young Englishwoman who had recently
married Will Godden, a cousin of Rumer's father, and come out to
India, they seemed an ill-matched couple. 'He had all the come-
hither,' Betty Godden recalled, 'but he was shallow. Rumer was
full of ideas and bursting to make her mark. All the Goddens are
single-minded; what they are doing is all that matters.' What
Rumer wanted to do, and what she was struggling to do whenever
she could find time, was write another novel.

She chose a subject and a setting near at hand: *The Lady and
the Unicorn* is about a Eurasian family's troubled dealings with the
Anglo-Indian community, part ghost story, part contemporary
romance, part social commentary, set against Calcutta's romantic
past. To write it, she had to look beneath the surface of British
Calcutta. She researched the historical and architectural details in
libraries but, more important, started to explore the city by herself.
She spent hours in the old cemetery in South Park Street, opened
in 1766, where the elaborate and beautiful graves and monuments
with their poignant inscriptions evoke most powerfully the drama
and danger of those early years; she visited grand old mansions with
classic proportions and pillared porticos like Hastings House, built
as a country residence by Warren Hastings in the 1770s. She
walked around the streets and lanes of the old Eurasian quarter off
Free School Street that stretched behind the New Market where

she went to shop; not very far, physically, from where she and the British community lived and played but socially and psychologically remote.

Rumer recalled writing most of *The Lady and the Unicorn* sitting on the verandah of the school building, among the waiting pupils, mothers and ayahs. Monisha Sen first realized that her employer was also a writer when she discovered that Phyllis Bourillon was typing a book for her. Rumer could type, but from the start wrote her books by hand, in small, cramped writing, with many crossings out, corrections and drafts. Her preoccupation with the book did not bring her closer to her husband; she felt 'more of a misfit in Laurence's Calcutta than ever'. He did not really approve of her interest in the Eurasian girls: 'Why do you have to teach those half and halfs?' he would ask. She found the round of golf and drinks and dinner parties more and more difficult: 'I might have been an iceberg spreading chill around me from the way people avoided me. "Can't you just be chatty?" Laurence used to say. Somehow I could not.'

As she saw more of Calcutta, and learned more about how the people lived – especially the vital, crowded, squalid and often cruel life of the poor – the blinkers kept firmly in place by most of her own community began to infuriate her. Calcutta's British residents were inclined to ignore what was going on around them and not even to try to share or understand Indian life. Of course there were exceptions: army officers knew their men; officials out in the *mofussil*, as the countryside was called, often became knowledgeable about the people among whom they lived, and by the 1930s both the ICS and the Army were open to the 'right sort' of Indians. But the bulk of the Calcutta business community lived, worked and played in its own world, from which all but a few rich and well-educated Indians were still excluded. Rumer was not the only one to notice: British life in Calcutta seemed desperately limited in outlook to a young woman, Margaret Martyn, who arrived there for the first time in the late 1930s, not long out of Manchester

University, with her ICS husband. She was bemused by the amount of formal entertaining and leaving of cards that went on, and appalled at the level of conversation among the Englishwomen she met. Dog breeding, the complications of their own pregnancies, and their ambitions for their children were the main topics. 'I have no place in all this nor do I want to have,' she wrote in a letter home. 'The social life, which is all there is to do, is so pointless. No one ever mentions a book or anything of interest. I just wonder what they do all day. I wonder, too, how long I'll last in this sort of set-up.'

Like Rumer, Margaret Martyn longed to find something constructive to do and to get to know Indians, but it was not easy. Except among exceptionally open and sophisticated circles, like the Simons and the Bonnerjees, contact tended to be formal and limited. Margaret was disappointed when an Indian colleague of her husband's and his wife entertained them in carefully European style. Things looked up when they went to Darjeeling where before long they met the Majumdars; Margaret was bowled over by their charm and brilliance. 'Lunch with the Majumdars, the first time I've been in an Indian home like this. A lovely family. He is a high-caste Hindu and a barrister. Mrs M and her sisters were at Girton and are Christians. She speaks the most beautiful English and it's just a privilege to be there.' The Majumdars, though, were far from typical.

What Rumer minded most was that Laurence and his cronies did not see the point of trying to learn Indian ways. 'They were still in Britain,' she recalled, 'adapting their exile to as close a British pattern as they could, oblivious to everything Indian except for their servants, to whom they were benevolent and of whom they were often very fond – and for their Indian clients. Laurence was popular with his but when, once or twice, we were invited to their homes it was to meet the businessman only, never his wife or wives and children, and I felt estranged.'

By this time their difficulties were becoming clear. Lenore

Johnstone was another young Englishwoman married to a stock-broker, who worked in the same firm as Laurence Foster. Johnny Johnstone was also a keen golfer, who became secretary of the Tollygunge Club, where the Johnstones had a flat. 'Laurence Foster was my husband's great friend. They worked together, and of course he was a wonderful golfer and a great sportsman. He was very well liked; he was completely sports mad, and Peggy, as we knew her, didn't know a golf ball from a tennis ball. She knew nothing whatever about sport; no one knew why they got married, they had absolutely nothing in common.' Lenore, at over ninety, was a willowy, good-looking woman, impeccably turned out and with plenty of charm; it is not hard to see what a success she must have been at the Tollygunge Club in the 1930s, not least because she enjoyed living there and everything about the Calcutta she knew. 'I loved every minute of it. We had such fun. Have you been there? Where did you stay? The Grand Hotel – I believe it's very good now it's run by Indians. It used to be run by Armenians and it was so dirty; one of the clubs used to have their annual dinner there and it would always end with a rat-hunt through the kitchens. And the Bengal Club? I hear it's full of Indian businessmen now, like Tolly. Of course, there were no Indian members at Tolly then at all, though sometimes very grand ones would be brought as friends. Did we have Indian friends? No, not in our position. It was too difficult.'

She remembered evenings with the Fosters all too clearly. 'She was so difficult! We used to be invited to dinner with them and Johnny would ring me and say, "We're in for a bad evening." Obviously Laurence would have warned him in the office, and when we got there she would sulk and hardly speak and we had to keep on chatting and smiling and try to keep things going ... Poor thing, she had three quite pretty sisters, who really were attractive and she wasn't, and that affected her very badly.' The Johnstones knew that Peggie Foster was also Rumer Godden, some sort of writer, but they did not read her books then or later; all they knew was that she plainly did not care for golf. 'Half the time she appeared to be thinking about something else, her books or her dogs. She was mad about dogs, and so were we, so that was something we could talk about. I think those dogs saved her life; she knew how to be affectionate with them.'

It is hard to like someone whose presence is a strain. 'Over dinner, she would just sit and scowl; Laurence would entertain everybody, make everybody laugh. She had absolutely no small talk. They weren't at all happy, everyone could see that – the whole thing was hopeless from the start. Somehow she didn't fit in and she didn't try to get on with other women. I was always thankful when the evenings we spent with them were over.'

Lenore Johnstone did not know that Rumer had written a book about Eurasians, but she was well aware of their problems. 'I used to feel very sorry for them. We knew one girl, a brilliant tennis player who went to Wimbledon; she was treated as a half-caste. I thought it was awful.' But to others living in Calcutta when *The Lady and the Unicorn* came out in 1937, it appeared that Peggie Foster had compounded her social error of associating professionally with Eurasians by having the nerve to write a sympathetic book about them.

When Rumer sent Peter Davies this second book, his response was wholehearted. He wrote to her, calling it 'a little masterpiece', and announced his intention to publish it without alteration that autumn. She was paid an advance of twenty-five pounds. *The Lady and the Unicorn* is not Rumer's best constructed novel; but her descriptions of the grand old Calcutta house and garden and the people who live in it, and especially her account of the Eurasian families clinging to the fringes of respectability, are well observed and beautifully written. What comes through most clearly is her understanding of Belle and Rosa Lemarchant's difficulties and her distaste for the smug, self-indulgent British businessmen who exploit them.

The story is a romantic fantasy, but Rumer did not romanticize either the squalor surrounding the Lemarchants or the corruption of the society in which they live. She has a disillusioned Catholic priest sum it up:

> I don't know which it is that is worse to have in this country, Mr Lemarchant, boys or girls. With the sons it is one thing: they cannot get work, the Indians squeeze them out from beneath, the English from above . . . before they begin they are failures. And with the girls it is another thing, they are too successful. Yes. There is always success for these girls, so smart, so nimble, so emptyheaded . . . They get money, they get ideas, they are taken up by men – men in Calcutta society, faugh! – and then when they are in trouble they are flung back on their people.

Nor does she over-romanticze the crumbling old house, for all its ghosts and fading frescoes and jasmine-covered carved sundial. She describes the filth that surrounds it, the dirty backyard where the children played, the noise from the street, 'the endless hum and chatter of people's voices: people spitting and hawking, and blowing their noses with their fingers, laughing, crying or splashing water from the street tap . . . the smell of drains and the threat of disease, especially in the summer heat.' She gives graphic descriptions of children sick with dysentery, and the hazards of the market:

> Round the car came the beggars, old and blind, dumb and deformed, led by boys who whined and called out, 'Mummie! Mummie!' They showed scales and leprosy and running eyes, tongues cut out at the root, and withered arms, and among them a sad old lady, dressed in a muslin dress and sand shoes and a toque, sold crocheted camphor balls on strings.

Such vivid writing about the side of Calcutta that polite circles preferred to avoid was bad enough; but what made Rumer most unpopular was her account, all too clearly based on observation, of how young Englishmen behaved with Eurasian girls. She had listened to the girls at her dancing school; she had listened to the

Arthur Godden

Katherine Godden

Rumer on her mother's knee,
and Jon

Rumer (*left*) and Jon in Assam

The house at Narayanganj

The Godden sisters as young women. Clockwise, from top left:
Jon, Rumer, Nancy, Rose

Laurence Foster, *c.* 1934

Paula (*left*) and Jane Foster

Right: Ears, Laurence Foster's bearer

Below: Jane with Ears's children in Calcutta

The Himalayan snows from Darjeeling

The house at Jinglam

Dove House, Bren, Kashmir 1943

Rumer at work, Dove House

Laurence during the war

Jane and Paula in the
mountains, Kashmir 1944

Jobara, the pony man,
Sonamarg 1944

men at clubs and cocktail parties. Both the Lemarchant sisters have affairs with English businessmen; Belle knows what she is doing, and uses her relationship with her crude employer to acquire money and pretty clothes and eventually, after an abortion, a ticket to England. Rosa, who is gentler, falls in love with the more sensitive Stephen, who has only recently arrived in Calcutta and does not understand its wicked ways. His seasoned cousin William tries to warn him about the party where he meets Rosa:

> 'It's a B party,' he said.
> 'What's a B party?'
> 'A and B. B girls.'
> 'Oh, I see,' said Stephen, and began to wonder about these Eurasian girls of whom he had heard so much, who were so alluring and so dangerous. 'What happens?' he asked.
> 'Usual thing,' said William. 'They behave very well and we behave very badly, and then they behave worse.'

When Stephen finds himself thinking of marrying Rosa his friends are horrified. He would lose his job, they tell him; he would have to resign from the club. When he says he does not care, they demur: '"It's hard to live in a community and not do as they do."' As for taking Rosa back to England, how would he feel if they had a black child? Rosa might be pale-skinned, but her little sister is pretty dark . . . Stephen is disgusted.

> 'God, what a muckheap this place is. Doesn't matter what you do if you're not serious, or what filth you commit to save your face.'
> 'Calcutta code,' said William pleasantly. 'You conform or you go.'

In the end, the fragile love between Rosa and Stephen cannot survive the Calcutta code: they each marry a more appropriate mate, and the house with its secrets is pulled down to make way for a cinema.

Looking back, Rumer wrote that she had a soft spot for *The*

Lady and the Unicorn. But, discouragingly, it did not sell well, and the few reviews it received were muted. It was not until 1969 that the *Hindustan Standard* remarked: 'This is the only memorable novel in English about Calcutta.' The *Times Literary Supplement* of the day remarked on Rumer's 'fanciful mind', while praising her 'unusually well-observed and convincing picture of those people whose claim to be Europeans is not accepted by Europeans', and referring primly to their 'unenviable state, conducive to idle sluttishness'.

In Calcutta it was not only the stuffier British who disliked the book: Monisha Chaudhuri remembered being upset by the sordid picture she felt it painted of Eurasians. 'A lot of people were hurt. It was very unkind.' Read today, the book has a touching eagerness: a first attempt by a writer learning her trade. There are themes and characters in *The Lady and the Unicorn* that recur in later, more accomplished books: notably a preoccupation with time and the patterns of the past, relations between sisters, and the love of a little girl for a dog.

Although Rumer maintained her composure, and later looked back with some pride on the faint air of scandal surrounding the book, it was not easy for her at the time. She was still keeping her journal, part diary and part notebook or commonplace book, where she described her thoughts and feelings, tried out ideas for stories or novels, and copied out useful or inspiring quotations. Jon did the same, and they acquired the lifelong habit of exchanging their notes and ideas. In one of the few surviving notebooks Rumer recorded, in March 1938, her feelings about the reception of her book. She realized she had made life in Calcutta uncomfortable and difficult for herself; she was ashamed that she minded:

> Is it worth it? It isn't only lack of courage, lack of confidence, though the little pickings of people, the 'ninety days and then forgotten' advice is undermining; it's laziness and a sense of inferiority in not having friends, not being smart (yet I should hate to be smart), being isolated in a party. Now after *The Lady*

and the Unicorn I am more peculiar than ever and very coarse.
I shouldn't mind, I shouldn't mind but the continual picking,
picking is like a swarm of ants ... and I have to be continually
sitting on the ant heap.

In the pages that follow, she records Jane's doings and sayings, the
heat – in April, it was 104° Fahrenheit in the shade – the charm of
the Pekinese, Wing, lying in wait to pounce on Laurence as he
came through the door. There is no mention of what she later
admitted had been making her even more anxious than her doubts
about her writing: she was pregnant again. The baby was due in
the early autumn; but Rumer felt uncertain about her relationship
with Laurence, their finances, life in Calcutta, her future as a
writer. She had another novel in mind, and it was some time before
she could bring herself to accept that the arrival of another child
was inevitable.

CHAPTER FIVE

Black Narcissus

1938–40

B Y THE SUMMER OF 1938, Rumer was back in England again, with Jane, awaiting the birth and working on her new book. Years before, near Shillong in Assam, she had wandered away from a picnic and seen the grave of a young nun, a small cross high up in the hills; it had lodged in her mind, and started her thinking of a story about a convent set beyond Darjeeling in the Himalayas. The book began to take shape before she left Calcutta, and she continued it on the ship that brought her and Jane back to England. Laurence had stayed behind; he was to join them in the New Year. To save money, they had given up their house; he moved in with Jon and Roland as a lodger, taking the Pekes with him. This time Rumer was able to make her base with her own parents, who had bought a house in Cornwall near St Breward on the edge of Bodmin Moor. Darrynane was a sizeable house built on the side of a hill with a drive, a lodge and a large wild garden full of rhododendrons and azaleas. It was cold, and quite remote, especially in winter, but the beauty of the countryside appealed to them all, local help was available, and Rumer was especially happy not to be condemned again to Esher. She told her father she was writing a book about nuns. His response became a family joke: 'Don't,' he said. 'Nobody will read it.' She had shown an early draft to Jon, who had been critical and made her rework it. However, on 1 August 1938 she wrote in her notebook: 'Finished *Black Narcissus* and a pair of baby's socks.' She sent it off to Curtis Brown with some trepidation. 'Can't imagine what they will say.'

Most young women within a month of giving birth, a new novel just delivered to their agent, would have allowed themselves a short pause. But Rumer was determined not to let domesticity and motherhood dilute her fierce need to work on her writing, to move ahead. Her notebook is full of quotations from books or articles she admired; she was reading Gertrude Stein, whose terse rhythmical prose appealed to her, and making copies for Jon. She had come across some lines in a letter Chekhov had written to his brother Nikolai that struck her with peculiar force. In August 1938 she copied them down for the first time; she was to refer to them again and again as a spur to Jon and to herself in the next few years. 'What is needed is constant work, day and night, constant reading, study, will ... Every hour is precious for it ... you must drop your vanity, you are not a child, you will soon be thirty. It is time.'

She was constantly devising plots for stories, plays, another novel; she wanted to try a book about the ballet, and had a working title for it, *Strange Cygnet*. She decided to learn German. There is something driven, even desperate, in some of her notes to herself.

> Resolutions. For the children. The best way to help them is to help myself. For this winter, to refrain from spending my money, to learn German and to keep Laurence satisfied and happy so that he will give them the things that I can't, and fail in. For myself. To pay attention. To try and feel it less hard to be gracious. To do as I have written from Tchekov [*sic*]. particularly in notes, German, plays and plots, and to go steadily with *Strange Cygnet* and to be careful, careful, careful: not to be unbalanced again.

She was in a self-scrutinizing mood and she was not particularly pleased with what she found. 'To come home again from far away is very difficult ... This question of identity, as Gertrude Stein would say, worries me; there are pieces of mine scattered all over the world.' She looked in the mirror, and did not much like what she saw. 'Myself,' she wrote, and then described herself as if she was describing a character in a novel.

The two halves of her face were divided into two distinct people: there was her weak little chin and undecided, easily sensual mouth, over-large and over-easy. Then there was the decided nose, the deep serious eyes and clever forehead. 'It's a clever face,' most people said, but the more discriminating noticed that mouth and were never, and quite rightly, taken in. It is a clever mind but with a weather-cock silliness which she is clever enough to recognise but which she despairs of ever being able to overcome. It is not easy to be this kind of a girl.

This is a revealing passage. Rumer knew, in her early thirties, that her 'sensual' side and her 'clever' side – her body and her mind – were at odds.

On 2 September 1938, her second daughter, Paula, was born in hospital at Wadebridge, Cornwall. Rumer asked Mrs Majumdar to be a godmother, and Paula was also given one of her names, Janaki, which means firefly. From the start she was a small, delicate, demanding baby. Rumer was enchanted by her, but found her fragility worrying, especially as it meant that she could not with a clear conscience turn back to her writing. She herself was fragile after Paula's birth, exhausted, apprehensive and yet unable to sleep; she remembered this period as a time when she felt near to despair. She had to struggle with her physical and emotional troubles after Paula's birth with only limited understanding, from those around her, of how serious such a reaction can be for a mother and child. Post-natal depression had barely been recognized; it does not seem to have occurred to Rumer, then or later, that she might have needed psychological help. The Godden sisters were not much given to self-analysis or admissions of weakness: they all had considerable reserves of vitality, and Rumer soon seemed to be getting over her bad patch. However, it is tempting to ascribe some of the later vicissitudes of her relationship with her younger daughter, which was never tranquil, to the unresolved emotional conflicts of the winter of 1938.

The response to *Black Narcissus* from Spencer Curtis Brown and Peter Davies had been positive, though not especially enthusiastic; Peter Davies planned to publish it in January, and Spencer Curtis Brown was busy trying to place her work in America. She was cast down to hear that one publisher interested in *The Lady and the Unicorn* did not like *Black Narcissus*. Towards the end of October, with Paula less than two months old, Rumer wrote to Jon:

> My eyes are so sore from lack of sleep that they burn ... I've been trying to work at *Black Narcissus* [proofs] but have given it up ... When will I write again I wonder? Have had Black Narcissus on my table for three weeks and done no good to it. Of course as it's impossible to find any time for them I have endless ideas, but whether they're real ideas or a kind of delirium I don't know. My whole being cries aloud for a nurse, a nurse, a Nurse ...

In due course a trained, uniformed nurse arrived and Rumer felt huge relief: she loved her children dearly but looking after a baby was not something that came easily to her. Paula was prone to infections, unusually pale and not gaining weight; the nurse told Rumer she had never seen such a tiny baby. Rumer tried to push her anxiety to one side and concentrate on her writing: she signed on for a short-story writing course, and took out a subscription to John Lehmann's *New Writing*; both were to be shared with Jon. 'I do quite a lot of work,' she wrote. 'Have started *Strange Cygnet* as I told you and keep a diary as you do, and the Course, but it seems to take ages to do anything these days ...' She worried about her appearance, and about the miserable letters she was getting from Laurence in Calcutta, and the fact that she was always short of money; the allowance Laurence had promised her had not arrived and she disliked being dependent on her parents for everything.

When the doctor came to see Paula, he told Rumer she should pay attention to her own health.

> Dr Bailey says I have some terrific long-name nervous affection of the heart and has given me masses of drugs (dope) which are probably worth their weight in gold. It explains all these bumpings and palpitations and sleeplessness. He says I must have no mental strain or worry Ha! Ha!!! Also not to work hard. I wonder where I should have been this year if I hadn't worked hard or where we shall all be (Jane, Paula and me) if I don't continue? Talking to Laurence is rather like talking to the wind and he simply can't care how we exist. This sounds bitter but I've had another white night. It isn't the money I mind so much, it's what lies behind it.

This time she was misjudging Laurence: he had sent the money to a bank in Bodmin, which had failed to notify her. She was immensely relieved, but her underlying doubts remained. Her letters to Jon seldom refer to him except over debts, usually small sums that he was supposed to pay on her behalf, concerning the dogs, or clothes she was having made in Calcutta, or books. The sisters were punctilious in such matters.

In January 1939 *Black Narcissus* was published. At first, Rumer would recall, it seemed as if nothing had happened; then reviews started to appear and the excitement began. *Black Narcissus* was the book that made Rumer's name, that turned her at the age of thirty-one into a professional writer and brought her, for the first time, solid critical and commercial success. It has remained in print for nearly sixty years. Like Daphne du Maurier's *Rebecca*, published the year before, or Margaret Mitchell's *Gone With the Wind*, *Black Narcissus* was one of those rare novels that combine huge popular appeal with emotional subtlety and literary skill. Its success changed Rumer's life, by proving to her and to all those around her that her writing was not some minor quirk or indulgence. Her talent and determination had finally been recognized and rewarded.

As a story, it has a pleasing simplicity. A group of English nuns travel up from the Bengal plains to start a convent, school and clinic in a deserted palace in the hills north of Darjeeling. They are full of confident good intentions, although they know that a previous attempt by monks has failed; even the scepticism of the Indian owner's agent, Mr Dean, and the rumours about the palace's shady history do not deter them. But gradually, their confidence and their skills desert them, as they come up against the complexity and intractability of local tradition and belief, and their own limitations. The weaknesses and fears within them grow, as long-repressed thoughts and emotions are brought to the surface by their encounters with the cynical Mr Dean, the handsome young General Dilip Rai (whose disturbing perfume gives the book its title), the knowing old ayah and the luscious girl Kanchi. Finally after encounters with sexual obsession, madness and death they are forced to admit defeat and go back down the mountain whence they came.

At the time, the novel was mainly admired for the authenticity of its setting and its insight into character. Rumer had drawn on her love of the landscape around Darjeeling, the forests with their sudden clouds of butterflies, the cold green water in the rivers, the tangled rose-bushes and azaleas and the distant snow-covered peaks; and her account of the minds and emotions of the nuns perhaps owed something not only to her convent schooldays but to her own experience as a teacher. Certainly the cool, authoritative Sister Clodagh, always apparently in control but inwardly unsure of her own heart, has qualities in common with her creator. To Rumer, after her months of seclusion with her family and her sense that neither of her first two books had really worked, the sudden outpouring of praise for *Black Narcissus* was astonishing. 'This is a marvellous book ... a novel of the highest quality,' wrote the *Observer*. The *Daily Telegraph* praised the beauty of the writing and imagery and called it 'a remarkable and beautiful book'. The *News Chronicle* hailed her as 'A great new talent'. Hugh Walpole wrote: 'Here is a new novelist of real importance. The writing is lovely, subtle, gentle, humorous and apprehensive.'

Black Narcissus was also one of those books that have an extra layer of meaning which becomes clearer over time. When Rumer wrote it, in the late 1930s, thoughtful people living and working in India could not fail to know that the British rule there was drawing to a close. The method and the timing of withdrawal were unclear, and there were still plenty of people with their heads in the sand who hoped and assumed that nothing would ever change. Rumer, unpolitically minded though she might be, was not among them. *Black Narcissus* is, in an unpretentious, unselfconscious way, a novel about why the British had to leave India, and why much of what they had tried to do there was bound to fail. All the nuns' attempts to impose order and method, to tidy up and disinfect and change the local people's ways are doomed: they are up against forces they do not understand, both spiritual and physical, against which they are helpless. Their dedication, their selflessness, their hard work count for little; it is not their country and they are not wanted. Rumer's novel conveys this message with sadness and humour, without ever stating it directly. 'You want us to go, don't you, Ayah?' the nuns ask at the end.

> But Ayah answered, 'Yes and no.' For once she did not seem quite certain what she wanted. 'I thought I would be glad and so I am,' she said. 'I hoped you'd go and quickly too, and now I'm sorry. Yes, in a way I'm sorry. But I'll soon get over that,' she added cheerfully.

When Sister Clodagh says to her, 'You don't remember things for long here, do you?' her answer is, 'Why should we?' Then she recalls her old Indian mistress, and how her presence has somehow endured. 'You are better to me than she was, but she belongs here and you don't.' No wonder Arthur Koestler wrote that Rumer's book bore comparison with *A Passage to India*.

As she tried to take in the success of *Black Narcissus*, Rumer felt a mixture of euphoria and panic. It seemed hardly real to her until, on a short visit to London with her mother, she saw from the window of a bus a bookshop with a large banner stretched across its front window with her name on it. Back in Cornwall, she wrote as soon as she could to Jon, the person she most wanted to share her excitement, whom she knew would understand her mixed emotions, and whom she knew had helped her make *Black Narcissus* what it was.

> This letter is all blots and emotion. I'm in complete chaos inside and can't settle to anything. The thing that's uppermost in my mind is that if all this is true and I can hardly believe it is true – I owe most of it to you. When I think how far off I'd strayed and how abominably cheap and strong it was, I simply shudder. You so very firmly brought me back again. It sounds like the parable of the good shepherd, but really it was rather like that. Never let me hear such things from you as of my being better than you. I'm a better technician, of course I am, how could I help it with the start I've had, but when it comes to critical faculty and original thought I retire. *Black Narcissus* proves it and I feel it should acknowledge it but I can't think how. 'Without resort to cheap device' says The Church Times. That was you. Please let this be a lesson to you and strengthen your arm; if you can do that to another person, what ought you not to be able to do yourself?

'There is one thing though which seems clear to me,' she went on, 'and that is, if the work is to be good, of any good, it's somehow necessary to write it all wrong first.' She had almost decided to scrap all she had written so far of her ballet novel. Like most young writers with an overnight success on their hands, she was worried about what would happen next, but her joy and renewed confidence shine through the doubts:

> Whatever happens let's go on and on and on. You'll think: it's easy for her to talk – but curiously it's very difficult. I'm now filled with a Holy Terror of taking a false step, of getting dull,

of being tempted. If this is success I could almost wish it weren't. I'd like to have a steadily rising temperature, not a leap. But if it is . . . I'm going to take twice as long over every piece of work, be twice as critical and ask you to rend me. This is a vow. I have never wished so much that you were here, or needed you so much. I know how fatally stupid I can be. Probably I am making a good deal of very little, but these things are so terribly important to us.

The realization that she might be about to make some money contributed to her euphoria. She sent Jon a cheque to spend on herself, told her of the new dresses she had bought in London, and planned to refund various debts for care of the dogs after Laurence arrived; he was due at the end of the month. 'I can't believe he'll soon be here. I long to see him but bang goes my precious peace . . . My summer seems beset with problems and Fosters but I am very, very happy.'

It seems likely from this letter that happiness for Rumer had everything to do with her writing and little to do with her husband. Even so, there are enough references to letters to and from Laurence in her correspondence with her sister to prove that they kept in regular contact, and that Rumer's hopes for her marriage were still alive. Even though her tone in writing about Laurence to Jon was always slightly defensive or apologetic this does not mean that they were not sometimes happy together, or that Rumer's romantic, frivolous side did not respond to him. But she could not share her writing life with him, and, increasingly she felt she could not rely on him. Professionally she did not respect him, as the point of his profession was to make money and he never seemed to make enough, while his achievements on the golf course meant little to her. His pleasure in her success with *Black Narcissus* inevitably included, she felt, relief that she had proved that her writing could be profitable. Their reunion at the end of February 1939, as described to Jon, sounds less than ecstatic.

I met Laurence in a shed at Plymouth open to all the rain and wind of the Atlantic; he was emerald green and looked all fallen in and thin and I expect I did too, but after a good deal of sherry on very empty tummies things were all right. We had a ducal and immensely expensive night at the Palace in Torquay and I danced for the first time for nearly a year. I have some nice clothes and if it weren't for Hinchley Wood [Esher] in the near future would be very happy. Laurence is nice and says he doesn't want to leave this place [Darrynane] but I don't know how long this will endure. Jane is entranced by him and Paula was very tactful. She went into peals of laughter, a thing she's never been known to do.

The next few months were hectic. Rumer and Laurence moved between Cornwall, London and Esher, sometimes leaving the children with grandparents so that he could play golf and she could write. She was still struggling with her ballet novel and had asked the legendary dancer and ballet teacher Dame Ninette de Valois if she might attend rehearsals. Together she and Laurence lunched with Spencer Curtis Brown: Rumer still found him 'disconcerting' although he was evidently confident in her future as a writer and gave her encouraging news about the American prospects for *Black Narcissus*. In the wake of the British success Little, Brown had made a good offer and were to publish in August. There was also interest in theatrical and film rights. For all the praise, only two and a half thousand copies of the book had sold by the middle of March, and Rumer's dreams of riches were receding. She and Laurence had some depressing financial discussions: his prospects were not good enough for them to plan the kind of family establishment in Calcutta she had in mind. She contemplated going back with him in August without the children: it might make sense to leave them in England for a while. Ever since her arrival in England in 1938 the threat of war with Germany had overshadowed all plans. Like many English families, the Goddens had felt relief mixed with shame in September 1938, when Chamberlain gave in to Hitler at Munich, but by the middle of 1939 it was hardly possible any longer to hope that war might be averted. Long journeys and long separations were unnerving prospects.

In the end, Rumer decided to stay on in England with the children. When Laurence left for Calcutta at the end of July without them, she was miserable. Laurence himself, she reported, had been 'more upset than I've ever seen him' at parting from his family, and 'I feel most dreadfully bereft as he has been delightful lately. It is particularly hard as we've no idea when we shall see one another again.'

As it turned out, it was more than a year before the Fosters were reunited. During the late summer of 1939, as talk of war grew louder and more ominous, *Black Narcissus* became a publishing sensation in the United States. Little, Brown ran a publicity campaign inviting comments from famous writers: praise flowed in from Margaret Kennedy, A. A. Milne ('enchanting'), Louis Bromfield ('a moving and beautifully written book') and Alexander Woollcott, who said he had bought a dozen copies for his friends. 'An avalanche of acclaim sweeps this novel overnight into fiction's forefront!' shouted large advertisements in the press. 'The strange story of souls in jeopardy high among the Himalayas'. The reviews were excellent: 'A real discovery,' said the *New York Times*, while the *New Yorker* praised the book's 'sensitive feeling' and 'distinction of style'. The dramatic rights were sold and an adaptation for the stage was already under way; by the end of August there had been several reprints and Rumer was told that nearly seventeen thousand copies had been sold, making it the fourth highest selling book in America that week. She estimated that she had already made about seven hundred pounds, but none of it had reached her yet. Her pleasure and relief were muted by the imminence of war but, as she wrote to Jon in late August, war or no war they knew what she had to do:

There's no use in talking about the war-fear – we all know perfectly well what we're feeling. But I would like to say this to you. It – if it comes and I still blindly hope it may not come – most definitely does not mean that writing is to be abandoned. In my view it will be needed more than ever ... In the worst times, if we can manage to get through to each other, even, it will keep something alive that is vital to us and I think too vital to the world. Naturally I don't mean our work is vital to the world but that the spirit of which we have a patch is vital.

To reinforce her message, she sent Jon the complete letters of Katherine Mansfield; those written during the First World War were, she felt, especially pertinent. 'I think this is the time you should have them.'

At Darrynane, as everywhere else in Britain, the household was suddenly busy with blackout precautions and gas masks. Rumer joined in, but in her letters to Jon she applied herself more assiduously than ever to discussion of their writing plans. She had put the ballet book to one side, and begun to write a quite different novel set in Normandy, *Gypsy Gypsy*. It excited her, but she was finding it difficult, and she knew how important it was for her to follow *Black Narcissus* with a strong book. She was also writing short stories, and on her last visit to London had discussed with Curtis Brown the kind of stories that she and Jon could hope to sell. She was advised to avoid Indian subjects, especially for the American market, and to read American magazines for guidance. Jon was working on a story about an Alsatian bitch that eventually turned into a novel, and she had finished, with Rumer's help, a story about a Eurasian woman's casual cruelties, 'Miss Passanah', which Rumer thought brilliant. 'If you can do that you can do anything,' she wrote.

After war was declared on 3 September little changed at first. Rumer was worried about her parents: Mop was not well and was fretting about Nancy, whose first son, Simon, had just been born in Calcutta; her father found inactivity more unbearable than ever.

'He is quite impossible poor soul, rabid war precautions, thinks every plane is a German bomber. If only Daddy had something to do ... It's all very dark at present except the children who are a saving grace.' She was writing regularly to Laurence, who was missing them more and more. It had occurred to her, in the wake of the *Black Narcissus* success, to go to India via America, perhaps giving a talk or two to pay her and the children's way; now she had wild ideas of taking her parents too. She had almost finished a draft of *Gypsy*, feared it was no good and proposed sending it to Jon for 'a rousing criticism'. During the autumn and the strange lull of the Phoney War, she spent some time in London, working on the draft of the stage version of *Black Narcissus* that was arriving from New York; she asked Jon to send sketches of authentic Indian costumes for the designers. It did her good to escape from Darrynane, and despite the war she enjoyed herself, staying in Dolphin Square with friends. She went out to dinner several times with Spencer Curtis Brown; in the glow of her success she was beginning to relax with him and to feel that they had a special friendship. At home, Jane was just starting school but Paula's health, although improving, still worrying. Rumer had made friends with the family of Michael Cardew, the potter, who lived nearby, and wrote to Jon, 'Paula is quite the most difficult child I have ever seen and I have never seen one like her anywhere. Mrs Cardew says quite seriously that she is a changeling and I almost believe her.'

Christmas was spent quietly in Cornwall, but Rumer was in turmoil. Laurence was starting to pressure her to return to Calcutta and she could now afford to make the journey. She also longed to see Jon. On the other hand, her mother looked agonized at the prospect of losing her, the voyage might be risky, and there was a chance that she would be required in New York to help with the play. Meanwhile, her agent and publishers were eager for her new book, but she knew that it needed work and was anxiously waiting for Jon's reaction. She felt, with reason, that she was at a crossroads. Should she rejoin Laurence and put first their chance of happiness as a family? Or should she stay where she was, support her parents and pursue her career? She wrote to Jon:

> You see Laurence and can judge a little if he is miserable. It isn't only that. I feel if I am going to have any married life at all I must make up my mind to it. I am getting most peculiar and set in my ways and I must choose; if I am to be any use to Laurence I must curb this now – if I am just going to be an author and a mother I can let myself rip.

Her painful indecision continued into the early spring of 1940, and brought her close to nervous collapse. Once she cabled that she had decided to come out; then she changed her mind. There was trouble over the play, as the New York producer wanted changes she disliked, and a trip to America looked unlikely. She was still fiddling with *Gypsy*, after Jon had sent her some suggestions for making it clearer and less impassioned. She was finding the children impossibly demanding, even though she had recently hired a trained nanny for them: 'I am very very tired of them just now and wish at times I had never had them. Jane is abominably naughty and Paula abominably tiresome . . . I simply cannot sleep.' Reproachful letters from Jon and Laurence made her feel even worse: whatever she did, she realized, would involve serious regrets.

> I suppose this dreadful division is to go on for the rest of our lives, and my heart sinks and my bones are weary when I think of it. It is a fact that while I should be down on my knees saying thank you for all I have, my amazing luck, no, while I am figuratively *there*, I am at the same time unhappy indeed in the fact that the two halves of my life won't be reconciled and never will be. Apart from you, my heart sinks at the thought of Calcutta, and all it will entail; in these two years I seem to have come so very far from it and I cannot imagine how it will all work out. I only feel that in fairness I must give it a trial and make it as fair a trial as I can . . . As soon as opportunity, in the way of a boat and reasonable weather, comes I and the children will sail . . .

Once the decision was made, she felt a little better. Spencer Curtis Brown told her he liked *Gypsy, Gypsy* better than *Black Narcissus*. Rumer, though, was not convinced: 'I am disappointed with it on the whole, but feel if I think about it any more I shall be sick.' Meanwhile, she sold a story to *Harper's* magazine for two hundred dollars.

Rose, whose marriage to C. D. had ended, arrived home; she was lost and unhappy but Rumer was pleased that one of them would be in England to look after their parents. The war was coming closer: she went to Red Cross classes and lectures on Russia, now Hitler's ally. She had decided she could now afford to take a nanny out to India with her, and early in April, through a London agency, a Swiss-Italian girl in her mid-twenties, Giuliana, arrived in Cornwall. At first she seemed very foreign and bemused by the remoteness of Darrynane, and Rumer wondered if they had both made a mistake; but it soon emerged that she loved children and animals and, though eccentric, was a girl of sterling character. Rumer had found that conventional nannies did not suit her; Guiliana was an original, and she liked the way she handled the children.

Rumer spent most of May 1940 in London settling her affairs with her agent and publishers. The new novel, *Gypsy, Gypsy*, was going ahead; it was no moment, Rumer knew, to express her continuing misgivings about the book, which she felt, rightly, showed signs of strain, with its melodramatic plot and uncharacteristically intense writing. The Phoney War was coming to an end: on 10 May the Germans invaded Holland and Belgium, and Winston Churchill took over as Prime Minister. As the Germans advanced through Europe, an invasion of England began to seem likely. Nevertheless, at the end of May, Rumer, Giuliana, Jane and Paula travelled to Southampton to board the P. and O. liner *Strathallan*, bound for India.

The separation from her parents was heart-rending. 'I cannot bear, even now, to think of our parting,' wrote Rumer, fifty years on. 'We knew it was more than possible we might not see one another again.' In 1914, not long after the outbreak of the First World War, Rumer and Jon had sailed back to India. Now, in the first week of June 1940, with the fall of France imminent and Hitler's armies apparently invincible, she began the long, hazardous journey to Calcutta with two small daughters of her own.

CHAPTER SIX

Thus Far and No Further

1940–42

IN JUNE 1940, for the first time and at her own expense, Rumer travelled first class to India on the best and fastest ship available. She was on her way back round the Cape of Good Hope to Calcutta via Bombay in what should have been a glow of achievement. She had left India two years earlier, anxious about her pregnancy, worried about money, and unsure of herself as a writer. She was returning with a second daughter, good financial prospects and a literary success story to tell. But, as Rumer often said of herself, although life provided her with plenty of ointment, she has always acquired innumerable flies to go with it. As the voyage progressed her mood was far from triumphant: England was facing invasion and all the horrors of war, and apart from her fears for her family and friends she knew that her writing career was bound to be affected. Returning to India seemed like taking a step backwards and she continued to wonder whether she was doing the right thing: 'It is my choice,' she wrote in her journal, 'then it ought to feel like choice; but it doesn't.'

The journal she kept on the voyage swings between introspection and unease as the ship sailed south, the heat began to build up and the news worsened. Rumer dreaded the bulletins and could not work. She read *The Tempest* and walked by herself on the deck at night, listening to the music from the dance floor, watching the sea, the night sky and the stars. One night she brought Jane out to join her. 'She came up in her dressing gown, her face beaming, telling all the stewards on the way up: I'm going on deck to see the stars.' Together they saw the Southern Cross.

France fell on 17 June: 'This date and day will never be forgotten,' noted Rumer, but a week later she was writing, 'It is more than extraordinary in these momentous times hardly to know the day or the date. There are three fears opening one from another, spreading like ripples and they seem to be increasing. First for Paula, second shipwreck, third the war.' Although she had Giuliana to help her Rumer found the tiny, fierce child more of a handful than ever on the journey. Disruption and tension affected her badly: she screamed and threw tantrums and refused to eat. Rumer found an ally in another young Englishwoman, whose small son was troublesome. However, the ordered life of a big passenger liner continued, war or no war: there were deck games and dancing, a fancy-dress party for the children, and first-class passengers naturally changed for dinner. But there were also alarming lifeboat drills, and after Italy entered the war Rumer had to protect Giuliana from officialdom. In Mombasa, a number of Indian refugees from Kenya joined the ship; many were ill, and disease began to spread. Jane and Paula developed ominous rashes and all Rumer's worst fears for Paula revived. She spent a fortune on the ship's doctor: their doctor in Devon had told her he thought Paula still too vulnerable to make the journey safely. Finally when they reached Bombay, after seven weeks at sea, they were unable to take the train for Calcutta immediately as Rumer had planned: a medical officer saw Jane's spots, suspected smallpox, and insisted she went to hospital. Mercifully Rumer's shipboard friend had good connections and a strong character: she soon extracted Jane from hospital, took the whole family home with her and looked after them until they could travel. Nevertheless, Rumer recalled wryly, the three-day train journey in the August heat across the Indian sub-continent was not easy, and 'it could not have been an attractive or endearing family that Laurence met at Howrah but he gave us such a welcome that I thought: this has been worthwhile'.

Once again, Peggie Foster took over from Rumer Godden as she assumed the role of the young wife happily reunited with her husband, running the agreeable house and garden Jon had arranged for them in Alipore; part of her probably quite enjoyed it. She felt entitled to spend some of the money she had earned and acquired a grand piano. She also reclaimed her Pekinese from Jon. Giuliana settled into Calcutta life well, and Rumer took on more servants to help Ears, Mrs Ears and Khokil, the handsome Rajput sweeper. They also had a car and a driver. Jon and Roland Oakley lived nearby, as did Nancy and Dick with Simon. The dancing school was handed over to Phyllis Bourillon. Rumer then decided to start a small playgroup in her house, with Giuliana's help, for English children of Jane's age. The Pekineses, Wing and Sol, were joined by a new white puppy, Moon; Rumer had always wanted to raise a litter, not an easy thing to achieve with Pekes, and found a white male to mate with Moon. The result was four enchanting puppies, to the delight of Jane, Paula and Khokil, who helped care for them.

Beneath the surface, though, Rumer was fretting. Her writing, yet again, had begun to seem irrelevant when it was the one thing she longed to do. She had some stories in mind, and an idea for a novel about a child and a spaniel had been with her for some time. On 15 August she wrote a stern instruction to herself: 'To write now – the humble Spaniel, easy to do while my mind is in such misery . . .' There was an empty room in which she could work, but she hated it:

> My writing room has nothing in it but other peoples' leavings – it has no shade or peace of any kind. It has an old gas pipe which is exceedingly ugly, patched yellow walls, an old electric meter. What can I do with it? The chair will not even go up to the table, the top of the table is rotten and dirty . . . The place my writing has in this house is exactly the place writing has in people's minds, a left-out corner. I do not mind but it's impossible to work like this. This town makes me miserably bitter.

In truth, she minded deeply, and when Laurence realized how she felt he took action. First he helped her to reorganize the room; then, when she still felt unhappy, he gave her his own. 'And now Laurence has turned out of his room for me so that I can have a perfect writing room. I feel ashamed to my heart but glad to the soles of my feet,' she wrote. It was not just that she preferred the room: by moving Laurence had acknowledged that her writing mattered.

He was trying his best, it seems, to make her happy; on her thirty-third birthday in December 1940 he and the children brought her presents when she woke up: a marcasite clip, silk stockings and flowers, and early in 1941 the whole family, including Giuliana and the dogs, went on another seaside holiday. This time they chose Gopalpur on the Orissa coast, some way south of Puri. They stayed in a hotel called Yatton Hall, where guests had their own cabins on the beach, the lifeguards wore pointed wicker helmets to protect them from the surf, and a donkey wandered in and out, to the children's delight. They all swam early in the morning, after which Rumer settled down to work.

In Calcutta, it was as if the Phoney War had not yet ended. After an initial flurry of alarm and preparations life went on much as usual well into 1941. When war was declared Owain Jenkins had hurried off to present himself to the Indian Army; he had been told there was nothing for him to do yet and went back to pigsticking. Margaret Martyn's husband, P. D., had worked day and night rewriting *The War Book for Calcutta and Bengal*, so that when the time came each department and official would know what had to be done; but she was struck by how little, at first, the social round was affected. There were guards at the post office, around the docks and at other strategic spots, ARP precautions were in hand, and many lists had been compiled of volunteers for war tasks, but there seemed little to do. During the hot weather the Government removed itself to Darjeeling as usual, the cold-weather parties continued as before, the Viceroy, Lord Linlithgow, arrived from Delhi with his wife and daughters; Lady Linlithgow inspected the recently formed Women's Emergency Service, intended to build up 'an efficient corps of women who may be of use to the community ... if war or internal trouble actually threatens Calcutta'. Margaret Martyn volunteered, and turned out on parade in her navy blue uniform and solar topee. A few days later the Viceroy's Garden Party was held at Belvedere as usual. As Margaret wrote home:

> With all these Christmas festivities you'd never know there was a war going on at home involving all our families. The pomp and ceremony of Empire out here has to be seen to be believed. It is argued that everything must go on as usual to inspire confidence and to show that we're not bothered. But PD feels very strongly about all the show so we're not going to the Garden Party.

Rumer, too, felt that she should try to do something. Jon was already helping the St John's Ambulance Brigade to recruit and train nurses; now Rumer began to work part-time in an Indian hospital in the docks and in a clinic for women and babies. She found difficult her sudden exposure to the cruelty and disease she witnessed there.

> It is on a day like this that I hate Calcutta [she wrote in her notebook]. For two days I have been in the hospitals, and I am sickened and saddened. The Indian, the Bengali, seems like a tree, so promising, green budding – but tap the branches and they are rotten inside. There is vice and indifference and neglect and ignorance and graft. I have seen a hospital ayah refuse to fetch a cup of water for a dying patient because she had no pitiful money to tip her ... It is the same everywhere from cooks to kings. I have never succeeded yet in learning the right price for anything, there is no true price, there is only the calculated amount of graft. And the women creep into the dispensary with the marks of the men's usage on them ... I

have dressed a wound for a woman bitten on the forehead by
her husband as savagely as any animal.

The screams of the babies with burns and abscesses were almost
unbearable.

Rumer took to getting up very early and writing on her verandah
while it was still cool, and sometimes she would walk in the early
morning or at dusk. Gradually she became accustomed again to the
sights and sounds of Indian life, where cruelty and beauty exist side
by side.

There was a corpse laid down on a litter in the road, a man
lying with his head turned on a clean white pillow, his forehead
painted with vermilion, a garland of marigolds round his neck.
He was quite alone. His bearers had gone to have tea in a
teashop ... Today I saw a man with a bunch of tuberoses and
a lemon, and another with a basket full of dead peacocks.

Before long, she found she had settled into another novel. Later,
Rumer would draw a distinction between books that she felt had
been 'vouchsafed' to her, which came to her with a mysterious
naturalness or spontaneity, and books with which she had to
struggle, which were a conscious effort from the beginning. *Gypsy,
Gypsy* had been one of the latter, which was partly why she never
felt happy with it; the book she wrote during 1941, *Breakfast with
the Nikolides*, was definitely one of the former. The story was set in
the Bengal countryside, and revolved around an English girl, an
Indian student, a spaniel, rabies and an unhappy marriage. The
links with her own experience are strong: the Greek family of the
title derived from some childhood neighbours in Narayanganj, her
time at the agricultural college outside Dacca informs her picture
of the Indian teachers and students, and her own passion for dogs,
the ever-present fear of rabies, and the memory of the terrier shot
by her father contributed to the sad end of the spaniel, Don.
Perhaps something of her own difficulties with Paula went into her
account of the battle of wills between Emily and her mother; and

it is impossible not to relate the estrangement between Louise, the wife reluctantly returning in wartime to her husband in India, to Rumer's own marital discontent. Through Louise Rumer gives a convincing portrait of a woman whose emotional and sexual dealings with her husband go badly wrong. Louise is a woman who finds India and Indians insufferable; her maltreatment of her stubborn daughter and the spaniel, both powerless to resist, is her displaced revenge on the place and the people she detests. No doubt Rumer had come across such women in Calcutta.

By the spring of 1941, *Breakfast with the Nikolides* was finished and had been despatched to London, where Peter Davies at once accepted it. In Calcutta, the fear of war was rising along with the temperature; there was talk of Laurence being called up, and the social round was beginning to seem more futile than ever. Margaret Martyn was struck by a sermon she heard in the cathedral in June: the chaplain

> outlined the situation at home – danger, privation, self-denial, sacrifice, courage, kindness and brotherhood – compared with us here. We may have taken off the frills and fringes but our comfort has not been touched. Convention is so strong that no one dares to defy it, hence extravagant parties all under the excuse of keeping things going to impress the Indians with our confident stance. But the Indian is not impressed. He of all people understands self-denial; he venerates the sadhu.

The chaplain suggested that the British community might refuse invitations to large parties, cut down on imported luxuries like whisky, and not dress for dinner, 'as a symbol'. For Rumer, life was indeed about to become simpler and more frugal, but for other reasons.

In the late summer of 1941, Laurence Foster found himself in serious financial trouble. The details of what happened are irretrievably obscure, but the general outline is clear enough; he had been speculating with money that he did not have, and was in debt to his firm, to other brokers and to moneylenders. He had also, without asking, used money given to him by Rumer for household expenses and had raised money on their insurance policies. His plight was revealed when he was called up: he left Calcutta for military training, without telling either his colleagues or his wife of his financial position. Soon after his departure, Rumer was told that her husband had large debts, that the money would have to be found somehow and that his future with the firm was in doubt. Although money matters had always been a difficult issue between them, this news seems to have come to her as a complete shock: she felt both humiliated and betrayed. She was also acutely worried about the future for herself and the children, and very angry. By returning to Calcutta she had shown that she trusted Laurence to look after them all, and this was her reward. Shock, anger and anxiety are a powerful mixture, and the débâcle of July 1941 left Rumer with a permanent sense of shame and injustice. Although it was not quite the end of her marriage to Laurence, it marked the beginning of the end.

Her own account of the episode was written forty-five years later and with reluctance. By that time, she had – as we all do with the dramas of our lives, and as Rumer was especially inclined to do – edited and shaped the sorry tale into a dramatic story in which she and Jane saw Laurence off at the railway station and returned home to find creditors waiting for them with bills and writs. That evening, she recalled, one of the directors of Laurence's firm came to tell her the worst. She at once decided that she would pay off his debts with what remained of her *Black Narcissus* money. At the time it was perhaps not quite as quick or clear-cut as that, but she was not exaggerating much. When she related what had happened to Jon on Friday 15 August 1941, she had retreated with the children and Giuliana to a house in the hills near Darjeeling, where they had already planned to spend the hot weather.

This is a pretty bad disaster and the definite end of it for me. Since Monday I have been falling through one hole after another – and on Wednesday morning the storm broke. I don't know quite what the position is but it appears that Laurence has just walked out and left me – and PSG [Place Siddons] to clear up the mess. He even pledged the furniture to the office. He never gave me an inkling except to say he had overdrawn at the bank and would I repay it out of my dollars. It goes to several thousands without any security – to Indian brokers – and I think even our insurances are gone. I imagine he will never be reinstated at the firm, or perhaps he will if I can hold off the worst debts – I have written to Donald [one of the partners] today saying that if it's possible I feel I should keep my capital and forgo the allowance (but of course it may be so bad that they will require both) and pay off the firm with that. I want to try and get a separation – a legal one with a maintenance order for the children – if it can be done without being made public so that at any rate while he is in the Army I can get his marriage allowance. Nothing must be done publicly as it will spoil his chances and the only thing that could help us now is for him to get his commission … I still feel too stunned to take it all in and further dreadful possibilities keep opening out. I have said nothing to anybody but you and Nancy … It is impossible to try and make any arrangements until I hear the full extent of it. It is quite possible, you see, that other brokers may appear as well with other claims. It is piteous to think how I kept the list of our debts and was patting us on the back for the way in which we were paying them off. Just as he left I told Laurence that he needn't worry any more about money because I could easily pay off his overdraft – 1800 r [rupees] he told me – and he let me say it! I just can't understand. There is no possibility he could not have known it was bound to come out. There has been no letter or telegram from him.

Inevitably, stories were told over the years around the Fosters' financial troubles of August 1941. Some versions painted Laurence very black indeed: hints were dropped that he had done something criminal, that he was lucky not to have been arrested, and that he got away with it only because the war soon blotted out all else. Rumer's immediate family prefer not to discuss the matter: pride and embarrassment linger, and what little she wrote in her autobiography and said thereafter in interviews seemed to some of them too much. If there was a case for Laurence's defence it is impossible to know what it might have been; but of the few people outside the family who can still recall the episode, the comments by two women with very different points of view are enlightening. Betty Godden remembers the scandal, and how the family always felt that Laurence 'had bled Rumer dry'. She always thought him a lightweight, and she was not really surprised by this turn of events: not because he had struck her as a bad character, but because both she and her husband came to dislike the corrupt, greedy practices they found typical of Calcutta business circles. 'So many of them were bounders,' she said crisply. 'They sat around in the clubs drinking gin and thinking of ways to fleece each other and the Indians.' To Betty, apparently, Laurence was not doing anything very different from the rest; he just went too far, and got caught. To Lenore Johnstone from the Tollygunge Club, however, the fuss simply seemed exaggerated. She and her husband, who had worked in the same firm, remained Laurence's friends; she knew there had been some difficulty over money but never heard that it was especially heinous. To the suggestion that perhaps Laurence might have been crooked rather than incompetent, her reaction was unfeigned laughter. 'Of course he wasn't a crook. He just wasn't a very good stockbroker. He really wasn't good at anything much except golf.'

For the next six months the house at Jinglam near Darjeeling where they had planned to spend the summer became Rumer's refuge. It was a bungalow on a tea garden belonging to Kilburn's, the firm by which Roland Oakley, Jon's husband, was employed; although it was only twelve miles from Darjeeling, it was rural and simple and felt, to Rumer, soothingly remote from Calcutta gossip. She badly needed time and space to collect herself, and Jinglam provided both. It was a valuable interlude for her, and it led to her most openly personal book, apart from her autobiography, an edited version of the journal she kept there. *Rungli-Rungliot*, subtitled *Thus Far and No Further*, is the only book she ever wrote that is not built around a story; there is no plot, only the notes, observations and thoughts of a young woman living on a tea estate below the Himalayas with her children, her servants and her dogs. Rumer's novelist's urge to shape, dramatize and invent is almost entirely absent from this book, which is perhaps why it demonstrates so well some of her other gifts as a writer, in particular her sharp-eyed, delicate descriptive talent. Rather to her surprise, for it never seemed to her quite like a real book and did not make much critical or commercial stir, some of her admirers have always ranked it high.

Rumer kept her Jinglam journal in the small hard-covered black notebook she had used on the voyage out of the year before. She sometimes dated her entries, but what she wrote was not a sequence of her daily doings or thoughts so much as a series of short descriptive essays on what was going on around her. She placed lemon leaves between the pages; fifty-five years later they were still there, although their scent, which to her was the distilled essence of Jinglam, had long gone. When it came to be published, she added an introduction, explaining the name and setting the scene. The house was part of the Rungolo tea estate; seven miles away was Rungli-Rungliot, a small settlement around a post and telegraph office high up on a spur of the Himalayas above the gorge of the Runglee river. Rungli-Rungliot, she explained, means 'Thus Far and No Further' in Paharia, the local language. The story was that in the dim past the waters of the mighty Teesta river, which flowed across northern Bengal, began to rise. The floods were so bad that even the ridge tops where the frightened people took refuge were threatened. A lama was at prayer in one of the hilltop temples

when the people came to ask him what they should do about the
threatening water. 'Tell it to go down,' he said. When they
demurred, he went outside himself. Rumer wrote,

> I think of him as looking Chinese in a stiff robe with a Chinese
> absorbed and peaceful face. He looked at the spines of the hills
> and the water swirling round them and the jumbled colours of
> the people and their frightened faces and silent horns and
> agitated flags; he looked up at the sky and the unmoving snows
> and back at the water, and he put out his hand and said:
> 'Rungli-Rungliot. Thus far and no further.' The flood immedi-
> ately stopped; the water went down and the lama went back to
> his prayers.

The drama of the legend appealed to Rumer and it carried an
apt message for someone who felt, as she did, that their back was
against the wall. She loved Jinglam from the first moment she saw
it and her account is suffused with an almost painful appreciation
of the beauty around her. There was something of her father in
Rumer: she always needed to be able to withdraw from people and
social life to feel fully herself, and to be able to write.

The house, she wrote, was 'an island entirely surrounded by
tea'. She loved its position, on a knoll 'thousands of feet high,
above the clouds, and from the lawn it looks down over the tops of
the trees and the tea to the river. It looks up to the mountains and
away to the plains.' The house itself was a shabby whitewashed
bungalow with a red roof sweeping almost to the ground; there
were only four rooms, but they were large and high-ceilinged with
big windows and wide fireplaces, and a deep verandah. 'Inside it
smelled of wood just sawn, which is what it was patched with, and
outside it smelled of roses and lemon trees and jasmine and growing
tea.' The garden was overgrown, but there were flowerbeds full of
'unpruned roses, orchids, zinnias and wild coffee that has thick
white flowers the shape of stars'.

Rumer used the assistant's office as a study; from the window she looked past purple bougainvillaea up the side of the tea-covered hill. She kept to her Calcutta habit of getting up early to write, and as soon as the summer rains cleared she moved out on to the verandah. She had brought some furniture, lamps, rugs and favourite possessions, up from the city; like most of Anglo-India, she was accustomed to moving household goods around. The house was lit with oil-lamps bought in the Calcutta Thieves Market, and she loved the soft light they cast on her particular treasures, some deep red Bristol glass, a set of three pink Chinese porcelain bowls and a Persian hunting carpet, depicting deer, leopards and flowers in soft reds and cream and blues. She brought four Pekinese with her and gave each a basket with willow-pattern cushions. Her account of the transformation of the bungalow has an undertone of defiance: despite debts and an apparently absconding husband, she was determined to make a proper home for them all. She loved the quiet, and it was a relief to feel far away from the war; they had no wireless, and newspapers arrived days late. She bought a pony: 'I like to come home from a ride and see the rooms in order and lit with this soft light; I like the windows showing blue squares of twilight outside and I like the children and Pekinese scampering to meet me and the servants coming along the verandah, white shapes in the dusk . . .'

Most of all, she loved the landscape and the astonishing views. Around Darjeeling the countryside is steep, hilly and intricate, with many mountain streams making pools and waterfalls; there was one near the house. 'In the crevices of the waterfall we find begonias, small ones, crisp, with heavy leaves; in colour and crispness each petal is like a delicate pink shell.' She soon had the garden cleared and replanted with sweet peas, forget-me-nots and snapdragons; the flowers attracted brilliant butterflies, black and crimson and yellow and blue, some with swallowtail wings six inches across. There was a small farm below them on the hillside: 'I learn it as I should learn a lesson. I want to know these people.' She noted the pale baked earthen walls, how the corn stook on a bamboo tripod was decked with marigolds, the orange grove, banana trees and pineapple bushes, the poinsettia hedge, the piles of baskets. Inside, the walls were washed a pinkish brown and all the family lived in one room with their possessions in trunks along the walls and their bedding rolled up during the day. 'If there is a baby it will have a basket slung outside on the verandah from the roof like the lost boys' cradle in *Peter Pan*.'

Best of all, as the weather cleared for the autumn, was the presence of the high Himalayas. She would walk alone up to the ridge and look at the distant mountains and feel instantly revived. 'There is nothing, no one to interrupt. Who could there be? Only I am there and the wind and the clouds and the snows.' Mostly the peaks were white as the clouds, though sometimes the Sikkim snows turned hyacinth blue in the sun; one evening she decided to see what happened as the sun went down. 'I leave my work and the children and go up to the Viewpoint to see if the sunset will turn the snows red.' As she walked along the road with the dogs she heard the gongs ringing to call the coolies to the tea factory. A crowd of workers passed her, laughing at the strange little dogs:

> I hear them still laughing as they go away and afterwards I hear a flute. It goes further and further away until I cannot hear it any more.
>
> I am quite alone on the hill: it is cold and the shade trees have the shape of winter; they are bare, their twigs black and a pale birch silver shines on their trunks.
>
> The dogs whine to go home, but I stay. The snows do go red: first yellow, then gold, not yellow – real pink – red. I leave them red and run all the way home.

Although she had wondered if she would mind the solitude, especially at night, Rumer found she enjoyed it. Although Jinglam was not far from Darjeeling, then as now the roads were rough, winding and steep, and transport was not easy to arrange. Her nearest English neighbours were the estate manager and his wife,

Billy and Marjorie Matthews. They were kind, but she did not like to ask them for help with household or transport problems too often. Billy was the boss of all the estate workers, including some of her servants; his support lent her extra authority, which a woman on her own was assumed to need. She managed the occasional visit to Darjeeling, to shop or to take a child to the doctor – Jane had troublesome tonsils – and also to call on Mrs Majumdar and her daughter Tara at Point Clear, but on the whole she felt little need of social life. It amused her, and made her feel, perhaps, slightly superior, when people told her how brave she must be to live alone.

> 'Don't you find the evenings awful? How can you bear all these coolies? How do you get to the Club?' ask the visitors. I try to explain that I do not need to be brave; that I am not lonely; that I do not like going to the Club, and that I like my evenings working and reading in my room with the children asleep next door and the dogs asleep in their baskets; with the smell of my own sweet-peas and the smell of the sap in the logs; and outside the dome of the Jinglam sky . . .

It was not so much that she was literally alone for, after all, she had Giuliana and the children with her, she had some dozen servants in and around the place and the manager's house was not far away, but that she had chosen for the first time to live outside the accepted framework of British India. She was not exactly breaking the rules, as she had with her dancing school and her Eurasian pupils in Calcutta, but she was certainly ignoring them; and she liked the feelings of competence and autonomy she felt as a result. Rumer was increasingly determined to live where and how she pleased.

The simple rural life she was leading depended, of course, on the servants. As well as Giuliana, Ears and Mrs Ears and their three little girls, she had brought an ayah from Calcutta. Then there were the local servants, some supplied by Billy, others she had hired. Rumer listed them in her journal: Khitmagar, Water-man,

Woodcutter, Bread Runner, Mali boy, Grass-cut, Washerman, Chowkidhar (watchman) and Sweeper. 'I had fourteen but sent the syce away,' she wrote. 'Then I had thirteen, but the cook left because he had Bengal foot rot and was rude . . .' Like most British people in India, Rumer found it entirely natural to have plenty of servants; what was less usual was that she was not only fond of many of the people who worked for her but genuinely interested in them. Her diary is full of observations, shrewd, affectionate and vivid. She appreciated them. 'Mrs Ears,' she wrote, 'is an avowed fool – we all know she is a fool – but she is a fine gentle tidy sensitive fool that lends a positive sweetness to the house. She never bangs, she never flounces, she never tries to control or contradict anyone . . .' After she had dismissed the cook, with Ears's help, the other servants came to see her:

> They gave me presents after the cook was rude – whether to show how good they all were in contrast or to make up to me for the indignity and unpleasantness, I don't know. Shoomi and Dicki [Ears's little girls] carried them in, dressed in their best clothes – apricot cross-draped saris – white blouses – red pigtail ties – and hair oiled to such a glossiness I don't how the ribbons stayed on – they gave me a bowl of eggs, a whole bunch of bananas and a platter of beans, broad beans in crimson pods.

Living at Jinglam helped Rumer, her journal shows, to discover her own children, to get to know them and appreciate them in a new way. As a mother, Rumer was always loving, punctilious and proud; but she made it no secret that the chores and demands of motherhood often bored her. At Jinglam she found it hard to write anything apart from her journal, which she felt might be publishable one day; as she reflected on her situation she realized that in Calcutta she had been drifting into attitudes and patterns of behaviour that she disliked. 'Now that I have space to think I know how ugly and complicated my domestic life has been and I hope I shall never fall into that ugliness again – on any excuse.' She realized that she had been too preoccupied to notice how fast her children were growing up:

> I look at them and it seems to me that I have not seen them for a long time. I thought I knew them intimately, but they are strangers ... What have I been doing this last year? I try to think and I do not know. I have been like a squirrel in a cage going round and round without any sense or direction, seeing nothing, missing everything. I can remember nothing of anything except my own work ...

Rumer set high standards for her children, and she was pleased that they seemed to be growing up attractive and interesting. As if to mark a new stage in their lives, she decided to give them new and more original names: Jane became, for a while, Miranda or Rafael, and Paula became Sabrina. She approved of Jane's metamorphosis from a 'plump baby' to 'a slim little girl with an erect back and red-gold hair', and she was particularly pleased that as well as an aptitude for painting Jane was developing an interest in words. Like all mothers, Rumer hoped her children would be talented and beautiful, and she typed out Jane's childish stories and poems, sent copies home and to Jon, and pasted one or two into her journal. It was too early to tell where Paula's talents might lie, but she was striking to look at, with her blue eyes, pale blonde hair and black eyebrows: she was certainly not a dull child: 'Her features are strongly marked and marked by temper as well. She is either going to be hideous or beautiful.' Rumer would make up stories for her daughters: their favourite opening was, 'Once upon a time there were two little girls, one with hair like marmalade and one with hair like honey.' She felt that Jinglam brought out the best in them, and that they were all learning valuable lessons about simplicity and routine. But for all the pleasure Rumer took in her children, she knew she could not submerge herself in them. When Jane came to her one day to ask whether, for a real treat, she and

Paula could have a picnic by themselves, their mother was delighted. A little of children's conversation, she was discovering, went a long way: 'I suppose children are intended partly as a discipline. Certainly mine are often that to me. It is compulsory stimulation, compulsory taking an interest in what does not interest you. They say it broadens you; but there is a danger of being so broad that you end quite flat.'

As for her own emotional state, there are clues in both the original and the published journal. Laurence is not mentioned in either; it is clear that the writer has recently been through a crisis and in consequence is reflecting on her situation, but by nature and still more by upbringing and the standards of her day, Rumer was disinclined towards intimate revelations. There is one passage, unusual for Rumer and for the times, which shows her thinking about the position of women in general and the woman writer in particular:

> I never long to be a man as much as in my writing, because I should have a man's wholeness. To me that is what a woman can never be; I think she can never be whole, whole physically or whole hearted. If she is whole then she is useless as a woman. She must be continually impaired; by marriage, by children, by duties and ties; drained, as she is drained by her menses each month ... complete wholeness is male, a woman cannot hope to achieve it and the lack of it shows in her work ... Men have this robust easy power and they do not even know that they have it; it is an unconscious lordliness. It is no use resenting it. I do not resent it, I can only recognise it and do what is within my power. Anything else would be hideous.

For Rumer, in some moods, then, marriage and motherhood were impairments, obstacles to be overcome if she was to be the writer she longed to be.

Her letters to Jon from Jinglam show that not all her preoccupations found their way into the diary. She was, not surprisingly, greatly concerned with money: soon after she arrived, she took on a small English boy from Calcutta, complete with ayah, whose parents were happy to pay her to look after him. When he went down suddenly with suspected appendicitis, Rumer had to rush him to hospital in Darjeeling and endure several anxious days before his mother arrived from the city; the experience made her decide, as she told Jon, that she would teach dancing or write articles for *Home Chat* rather than make money out of other people's children. She decided instead to do without Giuliana, who left them reluctantly to take up another job. Meanwhile, for all her passion for Jinglam, she constantly wondered whether it was really right for the children to bring them up in such isolation. She was in correspondence about a possible film of *Black Narcissus*, was trying to write a play, and *Breakfast with the Nikolides* was to be published in England early the following year, but she still felt that her earning power had been undermined by the war and her circumstances. The possibility arose of a job attached to a mission school in Kalimpong, a town a few miles away on the border of Sikkim, where there was an established European community and where she would be given a house and free education for the children in return for some teaching. Rumer knew that in many ways it would be sensible for her to accept, but something in her rebelled. She could not bear the thought of exchanging the beauty of Jinglam and her increasingly prized independence for a tame, safe existence surrounded by missionaries, and she feared she would not be able to write there. Her letters to Jon are full of her indecision. Jon wrote back, telling her that she should do what was best for her writing, which was what she both wanted and needed to do, and what she had hoped to hear – although she was also getting plenty of advice the other way. 'It's so queer,' she wrote. 'They all think I'm mad one way – you and Roland think I'm mad the other – I just feel I'm going mad anyhow.'

Nor was she quite as protected from war and rumours of war as the journal conveyed. Darjeeling was crammed with soldiers coming and going on leave and women bringing their children out of harm's way: Calcutta's extended Phoney War was over, and Rumer's sisters were both caught up in war preparations. Then, on 7 December 1941 Japan's attack on the American fleet at Pearl Harbor brought war in the Far East and India close to the front line. Rumer felt frantic with worry about Jon and Nancy, compounded by guilt that there was so little she could do; she wrote at once offering to take Simon and any other child who needed a refuge, and laid in supplies.

Meanwhile, she was once again in touch with Laurence, who had not disappeared after all: by early December he was pressing to come to Jinglam to see her. He was evidently not prepared to admit that the marriage was over; and Rumer remained more susceptible to him than she liked to admit, even to herself and certainly to her family. In the immediate aftermath of the financial drama in August she had been adamant: 'I have left Laurence,' she had written. 'I could not afford to support him a) mentally b) financially any more.' At first she tried to discourage him from visiting them, but Laurence persisted. 'He says he must and will see me, and he is in his rights if he is to pay me an allowance.' Laurence was hoping to join the 11th Sikhs, whose colonel had apparently asked for him, and he was trying to sort out his finances. He told Rumer that on his way through Calcutta he would talk to the firm. For all her reluctance, when it then looked as if, after all, he would not be able to come, Rumer was bitterly angry. As she wrote to Jon:

It is obvious that he is going to put all this out of his mind quite happily. He wrote me a letter of upbraiding and heroics and the last cheque he sent me was returned ... I am in despair as I can see that once he gets into regimental life and is popular as he is bound to be we shall be forgotten. I suppose I must take legal action. I can feel, though, in every man who is concerned a kind of stiffening against me ... I suppose in a man's subconscious mind the kind of wife they like is the

Hindu! I am so weary of them. It is obvious that I mustn't
count on him. Anything I get from him must be a lucky
accident.

As it turned out, Laurence came to Jinglam: he travelled for
seven days to spend barely twenty-four hours with them. To some
extent, he and Rumer made up. She felt very glad, she wrote, that
he had come 'and even more glad that he is going to see the firm
and really face things'. As they would inevitably be living apart
while he was in the Army, they did not have to decide their future
then and there, although he wanted to join his family when he had
leave. A few days later she summed up her feelings to Jon: 'I told
you I was happier after I had seen Laurence and that is true, only
it does not mean that I feel I can trust him or live with him. I only
feel that one day there may be a hope of my doing that again.' He
was trying to resolve the situation with his former employers so
that she would receive an allowance from them, and told her that
as his wife she would be entitled to various Army allowances. When
he was made a captain, he said, he would be able to support them
again. Part of her wanted to forgive and believe him, and she knew
that Jane and Paula loved him dearly. 'The children clustered
round Laurence like bees round a honeypot ... and it is easy to see
how fired he is with the work. He couldn't stop thinking or talking
of it.' Rumer's reconciliation with Laurence was only partial. By
letting her down in public, so that she felt humiliated before her
family and friends and Calcutta society, he had badly damaged her
pride. Nothing he could do or say after the summer of 1941 ever
quite restored her confidence in the marriage, although she still
found his charm and affection hard to resist.

Laurence left, and Rumer and the children spent Christmas
1941 at Jinglam; her journal is full of their excitement and
preparations. Presents were ordered from Darjeeling and from
Calcutta; a tree was brought in from the forest and set up in the
house, and all the servants and their children came in to admire the

decorations and receive their gifts. There was something peculiarly satisfying, Rumer found, about the comparative frugality and quiet of their celebrations: 'This is the first Christmas I have had as I want it. The Christmases I have known have been gross with fattening and killing . . .'

As the year ended, though, she was faced with yet another difficult decision. Laurence was to be stationed at Nowshera in the Punjab and wanted Rumer and the children to live, if not with him, at least within striking distance rather than on the other side of India. The Army would pay for the move. One possibility was Kashmir, and Rumer found herself gradually drawn to the idea. As the winter settled over Jinglam, she had begun to feel that they had been alone there long enough. In the published journal, she writes as if the decision to move was imposed on her – in a way, perhaps, it was – but her letters show that it was reached jointly with Laurence. By the New Year she had made up her mind. On 2 January she wrote to Jon:

> After a great many letters and telegrams and heart searching I have ended by deciding to go to Kashmir. Quite apart from being Kashmir it seems the best solution all round. I cannot and will not go to Nowshera and live with Laurence as if nothing had happened but I am willing not to bear rancour and be near enough for him to come on leave and be in touch with us – a complete impossibility if we stay here. He is twelve hours from Srinagar and gets passes. Apart from that it is healthy and very cheap. There are schools, a very good Convent and in the season I can just remove ourselves to a lovely place. And I can keep the dogs . . .

Suddenly she was submerged in a flurry of preparation and plans. Giuliana had sent a telegram asking if she could come back, she disliked her new job, and Rumer decided to take her with them. Then there were the servants to make arrangements for, and the furniture to dispose of, and the new warm clothes they would need for Kashmir; they would only be able to stop briefly in Calcutta *en route*, as Laurence was taking a few days' leave to meet them in Rawalpindi and take them on to Srinagar. As their last few days raced by Rumer realized how much she would miss Jinglam: 'I didn't know how much I minded about it until I came to tear it all up.' But she was certain now that her journal would make a book, and looked forward to showing it to Jon.

In the back of her notebook, Rumer had made three lists: things she had started 'of which I shall not see the fruit', things she had hated and things she had loved. In the first category she included the flowers she had planted, and 'the servants' manners'. Among the hates were 'a sordid bathroom ... the age telegrams take and the waiting for letters ... the smell of the pack-pony urine ... the solitude'. Among the loves: 'The solitude ... the singing of the coolies ... the walks up Teesta and the viewpoint.' When it came to be published she added, 'The effect that Jinglam had on Rafael and Sabrina and the getting to know them better.' She also listed in the notebook everything she had written during 1941: *Breakfast with the Nikolides*, four short stories, a play about a house and a family, and 'this journal. Next year I shall write – ?'

In the first week of January 1942, Rumer, her children and her dogs left Jinglam for Calcutta on the first leg of their long journey across Northern India to Kashmir.

CHAPTER SEVEN

Kashmir

1942–4

IN THE MIDDLE OF the fierce north Indian winter, Rumer and her household – Jane, Paula, Giuliana, and three Pekinese, Wing, Candy and Moon – travelled by road and rail from Jinglam to Darjeeling, down to Calcutta for a few days, across to Lahore, then Rawalpindi and north again towards the mountains to Srinagar. Rumer was 'depressed and apprehensive'. She hated leaving Jon in beleaguered Calcutta and the journey was arduous. It was a relief to see Laurence in Rawalpindi – 'a very smart, fat Laurence' – and to have him with them on the last stage of the journey by car on icy roads into the mountains. In the valley of the Jhelum, boys ran alongside the car offering bunches of wild narcissus; as they reached Srinagar eager houseboat owners had to be pushed off the running boards. 'Kashmir is the land of touts,' wrote Rumer crossly. 'I have never met such maddeningly oily persuasive creatures.'

Nevertheless, two days later Rumer took a houseboat, the *Dongola*, moored at the Lloyds Bank ghat in the centre of Srinagar and, once again, set about making her surroundings tolerable. 'We have taken this houseboat chiefly because the terms are so reasonable – the people so nice and the boat plain and simple. Most of them are horribly babu [lower-class Indian].' Rumer could never endure living with ugly, fussy things around her. She threw out 'horns and signed photographs, and beaded lampshades and eletroplated biscuit jars' and ordered her own simple walnut furniture and curtains and cushions made in local fabrics.

Half a century later, Rumer chose to leave Laurence out of this part of her story; at the time, she acknowledged how important his support was. 'It is a dreadful business getting anything done here in winter as the population are comatose. I don't know how I could have managed without Laurence.' She needed his help with the children, too: they had both been sick repeatedly on the journey, Jane was still ailing and poor Paula 'has what appears to be a nerve storm and is very unwell'. But at the end of their first week Laurence had to leave and was 'very sad at having to go', as Rumer wrote to Jon. 'He was extraordinarily nice and helpful while he was here, and he had to stand a good deal.' Paula promptly took a turn for the worse. 'She has been, or has made herself, I don't know which, exceedingly ill. I feel dreadful and eaten with remorse every time I look at her – this is getting to be a familiar feeling with Paula.' When a doctor arrived, he could find nothing specifically wrong and then said that he thought Paula would benefit from a month in a home away from her mother. 'I admit this is an alluring idea,' wrote Rumer wryly, 'but don't feel sure about the results for Paula.' It is interesting that a doctor new to them all should have decided so quickly that Paula and Rumer might have a bad effect on each other; sometimes it seemed that the harder Rumer tried the worse the results. She found the pathos of her sickly three-year-old daughter hard to bear: 'She is better today after a bad nose bleed in the night and I hired a push chair and took her out, a pathetic bundle of skin and bone and a dirty yellow hank of hair which she will allow no one to comb and a red nose and two enormous hollow blue eyes. Poor toad, what a future she is making for herself.'

The beauty and romance she remembered from the summer visit of 1917 with her parents was hard to discern in the winter of 1942, what with the cold, her domestic problems and the machinations of the Kashmiris.

At present we none of us like Kashmir one little bit. Everyone and everything in it seems to be frozen into a kind of petrification, we are surrounded by mountains which I don't remember being so close, the tops of them hidden in driving snow or mist ... Hundreds of huge suburban houses that might have sprung from Wimbledon all around and a large red-brick convent on the opposite bank; in between a dirty grey green greasy river like the Limpopo and all along the bund little shuttered shops with notices saying they will be open on March the 1st, and down below dozens of little tonga ponies shivering in the shafts and then being whipped and cantered down these glassy roads. Every day we walk along the bund and look into all the other houseboats ... I could not live like his for long, moored alongside a main street as it were ...

The family from whom she was renting the houseboat, a father and three sons, she found endearing, if unreliable.

The two eldest are very Persian, with large noses, pink cheeks and liquid eyes. They speak beautiful English and whenever I find fault with them, which is fairly often, they make a beautiful liquid deprecatory movement with their hands towards the floor and hang their heads and say, 'What can do, Madam?' and I feel a beast. All the same I know they need a stern control and that they and all of them would cheat you out of your own skin if they could. The greatest joy in life, though, is for them to show you that someone else is cheating you.'

But already she was beginning to notice another Kashmir, with distinct possibilities.

There are glimpses which show how lovely it may be; there is a village a little farther up the opposite bank, high houses with balconies in the poplar trees, there are wild geese on a sandbank in the river, there are the women with white veils and bunches of silver earrings and dirty filthy beautifully coloured blue and purple and prune coloured clothes. All the men stride about in enormous draped shawls looking like chieftains and every man, woman and child in Kashmir looks pregnant at present as they all hold a firepot in front of their stomachs.

Neither for the first time nor the last, Rumer found herself torn between what would be sensible for herself and the children, and what she instinctively preferred. It made sense for her to stay within the Srinagar community of other families with fathers caught up in the war; and yet she could hardly bear to settle for what seemed to her a depressingly conventional way of life. She was not like the others, after all: she was a recognized writer, or had been, and would be again, whatever it took. For the moment, though, she knew she had to do what was best for Paula, and opinion among the doctors – a female German-Jewish refugee with psychiatric experience had now been called in – was that the child was both physically run down and emotionally fragile, needed to be treated for worms and then to get into a routine of spending part of each day away from her mother. 'The German doctor really seems to know what she is talking of but how sick I am of them all,' wrote Rumer wearily. 'She says it will take months before Paula is really balanced again. They are strongly advocating that she should go to a school and I feel if someone doesn't remove them both from me for a little time at least I shall go mad. I am wandering around in silly circles unable to do anything but read the news and think about Paula.'

There were two schools in Srinagar to choose from: the Garden School, run by an English headmistress, Mary Groves, and preferred by the English community, and the Convent of the Presentation, which took Indian children from good families, including the son of the Hindu Rajah of Kashmir. The Garden School, Rumer told Jon, 'has several mothers in houseboats moored alongside, all very hearty and keeping together and with large hearty children ... I think I should go mad among them. Indians are rigorously excluded ...' Luckily the doctor thought the convent might suit Paula better, and Rumer liked the nuns. 'At least it is real and the bibis, the Kashmiri girls who go there, speak beautifully and seem nice.'

She also decided to move away from the centre of the town. She found a mooring further out at the point of Gagribal lake, where they would have an unimpeded view across the water to the peach orchards and the mountains. Her plan was to spend the spring there, then avoid the crowds who would descend on the lake in summer by sub-letting her houseboat and going into camp, not at Gulmarg, Srinagar's fashionable summer resort, but at Sonamarg, the meadow of gold, higher up among the glaciers and eagles. Already, well before the arrival of the spring, the beauty of the place was seducing her. 'Gagribal is the annexe of the Dal lake,' she told Jon. 'We went across it yesterday in a shikara [a flat-bottomed boat], taking Paula; it was very beautiful, frozen still with very pale dry opal colours, and the poplar trees looking curiously bleached. The sun came out just on the small island in the middle of the lake that has one house like a temple and a few peach trees, bare now, and turned the whole of it pale gold.'

When Jane and Paula started at the convent, dressed in green kilts and cream blouses, Rumer, reluctantly, went too. She needed to earn some money, and her only saleable skill in Srinagar was as a dancing teacher. Her moving and furnishing bills seemed huge, and she now had school fees to find as well as Giuliana's wages; her writing had stalled, communicating with her agents and publishers was difficult and payments from them were slower than ever to arrive. Laurence was trying to help, but her allowance from him was very small. She agreed to teach dancing, percussion band and rhythm 'to anything between 5 and 16 who cares to learn . . . It takes six hours a week for me but to balance it I should have stretches of peace, and it is peaceful there, and I shall see no mothers except the nun Mothers.' She bought second-hand bicycles to get them all to school; Jane rode her own and Paula sat on the back of Giuliana's. Jane, as Rumer admitted to Jon, would much rather have joined the other little English girls at the Garden School, but Rumer had been adamant: she and her daughters would keep their distance from the English community. 'I went out to tea with an old lady and spent the whole time in the corner with the cat. I shall live by my lake and go to and from the Convent in unfashionable silence.'

Despite her suspicion of Kashmiris with anything to sell, Rumer made friends with one of the leading merchants of the town, a Muslim called Ghulam Rasool with a shop near the third bridge. She took Jane to one of his workshops to see how the famous Kashmiri *papier-mâché* was made; they were both entranced.

> I had no idea it could be so beautiful or was so interesting. The paints are made from stones brought from Tibet, except red which is made from poppy flowers; the gold leaf is made from English sovereigns bought at great cost from the bank, and the lacquer is made from amber melted in oil and turpentine.

Soon Jane was taking lessons from their new friend, learning how to draw the tiny, delicate, jewel-bright birds, leaves and flowers. Ghulam Rasool's hospitality was more to Rumer's taste than tea at the Residency or bridge at the club: Jane was not sure.

> She [Jane] went out to lunch with my woodcarver friend yesterday and he gave her a white shawl all embroidered in white, but she said she couldn't eat the lunch because it was Persian. I went and lunched with him on Wednesday and thought the lunch was gorgeous myself. After lunch we sat wrapped up in long white paschmina shawls and looked at his collection of jades and agates. He is an amazing person; his only son is at school in Edinburgh, and he lives in a thin house by the third bridge surrounded by the most unutterable slums and comes and drinks tea in our cookboat with our boatman. Talking of tea, while we looked at the jade, we had spiced tea, the most delicious I have ever tasted, poured out of a teapot that is hollow in the middle, the hollow being filled with live coals.

Ghulam Rasool was a clever salesman: he soon sold Rumer a small jade figure of the Chinese goddess, Kwan Yin, holding a lotus with a bird at her feet and 'a very delicate, alive, gentle, humorous profile'. The Muslim merchant was the one new acquaintance she made in those early weeks in Srinagar who really amused and interested her. She admired his great knowledge of his trade, of the local crafts and all beautiful things, and was to be tempted, often, by his instinct for what would appeal to her. Later he found his way into her writing, and some of the things she acquired from him have stayed with her all her life.

Early in March Rumer arranged to spend five days with Laurence, who was now awaiting orders in Nowshera, two hundred miles to the east. Part of her wanted to have nothing more to do with him; he had hurt her pride badly, and she had punished him by rejecting him; but sometimes it seemed as if she was punishing herself as well as him. Rumer liked and needed male attention, and since her ugly-duckling childhood had not been sure that she was attactive enough to warrant it. Then there were the children: had she the right to cut them off from their father? Laurence was determined to convince her he was a reformed character. 'He is trying so desperately hard and getting on so well and I am always afraid I shall stop the train by not being able to buoy him up any more,' she wrote sadly to Jon on the eve of her departure. 'I know you think I am a fool but he is my husband and I was never light-minded as you know. I wish to God I were.'

She spent five days in Nowshera, and was struck by how much easier life was for the officers in the neat little garrison town than for their wives and children. She found the atmosphere reminiscent of a boys' prep school. 'I felt such an alien there in thoughts and speech and everything ... Jinglam has done something to me – perhaps it was the absence of talk, and reading instead ... Do I sound horribly superior? I don't mean to be and it fills me with grief for, however hard I try and bend it, I cannot see myself existing in an atmosphere like that, or only half existing ...' It was hard for her, after all that had happened, to write warmly about Laurence to Jon, but she described how they went for quiet walks in the evenings and studied Sikh and Urdu together. 'I was surprised how well Laurence was doing with his Urdu. He did everything on God's earth to make me happy and if I was not that was my fault. I was treated like a queen.' Laurence's efforts to please touched her, but she was only half won. 'Laurence does love me so very much. I wish he didn't, but he does however he has behaved. He seems to use me as a kind of mainspring and if I break it what will happen to him? Also I have no reason now to break it and anyhow this is not the time to think of it. There is only one thing to do now, keep quiet and wait.'

Back in Srinagar, she tried to settle into a routine but she found the dancing classes wearing: she was rusty after four years. She had nearly finished typing out the Jinglam diary, although she could not think what to do with it: 'Naturally I love it but doubt if it would interest anyone else and also think it far too personal for publishing.' She was working sporadically on short stories, but a new idea for a novel eluded her: 'I long to write but nothing comes.' She urged Jon to keep writing, and suggested they should do a book of short stories together. The beginning of spring lifted her spirits:

> The willows are turning a particularly limpid green and the almond blossom is out, and the plum; the snow is left only on the top of the mountains, and flower boats come round, rather like the flower barrows at home only more beautiful because they are reflected in the water.

She began to pay regular visits to the gardens at Shalimar, Nishat or Chashmishai, taking a shikara across the lake with a picnic and writing her letters in the boat or sitting on the grass while the children played. She especially liked going out early with a breakfast picnic, before anyone else was around. Nishat, she told Jon.

> . . . is as beautiful as I remember it. Quite empty, green green turf on all the terraces, bare trees and yellow and white pansies

and narcissus in the grass – the water channels and the fountains and the thrones are old grey stone and the walls are the colour of Maréchal Niel roses. Everywhere I take my children, I see us four through them.

With the spring, they were all feeling happier, although Rumer had days when she ached all over: it was lumbago, caused, she thought, by living on a boat. The children seemed happy at school, although Rumer worried about their accents, 'Jane braown caow and Paula chi-chi.' Jane, who liked to fit in, left her mother a note one day asking if she could become 'a catherlick'; Rumer regarded this as a passing phase. But Paula was a different child, full of energy and with an odd beauty and originality that pleased her mother, who so disliked the commonplace.

Rumer's occasional attempts to join in the social life of Srinagar were not a success: 'All these women come up and live in rooms that might have come from Hinchley Wood, bare new gardens, no view at all – a nest of children and governesses. They each have a governess and their children go to school – I found myself all tea trying very hard to imagine what they did all day.' No doubt Rumer appeared prickly and standoffish; to Mollie Kaye, another young woman with ambitions to write who found herself waiting for her husband in Srinagar in 1942, she appeared unhappy and insecure. Mollie Kaye did not know Rumer as a writer then; as she recalled, they talked about Pekes. She ascribed Rumer's unhappiness to an unsuccessful marriage and her insecurity to the fact that her position in the social hierarchy was uncertain: 'Her father was a box-wallah,' was how she put it. 'We didn't care, but a lot of people did.' Mollie and her mother, Lady Kaye, were well known in Srinagar and came from a long line of distinguished soldiers; they had no such problems. Rumer did, however, make some new friends: a Bohemian Dutch pacifist couple called Hopman, who were both artists. Clara was a sculptor of some reputation, and her husband Tontyn a painter. Rumer's friendship with Ghulam

Rasool continued, although she kept telling him that she was too poor to buy from him. She was especially charmed to come upon him walking in Nishat early one morning, 'wrapped in a pearl grey shawl with a spray of lilac in his hand'. He invited her to a picnic lunch:

> Kashmiris take a picnic boat for 24 hours, complete with cook, and fill it with carpets and quilts and hookahs and teapots (which are called samowars [*sic*] – more and more they remind me of Russia here) and flowers, and go out to Shalimar or Nishat. Our shikara must look decorative, it is full of Pekinese and lilac and lily-of-the-valley ... I see familiar Calcutta faces floating round – literally, in shikaras – but speak to no one.

At the same time, she was feeling acutely anxious at the war news – the Japanese were advancing through Burma after the fall of Singapore – and more guilty than ever at being able to enjoy so much beauty while her sisters were doing their bit in Calcutta, with air-raids expected and the city beginning to fill with wounded and desperate refugees. Her letters are full of concern for them: 'The news makes one disgusted – sick – impotently miserable – raging ... It is like watching lava creeping down and engulfing your home – and people in their homes – and being powerless to avert it.'

More urgently than before she began to plan how she could provide a refuge for her sisters, for Jon's Pekinese and, above all, for Nancy's little boy, Simon. The thought of them all enduring the summer heat in Calcutta, as well as bombs and refugees, was too much: she decided that she would have to move from the houseboat to somewhere with more room. Already Srinagar was filling up, the price of everything was soaring and she was afraid that the boat owners would want to exploit the situation. Through one of the pianists who accompanied her dancing lessons at the convent she heard of a cottage that was available; she decided to sub-let the houseboat and took it.

Savitri Cottage was a small wooden chalet with an enormous pear tree in the front garden, surrounded by orchards. In the garden – big enough for tents, Rumer told Jon – was a shed which the owner promised to turn into a two-roomed annexe while they spent the summer in camp. Rumer felt she had a bargain and began to plan colours and furniture all over again. 'I shall run it with three servants,' she announced. 'Cook bearer, khitmagar, and take up my poor old shambles of a sweeper from here.' A move always made Rumer feel better.

She moved into Savitri Cottage in May 1942, which took her mind off the war news: Mandalay had just fallen to the Japanese and more streams of refugees were heading north from Burma towards Calcutta. 'It is horrible being always days behind the news and being told rumours and truths all jumbled up together – and all garbled. Sometimes the loneliness of being always alone rises up in a crisis.' The move was hard work, but she relished the peace after the houseboat, and the garden was full of birds, bulbuls and hoopoes and the occasional golden oriole. Spring was turning into summer; the chenar trees were in leaf, the cherries were in full bloom and the sky and the lake were the same blue.

> There is still snow on the mountains and hills, and just behind
> our house are a tangle of wild roses and iris and in our orchard
> I picked thyme – scarlet pimpernels – buttercups and puffballs
> ... I am very happy, on the whole – or would be if it were not
> for the news. I would give a great deal, though, for someone to
> talk to – and a great deal not to have to do the dancing. Still, I
> realise very much how lucky I am.

She planted vegetables in the garden and stocked up on stores: she was preparing for Nancy to arrive with Simon, and it looked as if Laurence would have a month's leave before being sent overseas on active service. He wanted to spend it with his family. Rumer planned to leave Nancy in charge at the cottage to enable her and Laurence to go away together on a trek. Giuliana was still with them, but both she and Rumer felt that it might be time for her to move on.

As the date of Laurence's arrival at the end of May drew near, Rumer fell into a familiar state of doubt and anxiety: not, as she wrote to Jon, a very promising state of mind.

> Naturally, till after the war we must go one step after another, and if I withdraw my support of him now it will lead to no good. My dominant thought at the moment is to avoid having a baby! and that is not the spirit to welcome my husband. I am trying to welcome him; this is just a crack of dismay opened by writing to you. Don't worry about me financially; I am cutting any reliance on him out and Kashmir is cheap . . .

She was finding it impossible to work, but under Ghulam Rasool's guidance she was starting to take an interest in carpets and was tempted to invest in them. Meanwhile, without telling Laurence, she put some savings into war loans. 'If it were any good worrying about anyone's future ours would bother me a lot. It is obvious that what has to be done must be done by me.'

Laurence duly arrived, and they lived as a family again for almost a month. He was still struggling to learn Urdu well enough to pass the examination required before he could become a captain, and Rumer tried her best to help him. 'He doesn't seem to mind our peculiar poverty-stricken ways,' she wrote, 'no drink but beer, very simple meals – no thought of joining the club – we go out a great deal but only picnics – he reads a lot and we study Urdu together. Does this sound like Laurence? It is!' She was also touched by his 'passion' for the children.

After two weeks Nancy arrived with Simon. They were 'Calcutta pale' and in need of building up, but Nancy agreed to take over the household, and Rumer and Laurence went off to the mountains together in the middle of June. 'I feel Laurence deserves this,' she wrote, a touch defensively, to Jon. 'He seems to be living for it, and has been exceedingly nice and sweet since he came. I am aching and longing for it as I haven't had a moment's pause, it seems to me, since I came up.' They planned to drive up to Sonamarg and then set off with five ponies on 'a very ordinary trek but I am not well enough to do a very strenuous one'.

They were away for a week and the trek, she wrote later, was glorious,

> like a journey into another world. I don't think, ever, I could have imagined anything as beautiful or unspoilt – everything seemed to combine together to make it flawless (except the aftermath of money and even that was reasonable). The weather, the flowers, the people, the places ... we drove up the Sind valley to Sonamarg, then trekked up the Zojela, over the Herbavan Pass, down into Am and so home to Pahalgam. I never do have my ointment without a fly, though, and this one was that I had sinus the whole time ...

As for Laurence,

> I have never known him so nice and it is hard to remind myself that I must not depend on him. He simply loved every moment of it which is something and now if he goes overseas and anything happens I shall at least know he has had this and been with the children and been happy. I feel quite dead about any feeling for him except that it is nice to be cared for and thought of and I miss him.

Like many women in wartime, Rumer had decided to suppress her fears and reservations and give and take happiness while she could.

On her return to Srinagar, the heat and flies seemed intolerable: within another week she had removed the whole household, including Giuliana, the servants and the dogs, back to Sonamarg. She had hired a good local man, Jobara, to take charge of the ponies and run the camp, and had found an ideal site between a wood and a stream where they set up four tents. There were several other camps nearby but none was too close, and they knew no one, which was what mattered to Rumer: most of the other visitors were missionaries. At first, it was idyllic. 'Sonamarg smells of firs and honey and clover and is full of flowers, wild columbine on the hills, and forget-me-nots and clover and buttercups and bee orchids on the merg and down by the river.' She felt proud of herself as the children grew rosy and sunburned; but then Jane, usually the most robust, started to show the signs of what Rumer feared was whooping cough. She was generally worried about Jane: she had decided that the convent was not, after all, right for her, and that it would be better to teach her at home by correspondence through the Parents' National Educational Union (PNEU): she dreaded the work involved and wrote disconsolately to Jon: 'I am so distrustful of myself as a parent as I seem unfailingly to do the wrong thing . . .'

Before long it was pouring with rain and all the children were ill. Then everything began go wrong. In her next letter to Jon on 9 August, Rumer announced the sudden decision to spend part of the winter with Laurence at Nowshera before he went overseas, on grounds of Paula's health. 'The climate there is lovely in winter and Paula ought not to be in the bad cold if we can help it.' Then she related a disturbing event: some animal, either a huge wild cat or a small panther, had taken Wing out of his basket in Giuliana's tent in the middle of the night. She had run out in her nightdress and frightened the creature into dropping the little dog but he was too badly bitten to live. Two nights later a pye-dog was taken, 'a horrible episode as we could hear it being dragged away and could not help. No one here has a gun and we don't know what to do. A panther has never been heard of in Sonamarg.'

Then came the third announcement. 'The other news I can hardly bear to tell you. I am having another baby. I think this news needs no comment from me except to say there is nothing to be done about it . . . and that it will be born at the end of March, should be, at least, that I have enough money saved to pay for it and that I am stronger than I used to be.' Her first thought was of the effect on her work. 'I cut out, from the *Statesman* review of a Chinese book, a saying of Mencius about the scourging of ambition. Not that I am scourged but circumstances do seem to combine to make it as difficult as possible for me to prosper. Still – if I am visited with fifty children, still I shall be a writer – somehow. I swear it.'

Her pregnancy also led her to think that perhaps she should leave Kashmir. 'It is for this reason that I feel, if Laurence goes in December I should like to come back somewhere nearer all of you. It is a bit of an ordeal to face so far away and Giuliana I think will leave me. . . . When Laurence goes I shall be better off as I get Rs 600 a month.'

Rumer's letter was oddly emotionless, but she was plainly not happy. 'As you know I dreaded it. I can only say that I came over here and took Laurence back because I thought it was right – that there should not be rancour with war and because I knew, as I know now, he may quite likely be killed. At any rate, if he is now, I know I have done what I could.' A week passed: Rumer was feeling sick, the whooping cough had moved on to Simon and Paula, who was very ill, and the papers that reached Sonamarg were full of the political crisis of August 1942. In the wake of the Japanese triumphs Gandhi had launched his Quit India campaign, and the Congress party supported him. The leadership was promptly imprisoned and anti-British demonstrations were violently suppressed. 'I have a feeling Kashmir will get even more unpleasant than most places when Gandhi gets going,' she wrote. 'The Indian news makes me sick with misery. I expect you will disagree but I cannot help feeling it is a miserable mistake, though I know I am weak because I cannot see any solution. Whippings and so on! I feel we are back about thirty years.' She was still wondering where to go and whether it might even be possible to return to Jinglam: they were planning to trek back down the Sind valley in the last week of August.

A few days later Rumer began to bleed. After it was all over, she wrote again to Jon on 26 August: 'This will be a peculiar letter I expect because I am far from strong in the head ... it is of course the best thing that could have happened in the circumstances but it has all been so fierce that at present I just feel battered.' The bleeding had begun on a Wednesday evening; next day Nancy went to seek help from a missionary doctor in camp on the other side of the valley. The doctor arrived on Thursday evening with a nurse:

> It increased all Friday and she, the lady doctor, tried to plug me but it was of no use and early Saturday morning she had to operate, in a tent with dekchies [brass bowls] as sterilizers, on a low camp bed, of course nothing but brandy to help through. I shall not forget it in a hurry. She did it marvellously and I have no ill effects except weakness particularly of the head and coldness and pins and needles. They tell me cheerfully it will be weeks before I can do anything – at the moment I don't care.

After the operation Rumer was moved from the camp into a government rest-house with Jobara's help. 'I was carried here on a camp bed exactly like a corpse in a Bengali funeral.'

Rumer's letter turned then to other things. The new idea for a book that now gripped her was a determined attempt to detach herself from anything personal and emotional, to assert even in her state of weakness and shock that she was a writer with a future, not just a vulnerable woman with two children, an unsatisfactory husband and very little idea of how to shape and control her life. It also reflected her mounting sense that her fiction was trivial and useless, that she was merely indulging herself with it while others put all their energies into the war. As a writer she needed to apply herself to something more constructive. Underneath Rumer's detachment from politics and her dislike of the conventions and repressions of British society in India was a strong sense of pride in what people like her father had achieved in India and given to India. All this lay behind her idea, but something in one of Jon's letters had sparked it off:

Your quotation from Nehru's speech gave it to me. It ran something like this: 'My quarrel with the British is that they have left India a land of poverty-stricken wrecks.' I am going to try and write a book in answer to that. Not a challenge or criticism or anything like that, but by a reporterage [*sic*] of all and every sort of work that is being done every day, on all days, by English men and women in every part and corner of India, a great part of which is government inspired. I don't mean anything moving or noble, but just ordinary everyday English work and duty, and the extremely concrete results obtained . . . I only want facts; the book will be a portrait of facts and I shall not embellish them in any way, not even by beautiful writing. It shall be true, not coloured and it shall be 'real about real people'. . . I shall have to travel and look and listen . . . I mean every work, forests, agriculture, railways, irrigation, transport, medical, educational, missionary . . . it doesn't matter my being ignorant – I shall only report. I think I shall call it John Brown and Mary Smith or something like that and every man in it will be John Brown and every woman Mary Smith . . . I think it needs doing.

Nancy added a scribbled note to the back of this letter.

Peggie would type this but she has such a bad head I won't let her correct it. She has had a very dreadful time and has been so brave – she is so weak – am most anxious to get her back where I can get good food, medicine and more help if need be. It was a very near thing and never have I spent such a day. The doctor was amazing and saved her life – operated without anything, no instruments, nothing. I never knew anyone could lose so much blood and live. All will be well now if I can get quiet and rest for her.

Rumer appeared to recover from the miscarriage with remarkable speed. She had not wanted another baby, and so she dealt with the experience with brisk dismissiveness, annoyed at how weak it had left her but declining to acknowledge any emotional aftermath.

The return journey to Srinagar was made in pouring rain, partly on ponies and partly by car, with bridges collapsing behind them. Rumer always remembered how Jobara held her carefully on his pony, while Nancy rode up and down their caravan with Simon in front of her, rain streaming down their faces. But

> in spite of all this, we have never seen anything as lovely as the Sind valley. This extraordinary rain has made a bumper harvest and it was all like a valley of milk and honey, positively flowing with goodness, crops and crops of millet and rice and wheat, green and yellow and gold, and trees literally heavy with fruit and swollen little streams everywhere and very bright green walnut trees.

It was a relief to get back to Savitri Cottage, where the garden was bright with zinnias and sunflowers and the trees laden with pears and pomegranates. Nancy went to the hospital where she was to start training as a nurse and Rumer tried to recover her strength and make plans. Laurence, whose reaction to the miscarriage is never mentioned, was redoubling his efforts to persuade Rumer to behave like other Army wives and join him, with the children, wherever he happened to be. She was briefly tempted to go to him in Murree, where he had been given a job at headquarters and more pay, but after a brief visit she knew she could not face it. She described it to Jon as 'like Darjeeling only very much more sordid, a tin shanty town ... Laurence is very much in with it all and I find myself an alien in every way. I simply cannot do with the clique club existence and can see they think me a horrible prig.'

She tried to escape from her emotional impasse into her work. With the Jinglam diary almost ready, she decided that she must arrange for the illustrations she felt it needed. If Jon was unable, or unwilling, to undertake them, she felt sure that her Dutch friend Tontyn Hopman would be the answer. She asked Jon, who was about to go up to Jinglam herself to escape the heat, if she would send some photographs for him to work from, as he had never been to the Darjeeling area: she wanted landscapes, people, prayer wheels, 'coolie women with baskets plucking' and finally 'Could you send me a spray of tea? With flowers if possible . . .' She knew it was a lot to ask: her original plan had been to ask Mrs Majumdar's help but with the political situation so tense she was hesitant. Sometimes, indeed, the whole project seemed pointless: 'Now that Mr Hopman is all agog to illustrate the Jinglam notes, I have a disgust with them. They seem to me so flowery and feminine and trivial . . . perhaps I am so discouraged because I have been reading *New Writing* in Europe. It is the command of words of these men that leaves me dismayed . . .'

While she was worrying about her work she suddenly received a telegram with news from New York that astounded her and underlined the yawning gap between her literary success in 1939 and her present situation. The play based on *Black Narcissus* was to open there with Cornelia Otis Skinner as Sister Clodagh. 'I had no inkling of this at all,' she told Jon. 'Anyway, unless a calamity happens at the last moment I shall have been on the stage even if it is only for one night.' In the event, it was not for much longer.

The trees were beginning to change colour, and golden, red and amber leaves were reflected in the lake. Every morning Mr Honey, the fruit man, called at the cottage with huge pears, peaches, yellow plums and grapes, laid on chenar leaves in a flat basket. Rumer began to dread leaving Kashmir. There, she ran her own life in beautiful surroundings with one or two congenial friends and the chance to do her own work. She felt panic-stricken and rebellious at the idea of joining Laurence. She wrote to Jon:

> What can't be cured must be endured but it is <u>hateful</u> Quite apart from the problem of Laurence, to live in a hut with another forty yards in front and one forty yards each side, with no garden or separation and I expect each hut filled with females and children and wirelesses and dogs that will eat Candy. . . . No, Laurence did not pass his Urdu exam; I expect I am a fool to go on hoping he will ever do anything but for

Rumer Godden

the sake of the chidlren etc I must try again and there is no doubt that he is unhappy now, though whether to the same extent as I shall be with him, I can't say.

In the middle of October Rumer took what was supposed to be the first step and moved them all out of Savitri Cottage and back into a houseboat. A few days later, she made a decision: she would not join Laurence. Instead, she would start negotiating for a divorce. She wrote first to Nancy, who had not long returned to Calcutta leaving Simon in Rumer's care.

I have simply just not been able to make myself return to Laurence. As you know I had steeled myself to it . . . but now it comes to going back to live I can't. I feel desperately sorry for him – and incidentally for myself as there is going to be plenty of hardship and loneliness for me, but I can't go on tearing myself into tatters over this and we must both try and start again . . . It is all a horrible miserable situation and if it can be ended I shall be more glad than I can say . . .'

She wanted to leave the children with Giuliana and make a quick trip to Calcutta to start research for her India book; then, she thought, she would return to Srinagar, find another small house and perhaps start a nursery school. Meanwhile there was nothing to do but await Laurence's response to her decision and gather her strength. 'I am in old grey pieces.'

Ten days later she wrote again to Jon.

Tomorrow I am sending you a telegram telling you that I am divorcing Laurence – or vice versa; it doesn't matter which – and that I am staying in Kashmir. I have been for some reason quite unable to write to you while all this was going on – I don't know why – the unhappiness it stirred up was intense and I think perhaps I suffered for Laurence quite unnecessarily. (I have always been adept at being a fool.) After not answering at all he has answered today . . . He has given in about the children at once now that I have offered to free him from any

further financial responsibility – I could not have believed he
would do that – and even though I want him to it is a stab. In
the same letter he asks for his gold cigarette case! This must put
him in a terrible light and I confess it has startled me ... in
spite of everything he has done I shall miss him – he had very
nice ways as a husband and now that I have got so old and
unattractive there isn't likely to be anyone else. I know it is
right, Murree showed me that I couldn't have stood it – it is
just that I feel so unspeakably grieved – and a little afraid of
the starkness of being quite alone and solely responsible for the
two infants – I have borne that responsibility for years and far
more, but I suppose there was always a hope that one day
Laurence would turn round and help – perhaps he will now he
is free and has nothing to worry him.

She would look for another house, move Jane to the Garden
School and try to get some teaching there to help with the fees.
She also planned to give private dancing lessons 'and the rest of the
time write and write and write ... Don't worry about me. After
this has worn off I shall probably be better than for years – I have
enough money for now ... I hope to live on Rs 350 a month. I
think here I can.'

For all her brave words, as 1942 drew to a close Rumer was
uncertain and adrift. No sooner had she taken a firm stand than
doubts and uncertainties recurred: her letters cover the same ground
over and over again. It was soon clear that Laurence had not, after
all, accepted her decision. He was fighting back hard, writing her
'heart-rending letters – but they don't ring true at all'.

Before long she was finding that the classes she had started
giving at the Garden School were wearing her out, and she knew
she must leave the houseboat before the winter set in. When the
chance came to move into rooms attached to the Anglican mission
of St Faith's, she took it as a temporary solution. At least she was
still able to make regular visits to Nishat, where she found peace
and inspiration: with the leaves turning on the chenars and the late

roses in bloom it was as lovely as ever, and she would make tea on
a spirit stove and gaze across the lake. She began to wonder if it
might be possible for them all to find a house nearby. She knew it
would be more sensible to live in Srinagar, but once again she
could not bring herself to do the sensible thing. She missed the
lonely beauty of Jinglam, the independence and the sense of herself she had glimpsed there, and longed to find something like it
again. From Nishat she wrote to Jon,

> The great temptation is to come and live out here. It is
> surrounded by lovely Kashmir cottages with wooden lattices
> and cherry treees built under a huge chenar and no one for
> miles. I could send the children as boarders and write. What a
> pity I am not old enough or famous enough for the Govern-
> ment or the Authors' Fund to give me a pension. When I am
> old enough to have one, Nishat will be built over with weekend
> bungalows and petrol stations ... I wish I didn't yearn after
> things so – all the other women here seem content to live in
> hovels of bedsitting rooms surrounded by baby biscuits and
> napkins and other people's wirelesses. I just <u>won't</u>.

This time, Rumer Godden was not prepared to give in to Peggie
Foster, even though it sometimes felt like a losing battle.

> I keep praying for an answer to come from New York and
> rescue me ... but expect when it does it will be to say *Black
> Narcissus* was a flop and that *Nikolides* was too and that Story
> Magazine sits on its Mss and hatches them for a year before
> publication. I have sold my Kwan Yin (bitterness) and the
> piano which is a relief, also my bicycle.

Then, one day, she found the house. It was not far from Nishat,
in a grove of fruit trees half-way up the mountain above the village
of Bren, twelve miles round the lake from Srinagar. It was barely
finished and very basic, but Rumer loved the fretworked gables, the
solitary position, the views across the lake, and was agreeably
surprised by the rent. The owner and landlord was a young

Muslim. She wrote excitedly to Jon: 'I am sitting down and thinking seriously. The loneliness would not worry me at night, I do not think, though in a way it is more frightening than Jinglam. There I had Ears and a strong Billy not far off and a telephone. But I would love it. And might keep a faithful chowkidar if such is to be got.' As always nothing lifted Rumer's spirits more than the prospect of making a fresh start on the perfect place to live and work. A free hand to rebuild and replan her life always seemed to her exhilarating and positive, no matter what the cost in time, money and energy. Living at St Faith's had become oppressive, kind though the missionaries were: their rooms looked over a graveyard and, as she told Jon, 'the graves are so shallow that they split in dry weather like this and disgorge their dead. There has been a skeleton under our bedroom windows for two days.' She did not like exposing the children to such sights and knew that proximity to corpses could not be healthy.

But it was Rumer who fell ill first. Early in December she came down with a severe case of paratyphoid, running a fever of 105°F for several days. Luckily Giuliana was still with them and, with the missionary nursing sisters, she took care of Rumer; she was recovering fast, Rumer wrote staunchly to Jon, although she added, 'the gods seem to be loving me very much because they are certainly doing their best to slay me . . . just had a cable from New York to say *Black Narcissus* was unsuccessful. Not my lucky season.' She had thought the worst was over, until she developed jaundice, which kept her in bed, weak, yellow, thin, and convinced her hair was falling out. During her illness, though, she made two decisions. She took the house at Bren, near Nishat, for two years: surely, she thought, it would be peaceful and healthy out there. 'I am calling it Dove House,' she wrote on 1 December, 'because it is like a little brown and white dove sitting in the green.' She wrote more fully to Nancy and Dick, sounding, as she always did in her letters to them, positive and organized. Simon, she announced triumphantly, had stopped sucking his thumb, and

... it is not often that what one wants coincides with what one has to do but it seems so over Nishat. There is to be complete rest for a year which is impossible of course but I think out there I could achieve the nearest. I would just live there, do what looking after the children need – teach them a little – garden and write ... The house is a little paradise, set high above the lake with all the sun. It is small and white with a shingled roof and a vine and ivy upon it; it has orchards that lead into orchards where the children can play all day with no dirt or flies anywhere. It has no well but a spring that comes up into little streams and no fear of contamination as there is no one higher up the mountain. At present it has no ceilings, no glass, no electric light and no bathroom.

Her other decision concerned her marriage.

Laurence's stubbornness, on top of her own doubts and fears in the wake of her illness, wore her down. Rumer Godden might long to be a free woman supporting herself by her writing and in full charge of her own and her daughters' lives: Peggie Foster, however, still longed for support and tenderness from her husband, unsatisfactory though he might be. Her response to his pleas, however, was not exactly wholehearted: 'He asked me if I would go back on any terms. I said I might reconsider in a year's time, "if on the 1st of every month during that year you will send me a bankers' order for half exactly of your pay – no more but no less."' He must have given her an undertaking that satisfied her, for when he asked if he could come to Srinagar to see them before his next posting she agreed. The doctors had told her she needed various tonics to build her up: 'I wish they could also give me a new face, a new temper, some new ideas and a new husband,' she wrote to Jon grimly, adding, 'There were about fifteen funerals under our window this morning.'

Christmas 1942 was a subdued affair, spent at St Faith's as the new house was far from finished. Giuliana had left in floods of tears for her new job; all the children were in bed with flu and bad coughs; the new Kashmiri ayah regaled them all with folk tales of the Sisters of Death who carry away the sick in winter. Somehow, with the Hopmans' help, Rumer managed a crib and a tree with candles as well as small presents, but told Nancy she had had no sleep for four nights. Her spirits sank and for once she felt she could not face the effort involved in another move. Jon was worried enough to offer financial help, but Rumer was determined to cope:

> The only thing to do with a run of luck like this is to accept it quietly and proceed one foot in front of the other till it changes ... I can see now that I shouldn't have left Jinglam – or rather that I shouldn't have come out from home – but I tried to do what I thought was right. All my efforts seem to be each sillier than the last.

Looking back at this time, Rumer came to realize that she had been physically and emotionally at the end of her tether. She seldom allowed the extent of her anxiety and unhappiness to show, even to Jon; she always tried to sound resolute, not to make a fuss, but she admitted later that she had been on the verge of collapse. It was hardly surprising that when Laurence arrived after four days' travel, in time to help them move into Dove House on 31 December, all Rumer's reservations were suspended.

> I was so glad to see someone of our family – even if outcast – that I could not judge him properly at all. He was very charming, very helpful and very amenable, but I am sure he is still the same Laurence. Still, I have agreed to wait for a year before doing anything drastic and see how he behaves. He is now a Staff Captain and so should find it quite easy to behave in a monetary way.

To the surprise of the missionaries, Laurence arrived in style, driving a huge Plymouth coupé, laden with presents for the children and Elizabeth Arden scent and hand lotion for Rumer. 'It was bliss having a man over the move, but he had to leave too soon,' was Rumer's only other comment.

By the first week of January 1943 they were installed, after a fashion, in Dove House. The roof leaked, the carpenters were still at work, it was unpainted and very cold, but Rumer was euphoric nevertheless. 'Still it is lovely – utterly quiet, lovely soft air and lovely soft colours. The snow on the mountains comes right down to the garden . . .' She was sure that the fresh air and exercise would soon cure all their lingering ailments: already the children looked less pale and had better appetites. This alone, Rumer wrote to Nancy a touch defiantly, justified the move. 'If I had had any doubts over bringing them here (as poured into me on every side by my Srinagar friends) they would have disappeared after that. "You will be snowbound," they told me. We were, and I have seldom enjoyed anything as much.' They had brought the old Kashmiri ayah from Srinagar to help look after them although some of her opinions were, Rumer told Nancy, 'curious . . . such as that fruit gives cold, that honey should never be given to children, only pure white sugar, and that in no circumstances should a vest be changed in winter or a window be opened'. She had asked Jobara to come as chowkidar but he had declined; the bearer, cook and sweeper lived in their own quarters behind the house.

From the start, despite all the difficulties, Rumer loved Dove House. It was more truly hers, perhaps, than any house she had lived in before, because she had found it, she was decorating and finishing it, and she was in sole charge of the household. In everything she was to write about Dove House later she made it seem more remote than it was, although twelve miles by unmade road was further than it sounds. This impression sprang partly from her tendency to dramatize, but also reflected her emotional state and, perhaps, her sense of triumph that this time, all by herself, she had got away. She knew that what she was doing seemed odd to her Calcutta and Srinagar acquaintances, who were not slow to predict that trouble was bound to follow a lone woman living half-way up a mountain surrounded by Kashmiris, but she was all the more determined that Dove House should not only be a refuge for her family and a solution to her financial troubles but an idyll, a perfect place to live and work.

At first, it seemed that she was succeeding. To Jon she wrote,

> It is heavenly peace, even with the devilish behaviour of mistris [carpenters] – the grumbling of servants – with the worry over expenses – the question of Laurence – and the dreadful time I am having with Paula – the result, I suppose, of flu and this move . . . two days ago we had a lunch picnic in Nishat. We have narcissus and daises and almond blossom . . . the children spend their time discovering pools and copses. I at the moment drive the mistris but hope soon to get to work.

It was, once again, Paula whose troubles broke into Rumer's picture of how things ought to be: she was unwell and throwing unnerving tantrums. Her mother cut her hair as short as a boy's because she could not bear the exhausting scenes when it had to be combed. Paula's fierceness and pride reminded her of Jon as a child: even when she wanted to give in she could not. And much though Rumer relished setting her house in order, there were moments when she realized with alarm just how far removed her daily preoccupations were from anything to do with books. Her mother sent on to her an invitation to a party 'to meet a few literary people' from G. B. Stern, which prompted Rumer to write to Jon, the only person she knew who would understand how she felt:

> How much, how much I miss – I don't want to be like her [Stern] but I do want to be something. Now I spend most of my waking hours either ordering meals or administering them . . . and mending and teaching and walking . . . I get three hours a day for writing. Am re-reading *A Room of One's Own* – she talks of Shakespeare's 'incandescent, unimpeded mind'.

That's your and my snag – we are impeded in every direction – my mind is a jetsam of figures (I have a perpetual desire to check my passbook) of curtains and meals and entrance forms and name-tapes and codliver oil and Moon on heat and firewood – it is horrible.

Even so, Rumer had a strong practical streak and she was as perfectionist about the simple life at Dove House as she had been about the dancing school in Calcutta. She threw herself into choosing the colours for her walls, fabrics for curtains, planning her garden, planting hundreds of bulbs and flowering shrubs; she also ordered a large kitchen garden planted with potatoes, onions, carrots, pumpkins, aubergines, tomatoes and all sorts of green vegetables. Rather than rely on the expensive, unreliable Srinagar suppliers there was no reason, she felt, for them not to be largely self-sufficient. Chickens were available locally, and fish from the lake could be bought from the fishermen; an old man in the village kept bees, whose hives were built into the walls of his house. She learned how to make bran bread, and jam from apples and dried apricots. Alcohol and coffee were rare treats. When she began to think that the milk was being watered, she bought a cow; she also acquired a pony, Piccolo, and a small tonga – (pony cart). She was amused by her own transformation into a countrywoman: 'By the time you come up,' she wrote to Nancy cheerfully, 'I shall look rather like a mahogany and weatherbeaten scarecrow, with wisps of hair and nails full of earth and a raffia hat and seeds in my pockets.'

Just as Rumer's enthusiasm for a new start was always overwhelming, so it did not usually take long for the first cracks to appear in the brave façade. After the euphoria at the beauty of the snow came the reality of another long, bitter winter, in which the children, especially Simon, were often reduced to tears of pain by chapped skin. The ayah was terrified when they found a panther's paw marks in the snow around the house, which the other servants had decided was haunted. 'I have had to be very waspish about it or they would all leave, but the fact remains that in one room there is, about eleven, a peculiar feeling and one that I do not much care for, and the sound of a voice that I cannot account for, and also violent barking from Moon and shivering.'

There were other penalities to be paid for her independence: the post reached Bren only twice a week and she felt more cut off than ever from news of home or Calcutta. When she did hear from her parents there was bad news: Rose had fallen in love with a young airman, who had been killed. Rumer wrote at once, offering to have her to stay in Kashmir, and to pay her fare, if it would help. Her parents, not surprisingly, were uneasy to hear that she was now living alone on a mountainside: in their experience of India young women did not do that, unless they were missionaries or very eccentric. Her mother kept hoping for a reconciliation between Rumer and Laurence: in her view almost anything was better than a divorce, especially for the children. Laurence's parents tried to help, sending small sums of money, which always made Rumer feel guilty as well as grateful. Her own finances and dealings with publishers were dealt with largely by her father, with whom she had left power of attorney; when she needed money from her *Black Narcissus* savings for Dove House he handled it for her. Letters took three or four weeks at least to arrive, but during the war there was a steady flow of communication between Darrynane and India, and the three sisters in India would share the latest family news. Spencer Curtis Brown took the trouble to stay in touch with Rumer about her work, sometimes sending her a letter or a cable of encouragement even if there was no special need. She was always deeply grateful to him for reminding her that someone still regarded her first and foremost as a writer.

Although in some ways it was a relief to be remote from the war, Rumer suffered agonies of anxiety when the Japanese bombed Calcutta in the winter of 1942-3. She hardly ever saw a newspaper, and at first she had no wireless, so wild rumours reached her through the servants; she had to rely on visits from Tontyn Hopman to learn what was really going on, often days or weeks after it had happened. Full of fears for Jon and Nancy, she dreaded clear moonlit nights that might, she felt, be showing the Japanese planes the way. When the raids on Calcutta caused a panic among the poorer Indian population, who took to the roads in hundreds of thousands with all their possessions, she shared at first the indignation of most of British India at the pointless chaos of the exodus, but a letter from Jon made her think again. 'Poor hopeless creatures,' she wrote back. 'I think a small inkling of understanding is in us both.' Rumer, like her sisters, was quite capable of being outspokenly infuriated by Indian behaviour:

> Do you remember in *A Passage to India* how Forster says about the dinner 'they shouted that it was ready not because it was ready but because they hoped it was'? I was reminded of that this week when after every undertaking and promise of his had collapsed, I said to my young landlord, 'You don't tell me what is true but what you hope is true'; and he sadly agreed.

All her suspicions of the Kashmiris revived: 'The malis here are so awful,' she wrote crossly. 'If you remove your eye for one second from them they stop work and sit down with their hookahs. I am becoming a scold and a shrew. The servants are as bad; surely the worst, dirtiest, most shiftless servants in the wide world.'

Inevitably, too, she found the children's constant company demanding and the PNEU lessons a trial. The only answer, if she was to have any time to write, was to send Jane back to the Garden School as a boarder. Jane seemed keen, but as the new term drew near both she and Rumer felt increasingly unhappy at the thought of separation. Jane, now six, was a sweet-natured, helpful child and Rumer was afraid, sometimes, that she was beginning to rely on her too much; she was also taken aback when Jane asked her one day why it was that she had to earn money for them all by writing, when other families had fathers who provided for them. Rumer had tried not to make the children aware of what she thought of their father as a provider but, as always, they knew far more than she imagined. She resolved to be more careful, but Jane was growing up fast. She would get the other two up in the mornings and try to keep them quiet so that her mother could work. Simon, known as Chamba, was a happy, sturdy little boy but his high spirits and natural destructiveness drove Rumer to distraction. When he hacked at her new walls with his spade and dug up her plants she took to tying his hands behind his back. 'I admit I get very sick of children sometimes but then everyone has something.' She consoled herself by reading Jane Austen in bed: Jon had sent her the set for Christmas. Rumer, with her wariness of social life, identified strongly with Emma's misjudgements: 'I have behaved so like Emma so often, particularly those little stabs after an evening's behaviour when you look back on it.' She struggled to find two hours in the day for writing: the final version of the Jinglam book was being typed in Calcutta, she was starting to work on a new novel about a family and a London house, and wondering if a Dove House journal might work, but it was hard going. 'The book and the journal creep along, but at the moment it is in the dust and ashes stage . . .'

By the middle of February she was openly longing to get away. The ayah left: 'I think it was the panther that finished her.' She found another, after several days' relentless child care, a little Punjabi who was not, at first, much use. The house was still not ready – 'I am depressed by the enormous difference always between what I imagine and what reality is. I did think it was going to be sweet and it is just bare and dirty and rather ugly' – and she was beginning to feel lonely and nervous, especially at night. She thought she would have to get a large dog. 'I am so all alone at night here and if anything by chance did happen like a robbery I know the servants would all run away at once.' She missed Jane, who was miserable as a boarder at the Garden School and longing to come home. Sometimes she felt the irony of her position, although her letters never spelled it out: the only one of the four sisters with a record of professional success and work that she longed to pursue, she was also the only one bogged down in domestic chores looking after three small children. She sometimes wondered whether Nancy's war work was so vital that she should not be asked to come and take over the children for a while. She clung to the possibility of escape, if Nancy was willing, later in the year to research her book about British India, and she had another notion of visiting Ladakh for a travel book with Tontyn Hopman; she knew both projects were unlikely. She began to press them all, especially Jon, to come and stay with her in the spring and early summer when Kashmir was at its most beautiful. Jon had been ill and Rumer begged her to come immediately and convalesce. By mid-March the winter was almost over: 'We have had a week of clear sun and the hills and garden are full of wild violets and anemones and the blossom is beginning and my magnolia trees have large cream buds ... doesn't that move you?'

But her first visitor from her family was her husband. Once again, Laurence was due some leave, and was determined to spend it at Dove House before he was sent overseas. To Rumer's astonishment, he was enjoying the rigorous physical training: 'Surely they can't be making a commando of him?' she wrote to Jon, adding waspishly, 'Probably now he shows signs of being something of a comfort something will happen to him.' Clearly, it was going to be very hard for Laurence to win back his wife's respect. One thing is clear: he was not giving up. He spent a few days in Kashmir at the end of March, and was able to help Rumer with the mistris – who, Rumer admitted, worked much better with a man about. He was, she told Nancy, 'very taken with Dove House as it is now and he has helped me financially'. It does not sound, however, as if it was a particularly romantic reunion, as Rumer had a poisoned foot and a painful boil: 'I was either lame or unable to sit down all the time the unfortunate Laurence was here. He looked amazingly well and tough, utterly unlike the

Laurence of Calcutta . . .' She described their parting as 'harrowing
. . . for him': there is no reference to her feelings, or the children's.
Laurence kept two small black and white snapshots, one of Dove
House and one of Jane and Paula in the garden, to the end of his
life.

In the spring of 1943, as her garden burgeoned, Rumer was
seized with a new idea: she would start a herb farm. The Hopmans,
who were great believers in herbal medicine, along with the Tarot
and astrology, were encouraging. She envisaged a partnership and
was convinced they would all make good money. 'This probably
sounds cloudy and arty to you,' she wrote to Jon, 'but Clara
Hopman, with her haphazard tumbledown dirty methods, has sold
400 rupees worth of herbs since October and she will give me all
her knowledge and do the actual supplying and collecting for me.'
She asked Jon to find her a really good recipe for pot-pourri;
meanwhile she went on expeditions up the mountain slopes with
Clara, looking for useful plants and learning about their application. Rumer never did things by halves: soon she was busy
extending the garden, sowing and planting out the herbs, including
a thousand lavender bushes, and spending more than she could
afford on turning part of the Dove House outbuildings into a
workshop, complete with shelves and drying racks. She began to
look into possible outlets and agents in Srinagar and further afield,
and to order special baskets and jars for storage and packing. It all
cost money, of course, but she found it enjoyable, and was full of
herbal lore, recipes for liver-cleansing tea and rose-leaf jelly.

Meanwhile, after many changes of plan and anxious letters, the
moment Rumer had been truly longing for arrived: in April, Jon
came up to Kashmir to spend the summer with her. She seemed
frail and tired, and at first wanted only to rest and recover her
strength. Rumer tried hard to keep the children quiet and fend off
visitors, but as the weather improved people began to find Dove
House an agreeable destination for an outing. The missionaries
from St Faith's would sometimes call, or Jane's schoolfriends with

their parents; Giuliana was back working in Srinagar and came out to visit whenever she could, as did the Hopmans, who were so taken with Rumer's house and the prospects for the herb farm that they too were now thinking of moving out from Srinagar. Having Jon to herself, though, was a joy: they talked about books to their hearts' content, and Rumer found a quiet corner where Jon, who was working on her own first novel, could set up a writing table. Rumer was greatly impressed with its quality: she was always urging Jon to write, without a trace of jealousy or any sign that she would like to be the only writer in the family. Her childhood conviction that Jon was in every way superior – more beautiful, more talented, more original – was still with her; her own success, much of which she felt she owed anyway to Jon's critical acumen, only made her even more confident that Jon could do it too. 'I am sure as I sit here at my very substantial desk that you will succeed,' she had written to Jon before she arrived. 'I should like us to be the modern Brontë sisters (says she modestly), the Emily quite overshadowing the plodding Charlotte.' She saw herself, of course, as the Charlotte figure.

After Easter, celebrated in brilliant spring sunshine with four-teen people, including children, for an Easter egg hunt and a special tea with home-made cakes, they began to prepare for the arrival of Nancy and Dick in May. Nancy was pregnant again, and Rumer was determined that she, too, should rest; she wanted to make it up to her younger sister for the ordeal of the previous year in Sonamarg when she had looked after Rumer during her miscarriage. Nancy and Dick rented a houseboat nearby and, before they went off on a fishing expedition up the Sind valley, agreed to look after the household for a few days so that Jon and Rumer could also get away together. They took a boat on the Manasbal lake outside Srinagar and saw no one except the crew. There, Rumer read Jon the first draft of her book about the London house, and was told that it was not good enough. She knew her sister was right.

Later that summer they took Jane and Paula, with four Pekinese

– Rumer's and Jon's – up to Sonamarg and beyond on a long trek, over the Nichnai Pass, to the two lakes, Krishn Sar and Vishan Sar, fed by the great glacier. Jobara provided six ponies and ponymen. They all wore big straw hats and chapplis, the Kashmiri leggings of soft leather that fitted into strong walking sandals. As they climbed towards the tree-line they saw herds of wild ponies, and the red mountain marmots, small beaver-like creatures that sat on their hind legs and chattered as they passed. There were flowers everywhere, gentians and edelweiss and magenta primulas growing out of the snow, and huge eagles cruised between the high peaks. When they reached the lakes a sudden summer blizzard came down and they spent two nervous nights and a day confined to their tents, laced tightly against the storm and held down by heavy stones. Jobara and the servants somehow managed to produce hot tea and soup, crawling on hands and knees from one tent to another. Afterwards Rumer and Jon felt that perhaps they should not have taken the children, but the trek had been a most memorable adventure.

By the early autumn everyone had gone, and Rumer was left to face another long winter. The year ended on a subdued note. At Dove House the autumn was golden and beautiful, with the fruit ripening, the herbs gathered by children from the village and by the Bakriwars, the nomadic goat-herders on their way back down from their summer pastures to the plains. But Rumer missed Jon badly, waited anxiously for news of Nancy's baby, and worried, as always, about her finances. Running Dove House was not as cheap as she had hoped: the herb business was not making a profit, although orders were coming in from Srinagar, Lahore and Bombay, and the Begum of Bhopal and her household had placed a big order. In October, the Hopmans moved out from Srinagar to a house below Bren and Rumer was pleased to have them as neighbours, on hand to help with the herbs. Yet again she was having servant trouble – 'they are devils incarnate' – and feeling uneasy at night. She decided to get a watchdog and fell in love with a beautiful Alsatian puppy, a bitch she named Psyche. She had agreed to look after Jon's older Pekinese, Honey, a fierce little dog who pined for his mistress and fought with all the others for Rumer's undivided attention.

Rungli-Rungliot was to be published around the end of the year, but Rumer was beginning to feel that Little, Brown, her American publishers, were dragging their feet. 'I am horribly doubtful of my future,' she told Jon. 'The bogey of not being thought worth the publishing has always haunted me.' Meanwhile she was reworking the new novel, a complicated story of different generations living in a London home, which she was calling *A Fugue in Time*. Spencer Curtis Brown wanted her to change publishers; Rumer worried that this meant she was not wanted any longer by Peter Davies. Jon's novel, *The Bird Escaped*, was finished and Rumer plunged into doing everything she could to encourage its publication. Curtis Brown agreed to handle it, and although they could not place it in London it was eventually accepted in America.

In early December Nancy and Dick's second son, Richard, was born in Calcutta. Rumer wrote lovingly to congratulate them, but was unable to hide her own low spirits: 'Writing news from America is bleak and I am horribly lonely quite suddenly.' The approach of Christmas did little to cheer her, although she was delighted when Jon and Roland gave her, at her suggestion, a garden path lined with thyme. Laurence was coming for four days. Rumer failed to sound excited: 'I hope all goes off well and that I can manage to make things happy for him.'

CHAPTER EIGHT

Drama at Dove House

1944

RUMER STARTED 1944, her second year in Dove House, full of resolve. She was determined to run her household more efficiently and economically: she decided to get rid of all her servants, hire new ones and bring in Clara Hopman's mother as housekeeper and nanny. Old Mrs Hopman seemed a calm, sensible woman, and part of the deal was that the two Hopman boys would spend much of their time at Dove House; Rumer believed the arrangement would save her time and money. She had also decided, sadly, to get rid of the pony and Psyche: both were more expensive than they were worth.

Early in January she sent the revised *Fugue* to be typed and decided she had done her best with it; she was much encouraged to hear from Curtis Brown that Little, Brown had made an offer, after all, for *Rungli-Rungliot* although it was a small one. Spencer Curtis Brown was urging her to take the new book to the rising publisher Michael Joseph, who was offering good terms, and the herb business was at last starting to show a small profit. Although Rumer found it difficult to live on the monthly allowance she received from Laurence, and was always breaking into her dwindling savings, she began to feel that her finances were looking up.

As for her marriage, Laurence's short Christmas visit did not change anything. She was infuriated, she told Jon, at the way he and his parents seemed to think that everything had been forgiven and forgotten: 'It isn't a question of forgiving and forgetting, but of an utter inability, disinclination to continue.' Her own feelings had hardened: although she felt guilty about the children, she had decided to ask him not to come up on leave again 'as I don't think I can stand it'. She knew that the time would come when the question of divorce would have to be settled once and for all, but for now she just wanted to be left alone. The winter had its compensations: she loved the quiet, the soft pale colours and the crisp days when they could have the gardens of Nishat to themselves. She would always remember Jane and Paula in sapphire blue velvet trousers and hooded jackets made by the local tailor, brilliant against the snow. 'Possibly mine are the only children who have tobogganed in a Moghul garden. The water channels with their tilted slats made a perfect run and at the end of each, a dais packed with snow was a stop.'

But as the snow melted and the spring began to break through, Rumer's mood changed again. Later, she looked back at those months in the summer of 1944, which preceded the episode that changed everything for her, as a golden time, a dream come true. The trouble that came to her, she decided, arrived from outside, the result of changes that, against her better judgement, she had made to a happy household. In fact, her letters show that from early March she was beginning to feel physically and emotionally fragile. Some of this she put down to the usual stomach disorders common in India, and to the irregularity of her menstrual cycle since her miscarriage. She dosed herself with herbal remedies and practised relaxation techniques taught her by Clara Hopman but she still felt uneasy. Laurence, who had learned not to take no for an answer, was insisting that he was still coming to Dove House for his next leave. Rumer was reticent about sex, but she did not want to sleep with him, whether or not it might seem to be her marital duty. 'I don't see why he should provide for me while I refuse to live with him,' she wrote grimly, adding, 'I just cannot be Laurence's wife just now, nor am I sure about the future.'

After the effort of rewriting and finishing *Fugue*, she waited anxiously for some reaction from Jon; when, finally, the verdict was positive, her relief was immense. At the same time, both Jon and Roland wrote to her about the general direction her writing seemed to be taking: they expressed concern that she was becoming precious and unrealistic. Rumer knew there was some truth in this and she understood what Roland meant when he recommended 'a roll in the mud of human nature': but, she wrote back sadly, 'I don't see how it can be done. I am barred by so many things at the moment from being human at all. I think, and have always thought, that it is damaging for anyone to be cut off as I am, both by circumstance and nature.'

The first reviews of *Rungli-Rungliot* arrived and, on the whole, were good, which cheered her, but she was still feeling edgy and sleeping badly. She began to wonder if living alone was making her eccentric and peculiar; she knew that Nancy and Dick thought so, and were suspicious of the Bohemian Hopmans, with their herbs and magic mumbo-jumbo – perhaps Jon thought so too? And, rather to her surprise, lack of a sex life had begun to trouble her.

> For one thing I think I need a man . . . for years I haven't felt this need, now suddenly I do – and I have to make up my mind that it is a need that can hardly be fulfilled – quite apart from Laurence. I am 35 and have never been attractive to men. I am lonely, but I was just as lonely, when you were not there, in Calcutta.

This letter, for the first time, she signed Rumer, adding, in brackets, 'I have decided that is the nicest', but she still used Peggie in other letters. It was years before she habitually became Rumer to her family and old friends. In later life, she greatly disliked being reminded that she had ever been called Peggie. Rumer Godden had by then long superseded Peggie Foster.

Her insomnia continued: 'Try as one will, one is only half a person after nights such as these and it is very hard to keep sane over things . . . I don't mean to grumble and no place on earth is loved as I love this and I do rejoice in it but this trouble seems to destroy even my power of will and control.' The beauty of the spring failed to calm or comfort her, but there were consolations: the children seemed well and happy, she was writing poems and short stories with unusual fluency, she was suddenly full of ideas for books, and she was enjoying the company of a new friend who had come to live not far away. Helen Arberry was an Englishwoman some years older than Rumer, whose health required her to leave her husband for a spell in the hills. She was a painter, whose work Rumer admired, and who also loved books. Rumer felt they had much in common.

As summer approached, Rumer struggled to keep her equilibrium. She was hoping for another visit from her sisters, especially Jon; the new servants, including a rather superior cook, Siddika, seemed to be working reasonably well together, although they were inclined to quarrel with the malis, and Granny Hopman's presence was a help. Then two sudden dramas with the dogs upset them all. Once again all Rumer's pent-up emotion became focused on the plight of the Pekinese. They had provided some friends with a puppy, which suddenly went missing from his new home; it turned out, after much searching, that he had been sold secretly by his owner's servants. This treachery made Rumer disproportionately angry: 'Sometimes I think I just cannot go on living in Kashmir. It is evil...' Then Honey, Jon's much-loved Pekinese, became violently ill. Rumer called the vet, who diagnosed gastro-enteritis, and nursed the little dog devotedly, sitting up with him at night and administering chicken broth, eggs and nips of brandy. 'What is dreadful about it all is that I am beginning to suspect that he is being poisoned. I wouldn't put it in the least past these people.' Within a week, Honey was dead, but the post-mortem found advanced liver disease. Rumer was deeply distressed, but felt that everything possible had been done. 'Helen Arberry helped me and so did Granny and the sweeper and the cook. The vet says he was incurable. Poor little golden paws.'

Although Honey's death had been undeniably from natural

causes, it seems to have exacerbated Rumer's worst suspicions of the Kashmiris, so charming yet so treacherous. She had, she confessed to Jon, 'a great dark cloud over me and try as I will I cannot shake it off... One thing however emerges quite clearly, and that is that I must somehow change my life.' She loved Dove House but she had begun to feel that something was wrong. Sometimes she blamed herself, sometimes the Kashmiris.

> I never never want to leave it. That I may be driven out is another thing... I get frightened up here sometimes, Jon. Suppose unwittingly or by accident one ran really foul of these people. One would be stripped of everything. This morning is shining, full of dew, the garden is full of guelder roses, white iris, yellow tulips – forget-me-nots and golden orioles. In Kashmir I feel more moved to write than I have felt anywhere. It touches a spring in me, but I'm not sure I wouldn't change it all to live under a sane rule again. Is all India going to be like this soon?

The herb farm, she decided, would have to go: Dove House was too full of people coming and going. She was relieved to find that the Hopmans agreed with her: they could see that she was under strain, and offered to take over all the work and treat her as a sleeping partner. She went for a brief holiday to the Manasbal lake with Helen Arberry and felt better. On her return she decided to dispense with the services of Granny Hopman, whose presence had become oppressive, and found herself also thinking about returning to England when the war was over. Her reservations about the Kashmiris filled her with trepidation at the prospect of living in an independent India. On the other hand, though, Mrs Majumdar had written suggesting she return to Darjeeling. If she could manage that, would she be able to see more of Jon? In a letter to her sister, she said,

> The years pass and I see less and less of all of you I love, you and Mop, I seem to have gone wrong every time that I try to

renew things with Laurence and I have written and told him now that this is the definite end. He won't accept that at present but in time he may . . . I am so sorry for him but seem to be quite dead to his tears and pleas.

In the meantime, she thought she could see a solution to some of her immediate problems by pooling resources with Helen Arberry and sharing Dove House. Rumer knew that this plan would have drawbacks, but the advantages – both of them would save money and gain agreeable companionship – were so obvious that, despite misgivings, she decided to go ahead. It had become clear that neither Nancy nor Jon would be able to come up to Kashmir that summer, and she felt somehow that it was her duty to look after Helen, who herself had been having servant trouble and feeling unwell: 'She has had no peace at all for years and here there is such peace and she does things so beautifully that I both admire and love her.' By early June, it was all agreed and Rumer was rearranging Dove House to make room for Helen. She was once again ill herself, with fever and dysentery, and her eyes were bothering her; Jane had been nursing her with hot-water bottles. 'I feel that child will grow up to be a comfort.'

Predictably, on the eve of Helen's arrival, her heart sank. The weather was ominously thundery and hot, and she wondered if she was making another mistake. 'I feel horribly sad,' she wrote to Jon. 'She is being more than nice about it but the whole of Dove House will change, of course for the better I know for her things are far nicer than mine but it won't be mine any more.'

Helen Arberry moved in on 13 June 1944 and, after a few days of confusion, Rumer felt that all was well. Everyone was on their best behaviour except, predictably, Paula, whose worms had returned and whose temper had not improved. Helen liked children to be kept in their place and not to be noisy – 'I sympathise,' commented Rumer drily – so they were banned from upstairs and from certain parts of the garden. Already, though, Rumer could see that Helen's financial contribution would make life much easier.

What happened next brought Rumer's stay at Dove House to an abrupt, ugly and confused end, frightened her and her family profoundly, and affected the way in which she thought about India in general and Kashmir in particular for the rest of her life. Many of the details of what happened were soon to be disputed, obscured and lost in the aftermath of blame, evasion and guilt; Rumer herself was to mix fact and fiction in two versions of the episode over the next forty years, but the letter that she wrote to Jon on 2 July tells the story a few days after the event with complete clarity.

This will be a rather startling letter because we have been having more than trouble – a most horrid and surprising melodrama. Helen came to live here on the 13th and as I told you she is a very delicate person. I also told you I think that I had had dysentery and had got so thin and weak. The children too seemed to have got very thin and Paula was always having tummy aches. As soon as Helen arrived she began to get attacks of pain and diarrhoea – also we both had a curious sleepy stupidity and this began to affect her heart and she became really ill. On Friday 23rd while I was giving the children their lunch Jane bit on a piece of glass. I looked through the food and found several bits more. I thought naturally it was a careless accident especially as my good cook Siddika hadn't cooked the lunch as he was in town. (Actually it was the little Subhana whom you remember who cooked it. He is now in jail waiting trial.) As the children had eaten most of the lunch I took them to the Civil Surgeon after giving them cottonwool sandwiches etc. By the most incredible luck the old doctor was away and I saw the new young assistant Civil Surgeon Captain Clay who is extremely clever and energetic. He took a serious view, especially as regards Helen, and told me I must send stools for an examination and – this being Kashmir – go to the police. I didn't want to do this as it seemed so absurdly sensational but Tonteyn endorsed this and actually took me there. The police came and removed Subhana and one of the malis but as the food had been thrown away there was no proof. However next

day Captain Clay came out with the news that the stools were
found to be full of very finely powdered glass, so fine that it
was evident that it was no accident but a definite attempt – or
part of one. Since then life has been like an Agatha Christie;
police, doctors, the staff all but two removed, Helen going from
one heart attack to another. To add to this Siddika the cook
quite suddenly on Wednesday collapsed screaming with pain
and has been removed to hospital by Captain Clay with a burst
lung. It proves that he has TB and will probably die. The
people of course say that it is the finger of God but probably
the poor man is quite innocent. No one has any idea who did
do it.

Although Rumer does not specifically say that evidence was
found that she and Helen had been given drugs as well as ground
glass, her letters strongly imply it. Her main emotion as she wrote
to Jon was bewilderment:

It is all so incomprehensible as there appears to be no motive
whatever. As the police say, no case has ever been known here
of trying to poison children. As a matter of fact, though they
certainly got the glass they obviously didn't have any drugs as
they are perfectly well. We are all better, Helen able to dress
today but of course we feel very ravaged . . . Don't worry, Jon.
Though of course no solution has been found we are being very
well looked after.

The Hopmans were being wonderful, as was a new friend, Bob
Philipps, a young naval lieutenant on leave. He was based at the
Hopmans' but staying at Dove House every night. Rumer decided
to retreat to Sonamarg as soon as the authorities allowed them to
leave. After that, she was not sure. 'I naturally long to go away –
home if possible – but this may not be feasible. I have found great
difficulty in making my nerves stand this. (Actually whatever drug
they gave me was a good choice for me as it made me sleep heavily
for a few days.)'

It was not long, once the story was out, before all kinds of rumours were rife about what really had or had not happened. There could be no doubt whatever about the ground glass – Jane always remembered the odd grittiness of her mouthful of rice and dhal – but the question of what drugs or poisons might have been given to Rumer and Helen was more complicated: Dove House was still a herb factory where medicines were prepared and Rumer was known to make herbal remedies for herself and her children, which was an obvious source of speculation: maybe there had been a mistake in some preparation? Even the glass could perhaps be explained away as an accident: Indian cooks sometimes crushed light-bulbs into bait for mice and rats. Of course, Rumer had occasional difficulties with her servants but so did every employer sooner or later, and scenes were commonplace – but attempted murder? It was all very puzzling and unpleasant, but the general feeling was that although, of course, it had to be looked into, it was unlikely that the full truth would ever come out. As Kashmir was an independent state, the case was in the hands of the Kashmiri police; the specimens had to be handed over to them for further tests and there was no guarantee that the medical evidence would be consistent.

To some of the Srinagar British, it all fitted with what they had felt about Rumer for some time: that she should never have gone off in the first place to live up a mountain on her own, let alone start a herb farm and peddle strange potions. Mollie Kaye remembered how a friend of hers in the Forestry Service, Sir Peter Clutterbuck, was 'driven nearly mad' by the amount of advice Rumer required on herbs, and how when the stories of the strange drama at Dove House began to circulate no one was much surprised: 'She had been living on her own for too long; she caused such trouble, making complaints, bringing in the police, investigations . . . No doubt she believed it all, whether it was true or not.' Mrs Joan White, who spent the war in Kashmir as a girl, had friends not far from Bren who knew all about the strange household up the hill through their bearer: he had told them himself that it was all wrong for the memsahib to be there alone with two small children as Bren was full of badmashes (bad characters) and anything could happen. When something did, 'it was discussed over lunch for days. I'm afraid everyone thought she was rather a naughty lady and that something nasty had been going on in that little house.' In this version, the whole family were poisoned with drugs and taken to hospital *in extremis*. In fact, their physical recovery was rapid; the emotional aftermath was far more troubling.

Meanwhile Rumer, Helen and the children were allowed to travel up to Sonamarg, where Jobara was waiting to look after them, with the help of his young son Amah who had started work at fourteen as a bearer. There, in a tent on a green hillside under the fir trees, Rumer tried to make sense of what had happened. It had not been easy to get permission to leave Bren, and she had been told she might have to go down to Srinagar for questioning; meanwhile Sidikka, the cook, had been taken already for questioning by the police. Rumer, though calm, was still deeply shocked. Evidently Laurence had heard the news; she reported to Jon an exchange of telegrams. 'Laurence: May I come for a month's leave? MRF: Prefer you don't just at the moment. Laurence: Arriving Srinagar 12th.' Nothing makes the fundamental hopelessness of their relationship clearer than this exchange. 'I don't blame him for coming at this crisis,' she wrote wearily, 'but I wilt at the thought of more scenes and agonising. I think I shall leave him the children and take Candy and go to Leh and never come back.' At least, the children seemed well again and happy, and the beauty of the mountains was a solace, despite everything. 'It is so lovely here that I never want to leave Kashmir but they say if the police don't get a conviction I mustn't stay at Dove House any longer as it won't be safe. But where are we to go?'

By the time she next wrote to Jon, Laurence had arrived and was trying, pointlessly in Rumer's view, to activate the British authorities on her behalf. 'He is very stunned about the whole thing, and shocked, but I think myself it will all fizzle out without the police nor anyone else doing a thing about it.' He was trying to persuade Rumer to take the children to Bombay where he could arrange a house for them until they could take a boat back to England, but Rumer felt incapable of taking such a decision. She still found herself oddly reluctant to abandon Dove House. At least, however, Laurence seemed to have accepted that the marriage had to be formally ended and was not pressing her to sleep with him.

> Laurence is very much more reasonable and quiet over things and says he will do anything I ask, even a divorce – the financial side is the greatest difficulty but I think he can see now it will never never work. I have said I am content to wait as long as he will leave me alone and he is doing that and says he doesn't mind and perhaps he really doesn't.

She believed he had already found consolation with someone else.

Not surprisngly, Rumer's calm, almost detached frame of mind could not last. When she received loving, concerned letters from her family her composure left her. 'I have a dreadful affliction at the moment,' she wrote to Jon on 20 July. 'Every time I sit down to write a letter touching this affair I weep and I just can't help it. Your letters were so generous and good that I produced buckets!' She admitted that it had been good to have Laurence around, 'helping with plans and dealing with people', but it had also been a strain, for he could not help being emotional and tense – and the case had taken a new and unpleasant turn:

> ... what has transpired seems to me so foul that I should be glad if they would drop it (except of course when I think of the children when I go suitably savage and red in the tooth). They are pretty definite now that it was against me that the attempt was directed. It appears – as apparently often happens in Kashmir – that they think Siddika, my good cook on whom I own I was becoming more and more dependent, had fallen for

me and was trying to get me under his thumb – that's why the drugs. When he saw this was going to be interrupted – Helen coming etc – it all turned to revenge and being an unbalanced man of criminal type (as it is proved he was) he did this. It all seems so nightmarish and fantastic that I can hardly write it . . . I am afraid though it is probably true . . . It will also spread all over the place I expect and rows of people will say I told you so. Still, I say this, and always will. I should sooner encounter these risks than sit in a boarding house with all the sheep. Yes, still I would. When I think of Dove House I can't utter.

Even in these ominous circumstances, once in Sonamarg Rumer had managed to turn her attention to her own work and to Jon's dealings with Curtis Brown. To focus on their writing was, as always, a relief: she could detach her mind from her problems. Curtis Brown had raised the question of whether Jon should also use the name Godden, thus perhaps confusing readers and certainly inviting comparisons between the sisters. Rumer was in no doubt and urged Jon to keep their surname:

Perhaps there is a very personal bias in this, but for me it seems to be another good cement block in what is a very precious, intimate and joyful association, for me certainly the most precious and intimate and joyous of my life, ranking neck and neck with my relationship with the chidren, and free of the burden that is in that! I think you should invite comparison with your sister. It seems to me that unless one of us has a very bad lapse, it can only enhance each of us.

Her mood had lightened; she could even write cheerfully to Jon about Laurence: 'He has decided that I am a) mad b) frigid c) unnatural d) missing all the best of life. This last is surprising if he only knew it as it is precisely what I feel about him . . .' He had agreed to the divorce and to continue her allowance until she was back in England, and to arrange and pay for their passage home. 'I still weep, but that is passing; but my temper is dreadful. Jobara says I have "gone bitter".'

The police investigations dragged on. Rumer had to go down to Srinagar to headquarters 'to tell the whole miserable tale all over again ... there is no further development in the case. Siddika the cook is out on bail and so is Nabir Bat the mali.' Giuliana had returned to help with the children; Laurence, on his way back to Bombay, accompanied Rumer to Dove House to start the dreary business of dismantling it.

> I cannot tell you what packing up the house was like. I was a fool to love it so much. The end of all was very dreadful, fully thirty Kashmiris assembled to try and extort what they could from me, the landlord included. I let them rip because I knew what was going to happen. Siddika was leaning against the door with a laconic smile, the two young landlords were flinging their weights about, and an ex sweeper of mine was screaming and swearing at me when suddenly there was a sound of cars and two military police trucks swept round from Bren and up the road ... and an enormous Yorkshire Sergeant covered in red tabs ... walked into the room and said, 'Any trrrrouble here, Mrs Fosterrr?' You could have heard a pin drop. They stayed while I paid off everyone and then took me away with them, luggage, bearer, Moon and all. It was a wonderful moment to see those people's faces.

Perhaps, after what she had been through, Rumer was entitled to this small satisfaction but beneath it she was miserable:

> It is now all broken up and destroyed and done and I feel so completely ill and done myself that I must try and shut my mind tight and just exist in the moment here, which is beautiful, and try and concentrate on writing and the children and on Sonamarg. I have one great fear though: that they will bring the case to trial and won't let me go because they will want my evidence. They might do that.'

In the same letter, when she turns to writing news – 'I am so sick with anxiety over Michael Joseph and the book that I can't think of it' – she goes on to reflect on how she might write about the episode. Already, it was a help to try to shape it, to fit it into a story of her own devising; rewriting it would help her to come to terms with it.

> I ... have been wondering if it would help to take out all the thousands of little stings that seem to be festering, there really isn't any other word but this, if I made it all into a really horrid little murder story. It is all so vivid and only needs a very little embroidering and I have thought of a way to do it unusually ...

Meanwhile, she was much preoccupied with arranging for some of her household goods to be sold, some to be shipped home to England – her mother kept advising her to bring as much as she could as everything was scarce – and some to be sent to Jon in Calcutta. Jon and Roland were to take them in: Rumer was worried that her lack of clothes and battered appearance would let them down and also that her marital situation might be an embarrassment, but she intended to live very quietly and get on with her work.

Her plan now was to stay in Sonamarg through October, to enjoy one last, glorious Kashmiri autumn, and then make for Calcutta *en route* for England: but all at once this plan began to seem unwise. Word reached her that the state was indeed intending to bring the case to court, which would mean that Rumer would have to appear and give evidence, and that

> ... it looks more plainly as if the authorities might make us try and belittle it and hush it up for the sake of the State. They are afraid of losing visitors. This I will not do ... and if there are any signs of it I shall try and make a getaway, first to Pindi and then to Calcutta ... This all sounds theatrical and I hope it proves to be unnecessary but I will not be kept here and bullyragged by Kashmiri officials. They have taken my evidence about six times already ... How I wish now I had come straight away.

Jon was away from Calcutta, so Rumer consulted Roland about what she should do. He at once sent her a wire indicating that she could come at any time, which made Rumer feel much safer: 'It is such a relief,' she told him and Jon, 'to know that there is a door open for me to get away if things here develop and I fear they are going to. It feels like sitting on a volcano and I often panic and feel, heat or no heat, I should run now.' She now had convincing proof that Siddika, the cook, had been at the heart of the episode: she had received a letter from a woman in Gulmarg who had also employed him. 'Her house was burned down and she was very nearly killed and also very severely robbed. Siddika was acquitted, her mali and driver got ten years. She says Siddika was a thoroughly bad man.' Her decision to leave sooner rather than later was strengthened when, not long after receiving this letter, she saw Siddika in Sonamarg. He had taken a job as cook in a large RAF camp nearby, and she told Jon,

> He is out on bail and seems to have taken this service deliberately as he knew where our camp was. However I thought this ought not to be left just as it was and reported it to the police and they have come and seen him away from this place and warned him not to come back . . . Helen went into complete panic . . . she is completely terrified of him. I saw him this morning and explained to him that apart from anything else he was a fool to come here so near to us. He is so extremely odd about the whole business; he just smiled and said in a sly voice, 'I haven't done anything wrong.' Where else but in Kashmir would a man out on bail for suspected murder be allowed to come and live next door to the ex-victims?

Helen's husband was coming up to join her, which was a relief to Rumer as she didn't like the thought of leaving her friend alone. Meanwhile, she told everyone except Helen and the Hopmans that she was staying until November. She had, in fact, made bookings – in the Hopmans' name – to travel on 3 October.

Roland followed up his telegram with a firm letter to Rumer, advising her strongly to leave as soon as she could. Rattled, she plunged into an attempt to do so, only to find that the earliest train she could book was for 22 September. Up until the last minute – although she admitted to Jon that the tension was making her feel ill – she kept up a normal routine of writing and looking after the children; Paula had her sixth birthday party on 2 September.

Rumer spent her last few days in Sonamarg in wistful, slightly puzzled appreciation of all she was about to leave behind.

> Now the crops are turning red and gold and all the cherries and the birches. The children have found a beach to play on by the Sind; a beach edged with gentians, big blue ones, and immortelles. It is so unutterably lovely but the trouble goes on and it is somehow all poisoned. I ache to get away from what I think is the loveliest place on earth.

At the end of August she had finally heard from Michael Joseph: 'Delighted your brilliant new novel. Please accept our congratulations.' Rumer was so preoccupied she almost forgot to tell Jon the news, but when she did: 'I feel a hundred and one years younger.'

On 22 September, very early in the morning, Rumer, Jane, Paula and the pekinese left Sonamarg by car for Rawalpindi, and the trains for Delhi and Calcutta. Half a century later, Jane can still remember the relief as they crossed the border, leaving the state of Kashmir for the British North West Frontier Province. Once they were safely installed in Calcutta, Rumer wrote: 'As soon as we passed the signpost I fell peacefully apart inside and that night I slept and have slept practically ever since.'

With her arrival in Calcutta, her letters to her sister naturally ceased, and the story of the drama at Dove House, as she experienced it at the time, ended. Forty years later, she wrote in her autobiography that the case was heard eventually and went very much as expected: Helen Arberry gave evidence, but Siddika was let off. She added that charges of defamation had been brought against her and Helen and that she could never go back to Kashmir. Afterwards, Rumer learned, Helen felt she had been humiliated and became angry with Rumer for running away; they lost touch and never met again. Rumer has told the story twice, once in a novel, *Kingfishers Catch Fire*, published in 1953, and then in her autobiography in 1987: both accounts combine fact with fiction. Once she had re-imagined what happened, the borderline between what was literally true and what was imaginatively or emotionally true dissolved.

Kingfishers Catch Fire is full of clues to Rumer's view of herself and what happened to her in Kashmir. In the ways in which it diverges from the facts, it reveals most strikingly her need to explain in fiction what remained inexplicable in life, to bring to a conclusion an episode that remained disturbingly open and even, through rewriting the story, to expiate some of her own actions. *Kingfishers Catch Fire* has to be regarded as an aspect of autobiography, one of the most autobiographical novels she has written. Perhaps for this reason Rumer came to dislike the book and to wish she had never written it.

She did not, in the end, write it as an Agatha Christie detective story but as something much closer to home. The novel's brief prologue is set in England: a young woman, Sophie, recalls with her slightly disapproving husband a strange episode that had taken place two years previously in Kashmir. She had found herself at a low ebb in Srinagar one winter during the war. She was with her two children, the older a sensible little girl, Teresa, and an original, vulnerable small boy, Moo. There is an unsatisfactory first husband elsewhere in India, who dies soon after the novel opens leaving them short of money. After a serious illness, when she is looked after by missionaries in a house overlooking a graveyard, Sophie decides to solve her problems by living as simply as possible in a small wooden house on a mountainside above the lake. Everyone advises her against it, but she is determined: 'It was her own idea to go and live there. When Sophie had an idea her child Teresa trembled.'

In the novel, Rumer draws a striking contrast between the romantic, wilful Sophie and her practical daughter: the mother is shown as unrealistic, even foolish, while the child sees things as they really are. Thus Sophie is enraptured by the primitive beauty of the peasants and their village, while Teresa sees it rather differently. '"How picturesque they are!" said Sophie admiringly. "And dirty," said Teresa. It was true. They were very dirty.'

From the start, Sophie appears dangerously oblivious to how she is really perceived in the village, and unaware of the tensions her presence stirs up. Although she feels poor, to the villagers she is enviably rich; her employment of some and not others causes trouble, and when she sets up a herb farm, employing local women and children and treating their ailments, the men, especially the local barber, fear that her influence will undermine their authority. The two leading local families, the Dars and the Sheiks, compete for her custom and her favours; she does not understand their traditional rivalry or why there is constant trouble in her household. She has two servants on whom she relies: Nabir, the gardener, a proud, independent young man, and Sultan, the cook, who is desperate to please her. They are both caught up in the struggle for her patronage.

During a sultry summer she starts to feel both ill and oddly elated, and to have strange, erotic dreams:

> . . . she dreamed about the lotus flowers and for days the dream seemed to stay with her so that she was by turns exhilarated, then sleepy; in her dream the male flower was a man and when he seized the female flower it was herself . . . In the night she would wake throbbing and for a long time she could not believe she was alone.

One evening, she shares some of her supper with Teresa who finds ground glass in the food; Sophie sends specimens for analysis, but before the results arrive something else happens. She sends a reluctant Teresa out to look for Moo, who has been playing up the mountain with some of the village children. Even the children have been affected by local feuds, and they turn on Teresa and injure her badly, leaving her unconscious. Nabir, who finds her, is accused of the attack, and when the specimens are found to contain drugs as well as glass he, along with Sultan, is arrested. Sophie feels sure they are innocent.

With Teresa recovering in hospital, Sophie decides to act. She visits Sultan in prison and he tells her he was only trying to give her a potion that would make her do what he wanted; she had once told him the legend that a pearl dissolved in a drink would have a magic effect and so, in the absence of pearls, he used ground glass. The village barber had supplied him with herbs. Then she extracts the truth from the children about what they had done to Teresa; one of them throws a stone at her and cuts her head, but she is able to get signed statements that will exonerate Nabir. An old admirer, Toby, a solid English doctor, already alerted by Teresa, arrives to rescue Sophie; she succumbs to his familiar, comforting presence and thinks that perhaps, after all, she will go back to England and live a quiet suburban life. The book ends with Sophie running away from Toby, but only temporarily: as the opening has shown, she settles in the end for him and safety.

In her novel, Rumer makes her heroine, Sophie, largely responsible for bringing disaster on herself, her daughter and the village, and it is Teresa who pays the price for her mother's romantic, unrealistic view of the place she has chosen for them to live in and the people around them. The attack on the child by the local children is savage, and distressing to read: although it was not a sexual assault, in the book rumours soon spread that it had been. It is hard not to feel that, through Teresa's ordeal, Rumer was expressing her fear of what might have happened to her children, and her guilt at having exposed them to danger. In the book, the fear and revulsion Rumer felt towards Siddika is not transferred to

Nabir or to Sultan; strikingly, the novel lacks a villain. Some Kashmiris are depicted as devious and greedy, but others are not; the village children's cruelty is linked to poverty, ignorance and fear. Sultan is venal and pathetic, but has no intention of harming Sophie, and Nabir, the gardener, is the hero of the story. Indeed, in Nabir Rumer creates a Kashmiri full of dignity, whose natural decency and goodness make him vulnerable both to the villagers' envious conspiracies and Sophie's naïvety and wishful thinking. The relationship between Sophie and Nabir is potent, emotionally charged but not overtly sexual: 'Nabir is wiser than I am,' Sophie tells Toby. 'I wasn't fit to be with Nabir.' Toby protests: 'Really, Sophie . . . I hate to say it, but you make me wonder if there isn't something in what people say.' Sophie does not argue; instead, she defuses the innuendo by changing its meaning. 'What they say is true,' said Sophie . . . 'They have had their way. I love these poeple and this place.'

Perhaps the most striking difference between the factual and fictional versions of the Dove House story is the way in which, in the novel, Sophie is able to put things right. Neither the Kashmiri police nor the British officials can disentangle what has happened; it is Sophie, on her own, who ensures that Sultan and Nabir are eventually set free. Her paradise is spoiled, she has upset and humiliated people she respects and she has to leave the house, but she leaves with the respect, even gratitude, of her former servants and the villagers. Sophie, unlike Rumer, is able to look back at her time in Kashmir with affection and appreciation rather than with fear. The book could be seen as an extended tribute to Kashmir and the Kashmiris, a country and a people whose beauty and natural nobility are shown in striking contrast to the drab, conventional nature of England and the English.

Kingfishers Catch Fire is a remarkable and unusual book, because it was written from personal experience by a woman brought up in British India, and touches, lightly but effectively, on one of the central and most potent fears of the British community. Without the loyalty of their Indian subjects and subordinates, India would always have been ungovernable. The fear of the treacherous servant, who abuses his or her trust and turns on master or mistress, was profound, but it was seldom publicly acknowledged let alone written into popular fiction. The memoirs of the British in India are packed with loving stories of devoted servants, of heart-rending partings after many years, of lingering memories of an ayah singing lullabies or the syce's riding lessons. Less often written about are the darker stories of theft, exploitation, rape or murder although they circulated busily: Rumer's sister Nancy always insisted that what happened to Rumer was nothing exceptional, especially in Kashmir – 'It happened all the time.' Much of the instinctive disapproval that surrounded Rumer's household was provoked because she was a young woman on her own running a staff that was mostly male. Again, among Indians there were always plenty of stories about handsome young Kashmiris taking the fancy of the bored, neglected memsahib: the looks of the Kashmiris, with their fine, hawklike features and light skin, were much admired and their prowess with women was legendary. It was an easy and obvious way for both communities to discredit Rumer, who had offended the customs of both, to imply that perhaps her relationship with Siddika had been closer than it should have been, perhaps as a result of drugs, perhaps not . . . The idea of a native servant having his way with a drugged, compliant white mistress tapped the deepest taboo of all.

Rumer's novel deserves to be considered alongside the two best known books by British writers about life in British India. E. M. Forster and Paul Scott were outsiders who spent comparatively little time there and their books revolve around a mysterious destructive episode involving an Indian man and a British woman. In *A Passage to India*, well-meaning Adela Quested causes chaos by encountering something she could not understand in the Marabar caves; and in *The Jewel in the Crown* all Daphne Manners's courage and good intentions cannot prevent the destruction of her lover

Hari Kumar after the rape in the Bibighar Gardens. Both books revolve around the realization that the intense, intricate relationship between Britain and India had a dark, mysterious side, and that all the formality and ritual evolved by Ango-Indian society was largely an attempt to keep out the darkness. What happened to Rumer Godden in Kashmir belongs in the same category. It is as unlikely that the full truth of what happened at Dove House will ever be known as that the mystery of the Marabar caves will be resolved once and for all.

CHAPTER NINE

Return to England

1944–8

BETWEEN OCTOBER 1944 AND JUNE 1945, Rumer, Jane and Paula were based with Jon and Roland in Calcutta. It was a time of transition: the war was entering its last phase. In India it was evident that once the war was over, independence would come. For herself, Rumer knew that the next step was to return to England. The joy of being with Jon again, sharing her exquisite house and garden – East Lodge at Tollygunge – full of bright birds and flowers and gambolling Pekes, with Nancy and her two small boys nearby, was intense, but so was her need to take charge of her own life, re-establish her writing career and move on from her failed marriage. Jon and Nancy were well-established and popular young wives in Calcutta; Roland and Dick were prospering in their respective companies, Kilburn's and ICI, and even in wartime their wives could afford to dress well and entertain their friends. Rumer's position was in some ways awkward: she disliked feeling dependent and dreaded being in the way, and although she paid her expenses scrupulously and avoided the social side of Calcutta as best she could it was hard to be, once again, the problem sister, the one who wrote rather undesirable books, who was not easy at parties, whose husband's job had gone wrong, who was getting divorced and who had recently been involved in something unpleasant in Kashmir.

Her way of regaining her self-respect was to plunge into a new and demanding project. She had never quite let go of the ambitious and somewhat unlikely idea that had seized her in the summer of 1942 for a book celebrating the range of work done by the British in India. Back in Calcutta, where she soon realized that the demands of the war had greatly altered the easy, pleasure-seeking routines of the British community, she wanted more than ever to find a way to write about what was going on as her way of making a contribution before it was too late. She was lucky that an opportunity opened up for her soon after she arrived. As it happened, great exception had been taken in British Calcutta to recent comments relayed from London about how easy life was for the British in India, especially for women, compared with the grim struggle endured by those at home. The Bengal office of the Women's Voluntary Service was thinking of producing a pamphlet in response to this allegation; when Rumer heard about it, she offered to help. The pamphlet grew into a short book sponsored by the WVS, who arranged for Rumer to spend time, in uniform, with the various organizations around Calcutta and to travel the length and breadth of Bengal during the winter months of 1944–5. The result was *Bengal Journey*, certainly the most obscure and least polished of Rumer's books but one full of observation and effort, in which she tries valiantly to restrain her natural inventiveness and stick to the facts.

Before launching into her account of the organizations she visited, Rumer wrote an impassioned introductory description of wartime Bengal:

> The last six years have bitten deeply into the life of the Province; they have been years of war and hunger and pressure and sickness and misery; to meet their danger and distress the work of women living in Bengal has risen too, not all the women but very many of them; this work has swollen from tributaries, thousands of small initial efforts, to a stream that is bearing its burden steadfastly and purposefully towards the common sea in which nearly all the world has pooled its hopes. It is of these women that I wish to write.

She knew that it was important to include Indian women in her survey, and she pointed out that even before the war started many had volunteered for service along with the British; but although encounters with Indian and Eurasian volunteers are sprinkled through the book, the main emphasis remains on the British. Her own experience, and what she knew from Jon and Nancy, comes through emphatically, sometimes tinged with indignation.

> There are certain things to be said about British women working in India that are facts, but however plainly stated they do not appear to be sufficiently understood ... this is India, not Europe nor America, and it has a climate – *a climate* – yes, a climate – that makes it highly unsuitable to European and American ideas of work, and office hours, and meal hours. (Have you ever served canteen steak and kidney pudding with a heavy suet crust by the hundred platefuls at 1.30 p.m. at a temperature of 100 degrees in May?)

Determined not to write a drab, impersonal report, in *Bengal Journey* Rumer devised an idiosyncratic mixture of hard facts and vivid glimpses of individuals going about their wartime activities. She worked hard: she lists dozens of groups, noting doggedly how the Ladies' General War Committee was set up to co-ordinate and expand pre-war good works, how the Literature for Troops Section of the Red Cross turned itself into the Amenities for Troops Section, how the St John's Ambulance Brigade Overseas Nursing Divisions (Bengal) expanded its training role, and the ARP (Women's Section) organized lectures. To set the scene, she summarized events since 1939 and described in particular the disastrous year of 1942, the retreat from Burma and the arrival in Calcutta of the battered survivors with their terrible stories, the air-raids, the panic and

> the wild rush among many of the Indian community to get away ... Women, with their houses full of refugees, themselves nursing, or driving or working in other ways, found themselves servantless with the food shops closed ... of course they used

bicycles, but have you ever cycled eight miles daily in a
temperature of 110°?

Tentatively, she tackled the political difficulties of August 1942
after the Congress party leaders were arrested. Most British women,
she wrote, ignored politics and carried on with their jobs, 'going
out daily among hostile sullen faces . . .' She described the onset of
the terrible Bengal famine of 1943:

> The authorities kept repeating 'there is plenty of rice; plenty of
> rice . . .' In that case who, women were beginning to ask, who
> were these people flocking into the towns and the city? Men
> and women and unclothed children, all the scarecrow legs and
> arms and ribs and strange sunk eyes and swollen stomachs?

The scale and horror of the 1943 famine had been bewildering
to a community used to pre-war prosperity and administrative
competence, and worse was to come, but this first man-made
Calcutta disaster had a special impact: 'No one could discover the
truth or the remedy, and what could the women do? Some did
nothing, but the voluntary effort was magnificent.'

Both the tone and structure of *Bengal Journey* are eccentric, less
a report than a collage pieced together from Rumer's investigations
with her notebook. It was important not to leave anyone out:
dutifully she attended on the ARP, the YMCA, the Red Cross, St
John's, the Women's Voluntary Messenger Service, the Calcutta
Hostesses Club, the Nursing Divisions, the Convalescent Hostels,
the Canteen Services, BESA, ENSA, the Three Services Entertainment Committee and more. She tried hard to enliven the statistics
with individuals: 'Here is a Red Cross Almoner come to indent for
her week's supply; she walks around with her list in her hand.
"Sweets," she murmurs, "pingpong balls, blotting paper, tablas
[Indian drums], darts."' Occasionally, a novelist's device is applied.
'Shila and Sheila have never heard of one another; they are quite
different and they are the same. That is, they are both Indian Red

Cross Hospital Welfare Workers.' One is Indian, one is Scottish. No one is named, but 'Mrs X' of the St John's Ambulance Brigade has overtones of Jon, working in a military hospital, helping at a canteen, meeting casualties and refugees at the docks and railway stations; Jon and Nancy may also be characters in a vignette of a typical volunteers' committee meeting, which Rumer wrote like a short play: 'Scene: a small room lent for the occasion in one of Calcutta's leading clubs... Characters: twelve women, in mufti, all well groomed... Time: Dusk of an Indian January day... It might be a cocktail party but for two things – there are no cocktails and an amazing amount of business is proceeding.'

The last section of *Bengal Journey* describes the long tour Rumer made all over the province, from Kalimpong and Darjeeling in the far north to Chittagong and Cox's Bazaar on the Burmese border in the south. To be back in Darjeeling as a reporter in uniform must have been odd, as she looked back to her quiet, introspective months at Jinglam. Her descriptions of the landscape are loving:

> The road to Darjeeling winds down past terraced fields of millet and rice and Indian corn; the hillside is red with poinsettias and yellow with sunflowers ... the road drops to the Teesta River, rushing down from the Himalayas in its winter colour of ice green and jewel blue ...

The Gymkhana Club had turned its theatre into a Services Canteen: dances were held for servicemen in the Durbar Hall of Government House. As she travelled down through the plains, she was impressed by the efforts made in some of the remotest corners: 'British women in the Mofussil (the country) in India are scattered like tiny grains in the loneliness of the Indian plain and in the blank indifference of the largest part of the Indian community. Neither side is good at making friends with the other.' Paksey, a railway community in the middle of Bengal, miles from anywhere, particularly struck her. She rode into the town on a railway motor trolley, through the rural landscape she loved,

> ... an exhilarating way to travel, flying along the rails ... rice
> fields unfold in the sun with a pattern of white clouds, white
> pampas grass and white paddy birds ... there is a smell of sun
> and dusty grass and honey from the mimosa balls on the trees
> along the way ... The Paksey-Ishurdi Work Circle from 1940
> to 1945 sent more than 1,500 knotted garments, 1,200 hospital
> supply goods, 2,000 books and magazines to the Red Cross ...

Slowly she made her way back to the river country of her
childhood. She went part of the way to Narayanganj by boat,
watching the porpoises roll and listening at night to the paddle-
wheel turn and the leadman's sleepy, rhythmical call.

The US Navy was installed along the river, and Rumer found
the five European women who were still in Narayanganj organizing
weekend leave in private houses for men from the 14th Army based
in Dacca. She found little to record there but she managed, she
later wrote, a walk through the town.

> As I walked through the bazaars and the jute works, along the
> river, past the Club, the bamboo-built church and school, the
> houses I had known, it was as if I had gone back thirty or more
> years and was seven, eight, nine, ten, eleven, twelve again.
> Everything was the same; I had lunch on the verandah of one
> of the houses, waited on by whiteclad servants who might have
> been our own. On the way to the ghat we passed the gate of
> our house; I could see the top of my cork tree over the gate ...
> the tree was in flower. For a moment I hesitated. 'Go in, go in,'
> the Babu urged but I could not bring myself to do that.

She left by a steamer that could have been her father's. Watching
the town was like looking at her past down a telescope, 'smaller but
more and more clear until it was out of sight'. She came to regard
this as the moment when the final version of *The River*, her novel
based on her childhood, was born.

The interest of *Bengal Journey* is not so much its factual account
of what women were doing in Calcutta during the war as the

sound of Rumer's own voice describing a society she knew well under pressure. When she writes a humorous description of how a series of domestic disasters fails to prevent a determined memsahib from turning up for her shift at the canteen, despite her demanding husband, her small boy and her imperious servant ('You must remember there is a war on, Abdullah'), or shows, through a monologue, how some other memsahibs continued to justify doing nothing ('No, I admit I'm not doing a war job. Well, really, I haven't got time. You see, there's the house and the servants . . .'), the idiom and atmosphere of the time are re-created, without artifice. However, Rumer never felt satisfied with *Bengal Journey*: she realized that her first attempt at non-fiction showed that her natural talent was for fiction. Nonetheless it was a valuable record of an exceptional time and place.

By the end of June 1945, Rumer and the children had arrived at the Homeward Bound Trooping Depot at Deolali, where they waited in the intense heat and monsoon rains, along with hundreds of other families, to board their ship from Bombay. The rows of little huts festooned with washing, the communal dining room, endless queues, the mud and the flies and open drains were Rumer's idea of hell. Also, Paula was ailing again and Rumer was afraid that they might not be allowed to sail. Fortunately the camp doctor decided that she was not infectious and that it was important to get her home as soon as possible. When they finally got on board some two weeks later, Rumer found the clean, well-ordered ship a relief. Soon, though, they were all in bed with diarrhoea and boils. 'The hospital is blessedly cool and quiet,' Rumer wrote to Jon. 'Outside the noise and the crowd just stun me and I had a cracking head all the time and felt continually faint.' Already she was missing Jon and the civilized comfort of East Lodge, and pining for the Pekes she had reluctantly left behind. As for Laurence, she noted that he had not come to the camp or the ship to say goodbye to the children, though she felt he could have easily arranged to do so. 'Perhaps he doesn't want to see me. It seems obvious he doesn't care much about them in spite of his protestations...' Jane, however, never forgot an earlier moment, 'saying goodbye to Daddy at East Lodge'. She remembered him in uniform, having come from Cox's Bazaar and the fighting in Burma.

As the long, hot, crowded voyage went on, Rumer worried about Paula, who seemed more vulnerable than ever, and about what awaited her in England. She had planned to go first to London but changed her mind and decided that they would all make straight for Darrynane. From Liverpool, where they docked in the last week of July, they travelled on by packed trains to Exeter and Bodmin Road. She had dressed Jane and Paula in their best Kashmir woollens, forgetting that it can be hot in England too. They sweltered all day and then had to spend a night in a hostel at Exeter. By the time they fought their way off the train at lunch-time the next day they were bedraggled and exhausted, but Mop and Fa were on the platform to meet them. After five years, they were back.

It was not exactly home – none of them was sure where home really was any more – but it was reassuringly familiar. The house was shabbier and the garden was overgrown, but the hydrangeas still lined the drive with brilliant blue and the moor was still wild and beautiful. The war years had been hard on the Goddens: Rumer admitted to Jon that her first sight of them had shocked her. Their father was bent and slow, and his eyesight was poor; her pretty mother had become wrinkled and toothy and 'terribly careless of herself, poor darling...' Their standard of living had slipped noticeably: Rumer was determined to find them more help and to reorganize the house and garden. Nancy and her family were expected soon for a long visit, and Jon would arrive the following year. Rumer decided to try to make a donkey hut into a proper study where she and her sister could write. She put off all plans for London and her career until after the summer. For the moment, Darrynane was to be the Godden family base, where they could all gather to celebrate the end of the war.

It was not very long before the euphoria of return and the family reunion faded. Rumer tried hard, but found the unfamiliar domestic chores profoundly uncongenial; in India, even at her lowest ebb, she had never had to cook, wash or clean for a household. After Nancy and the small boys arrived in mid-August, she retreated to the hut where she wrote increasingly desperate letters to Jon, worrying about their father's gloom – which was deepened considerably by Labour's 1945 election victory – deploring her domestic inadequacies, and fretting about her enforced inactivity. *A Fugue in Time* had sold around fifteen hundred copies, and been bought by the *Ladies' Home Journal* in America, but it had not been particularly well reviewed. She was concerned as to what Michael Joseph would think of her new book *The River*, which she was now revising again in the light of her visit to Narayanganj. She knew it was unfashionably short and that they had hoped for a full-length novel. As soon as she could arrange schools for Jane and Paula she intended to go to London, where agents and publishers were waiting to talk to her: there was talk of a film of *Black Narcissus* and *Vogue* magazine were suggesting she write articles for them. It was all, potentially, wonderfully exciting and more than she had dared to hope for; but she felt restrained, once again, by her obligations to her family. Her mother was exhausted from running the house, her father more difficult than ever, money was a constant worry – and Paula had developed a badly poisoned thumb that landed her in hospital. No wonder Rumer herself felt, sometimes, as if she was going mad: 'I know how very lucky I am and odd though it may seem I appreciate that deeply but fundamentally I am not very happy,' she told Jon. 'I can't explain it . . . I only know that I am intensely lonely, that Mop and Daddy and Nancy regard me as something cranky . . .' She knew that she needed to find an independent base. 'Somewhere of my own I must have and get fundamentally straight in it. Somewhere where I can get back to living, not perching on the edge of things.'

By mid-September things were looking up. Rumer found a

boarding-school in Oxford for Jane, and planned eventually to send Paula away to school as well, but for the moment she would stay at Darrynane. But first she had a painful encounter with Laurence's parents, who were still hoping against hope that the marriage could be mended. There are few references to Laurence in Rumer's letters from now on, still fewer in her autobiography and those few are bleak, almost dismissive. The hold he had kept over her for most of the five years she had spent in India had been finally broken; but there was still the divorce to be arranged, which she dreaded, and there were the children. Paula, she told herself, could barely remember him, but Jane was another matter. Jane was a loving, determined child, who could never dissemble and hated seeing those she loved in distress; she was also very fond of her Foster grandparents. Rumer feared that when Laurence came back to England there would be trouble.

It was with a sense of liberation, mixed with guilt, that Rumer went to stay in London with Gilbert and Jimmie Simon, her friends from pre-war Calcutta, who were now living in Pont Street in Knightsbridge. She felt shabby and unattractive, unable to face her agents and publishers until she had bought new clothes and been to the hairdresser's; her appearance, and being properly dressed, always mattered to her. She was not impressed with the war-starved London shops, though, and advised Jon to bring most of her wardrobe from Calcutta, where it was still possible to have clothes made well and cheaply; indeed, she asked Jon to bring underwear and blouses for her and their mother too.

Jimmie Simon was as gay and amusing as ever, and for the first time in years, Rumer found herself having fun. She went out to lunches and dinners and even danced one evening at the Mayfair Hotel, wearing a long skirt made from a velvet curtain and a Kashmiri embroidered jacket. There were to be other evenings when she dined and danced with the Simons, who would find a partner for her from among their many friends; one, who danced remarkably well, was a civil servant called James Haynes-Dixon, described by Jimmie Simon as 'a nice, ugly man'. He was immediately taken with Rumer and started to ask her out; she bought a new evening dress made of rose-coloured chiffon. He was not her only admirer: Anthony Bent, one of the young men who had joined in Sunday lunches at Narayanganj nearly twenty years before, remembered meeting Rumer in London after the war and thinking that she was a little sad; he liked her as much as ever – she had always been his favourite of the sisters – but they were never more to each other than friends. To Jimmie, too, Rumer seemed more anxious and driven than ever, and she felt that the break-up with Laurence had affected her friend more than she would ever admit. She longed for Rumer to recapture some of her old gaiety and sparkle. In Jimmie's view, the only man Rumer cared about at this time was her naval-officer friend from Kashmir, Bob Philipps, now back in London. He had looked after her during the Dove House drama and they had become close; he was bookish and an aspiring writer himself, so they were able to talk about work, always a way to Rumer's heart. But he was married, and after Rumer met his wife she knew there was no future for them.

Rumer liked male admiration and she needed some romance in her life; she was also increasingly aware of the danger, spelled out to her not long before by Roland and Jon, that living alone could cut off both her and her writing from reality, from human warmth and muddle and complexity. But she also knew that, with divorce proceedings pending, she needed to be careful. It was proving difficult to pin down Laurence and the lawyers; she intended to have custody of the children and to ask for maintenance. Since she had left India, Laurence had made no secret of his involvements with other women, but nevertheless, urged on by his parents, he was still asking Rumer to give their marriage another chance. She knew this was impossible, but it was important to her to arrange the divorce discreetly and amicably. In late 1945 she still hoped it could be managed within a year; it took nearly three.

Rumer's professional life, though, was looking promising. She had several useful meetings with Spencer Curtis Brown: his regular communications with her during her time in India, especially while she was in Kashmir, had meant much to her, and although their relationship was volatile she knew he was on her side: he had a soft spot for Rumer. She met Alan Collins, her New York agent, who urged her to visit the USA, and Raymond Everitt, her editor at Little, Brown, who was asking to see her next book. She had lunch with 'a delicate but stubborn little Hungarian', Emeric Pressburger, to talk about filming *Black Narcissus*: 'I think he would treat *Black Narcissus* right if he ever gets it past the censor.' There was talk of a play for New York, of demand there for her short stories, of writing for *Vogue* and *Time and Tide*, of another film based on *A Fugue In Time*.

She returned to Darrynane exhilarated, nervous, and determined that, if she was to grasp these new opportunities, London had to be her base, at least during term-time. 'It is the breath of life to me at present; I need it, and I think it is necessary,' she wrote to Jon, a touch defiantly. Neither her parents nor Jon, she knew, regarded the Simons with much enthusiasm: the Goddens were profoundly clannish, and any strong influences outside the family circle tended to be suspect. Her parents, especially her father, found Rumer's wish to live alone in London hard to understand, but she was adamant. She would still be part of life at Darrynane, and try to do her bit, and use the hut as her study in the holidays, but she was quite certain that her career now required her to be in London.

In all her discussions with her advisers, she assured Jon, she had brought up her sister's work. 'Don't be afraid. I didn't eulogise.' In her eagerness to convince Jon that she, too, could be a professional success, Rumer failed, perhaps, to realize how sensitive her sister was about her position. She relayed a remark of Spencer's about 'naïve faults of construction' in Jon's work: 'I said I hadn't seen these faults to which he replied, "Yes, but you often have naïve faults yourself."' Yet for all Rumer's fierce belief in her sister's talent it had not yet been publicly recognized. Rumer loved and admired Jon so deeply, and had such a profound need for her love and approval in return, that she, perhaps, failed to realize that she was treading on dangerous ground. Rumer was always oddly humble where Jon was concerned: any thought that she was clearly, in professional terms, far ahead of her sister would have been quite alien to her. She urged Jon continually to work harder, to finish her novel, to let nothing stand in her way: 'We must have the courage to go on, both of us ... Maybe you think I don't need courage any more, but Jon I do. The opportunities have to be grasped and I am so uncertain – so unfinished – so over-enthusiastic and under-intelligent.'

By early November, back at Darrynane, Rumer had finished her revision of *The River* and sent it to Michael Joseph. While she waited to hear if they liked it, she found herself, for the first time, gripped by an idea for a children book, which she tried to resist. It would not go away. Within a fortnight, she heard that Michael Joseph liked *The River* very much and would publish it the next spring. Her spirits rose: in the same week she was told by Jimmie of a small house in a Belgravia mews and took it at once. It was tiny, white with blue shutters, 'like a doll's house', she told Jon, but there were three bedrooms and a cupboard-like study and 'there is something very gay and happy about it'. It was furnished, which should have saved her money, but she immediately started thinking of new rugs and lamps. She was feeling rich again: a cheque from the producers of *Black Narcissus* had arrived, and the film would go ahead in the New Year. But Rumer's pleasure in all this exciting news was muted. Jon was infuriated by the criticisms of her work, and still more by her sister's attempts to relate her difficulties with her writing to the circumstances of her life in Calcutta and her emotional ups and downs. It transpired that she had felt for some time that Rumer asked too much of her, and especially that the aftermath of her departure from India had left Jon with innumerable chores over the publication of *Bengal Journey* and the despatching of her sister's possessions from Kashmir and

Calcutta. After making her feelings plain in a letter to their mother, Jon stopped writing. Rumer wrote anyway; eventually Jon relented and Rumer was forgiven. She, of course, felt the trouble had been all her fault: 'I was very miserable over it,' she wrote, 'and it seemed to me that I did nothing but make the very people I cherish most, most unhappy.' It was not the first time, or the last, that Rumer's single-mindedness caused trouble in her family.

It was not only Jon who was making her feel guilty: Laurence had arrived from India and was staying in Esher with his parents. Before long he told Jane that although he wanted them all to live together, her mother did not as she no longer loved him. Caught in the classically painful position of being asked to choose between her parents, Jane wavered: perhaps, if her father was so unhappy on his own, she should stay with him and look after him? The thought of losing Jane, even of sharing her, was impossible for Rumer to entertain for very long. She soon regained control, for Laurence's plans were vague and his resources limited. As Jane recalls, after one or two more awkward meetings her contact with her father faded away, her mother having decided that 'a clean break' would be better for all of them. But Jane never stopped loving her father, whom she remembered only as gentle, kind and affectionate. Rumer could control her daughters' lives while they were growing up, but she could not control their thoughts and emotions – and, for all their love for her, she was not the easiest of mothers, which they both realized as they began to grow up. The return to England was altogether a painful time for Jane, who never forgot how hard she found it to settle at school, where she felt out of place and the other children teased her relentlessly for not knowing how to behave like a proper English schoolgirl.

After Christmas at Darrynane, with Jon the only missing sister, Rumer was unable to hide her excitement at her forthcoming move to London. Somehow, despite the cold and the mud and the family, she had finished her children's book, a story of dark doings in a doll's house – although, as she wrote defensively to Jon, 'I know I should not have written it. I know I should eschew, violently, the teenie weenie and the precious but I just could not help writing it and after all I can suppress it if I think it wiser.' On the last day of January 1946 she took the night train to London to start her new life. 'I am scared stiff of it: of the immense amount of money I shall have to make to live there at all, of the writing part ... and the thought of answering the door at night and finding that it is a postman who isn't really a postman but a bandit who will knock me on the head ...'

Her London venture started in style. It was not long before she decided that the rented furniture was too hideous to live with and spent more than she could afford on a pale blue Persian rug and Regency furniture, including an inlaid table to use as a writing desk. She went out and about with the Simons and their friends, including James Haynes-Dixon, to concerts and exhibitions, and bought new clothes. Publication of *The River* was imminent, but Rumer was more excited by the plans for the film of *Black Narcissus*, and her meetings with Pressburger and the director Michael Powell, whose initial choice for the key part of Sister Clodagh was Geraldine Fitzgerald. When *The River* came out, in the spring of 1946, to her best reviews since *Black Narcissus* in 1939, Rumer was taken by surprise. She remained modest about *The River*, and almost bemused by the praise it continued to receive.

The River is only a hundred pages long but it contains the essence of what makes Rumer Godden a remarkable writer. It had taken her years to get right, and yet it reads as easily as if it had been written in a week. Firmly based in her own childhood, it has universal echoes of all childhoods. It is a simple story that unfolds in a few months, in a backwater in India, among children and adolescents. In characteristically clear, unaffected prose, the writer touches on deep truths about the ways in which we all learn about love, death, guilt and loss. It is not just a brilliant evocation of the passage from childhood to adolescence, but a classic reworking of one of the greatest of fictional themes, the theme that underlies all of Rumer's best work: the loss of innocence. Written as Rumer was finally leaving the India in which she had grown up – for although she returned on visits she never lived in India again – it is more than just a personal celebration of a lost world: by the time it was published in 1946 the British withdrawal from India was little more than a year away. There is not a political thought or word in *The River*, and Rumer never wrote directly about the British departure or how it affected her family. (In fact, for the Goddens, Indian independence in 1947 did not mark the end of their involvement with the country: unlike the army officers and administrators whose occupations were removed overnight, many businessmen remained in their jobs for twenty years. Jon and Nancy and their husbands continued to live and work and prosper in Calcutta. Yet it is impossible to read *The River* now without relating its theme to the realization among countless British families that their life in India was over, that the ever-rolling stream of time was carrying them away.

The setting of *The River* was a barely fictionalized Narayanganj and a household very like the Goddens'. Four English children are living with their parents in Bengal. 'They lived in their house beside the river, in a jute-pressing works near a little Indian town; they had not been sent away out of the tropics because there was a war; this war, the last war, any war, it does not matter which war.' On the first page, Rumer shows, lightly but unmistakably, that she intends the story, though told through a child, Harriet, to have universal overtones. Harriet is struggling with her lessons. 'It is strange that the first Latin declension and conjugation should be of love and war.' Harriet is Rumer, with her private diary and her poem book kept in a secret place, her determination to be a writer one day, her longing to be pretty despite her big nose and her devotion to her beautiful, accomplished, enigmatic older sister, Bea. Their father runs a jute factory rather than a shipping line, and they have a younger brother, Bogey, as well as a little sister,

Victoria, but the details of the large grey house with its flat roof and flower-filled verandah, its wonderful garden with a big cork tree and brilliant creepers, the servants of all faiths and, above all, the wide river with its constant traffic of steamers and sailboats and rolling porpoises, the kingfishers flashing among the water hyacinths, are all recalled with piercing accuracy.

The story revolves around Harriet's reluctant discovery that growing up is inexorable and means encountering the facts of life, love and death. She watches, jealously, as Bea moves away from their childhood alliance, drawn towards maturity by a sophisticated friend and the admiration of a young man crippled by the war. Harriet can still escape these confusions to join her brother Bogey in his secret world in the garden, but when she breaks a household rule and allows him to keep his biggest secret the result is tragic. The cobra that kills Bogey one hot afternoon is real enough (and Rumer later said that she remembered Nancy playing with a snake among the flower-beds), but it also represents the dark side of life, the reality of evil that no paradise, no guardian angel, parents or servants can keep away, in India or anywhere else. Harriet's guilt and pain are the price she has to pay for her fall from grace; but by the end of the book she has learned the two vital truths that enable her to go on with her life and follow her calling. The first is personal to Harriet, as it was to Rumer: for a writer, all experience, no matter how terrible, can be used. '"No. No, I can't, I mustn't. *Write* about this? No. No. I can't", but it was already forming inside her head . . .' The second is universal, and it is the message of the river, flowing calmly on, inexorable, impervious, like time, to love, hate, sadness, joy: '"How beautiful it is," said Harriet. It's beauty penetrated into the heat and the ache of the hollowness inside her. It had a quiet unhurriedness, a time beat that was infinitely soothing to Harriet. "You can't stop days or rivers."' Harriet's realization has everything to do with the impact of India on Rumer, learned in her childhood and youth not deliberately or intellectually but through her eyes and her emotions. India taught her, as it has taught many Westerners before and since, that acceptance is a form of understanding and that not everything of value is achievable by conscious thought and effort.

Not everyone instantly saw the point of *The River*. Rumer never forgot that one critic said that 'There is not enough meat on this book for the library cat.' At first, in America, Little, Brown were cool, regarding it as a 'novelette'. But when it was published there in the autumn it was well received, and one short review in particular proved important. The *New Yorker* called *The River* 'a beautiful written long short story' and 'A brief moment in the unfolding life of a little girl growing up in India that catches, because of the author's exquisite delicacy and wisdom, the wavering, elusive lights of childhood.' The revered French film director Jean Renoir, by this time living in Hollywood, was so struck by the *New Yorker*'s remarks that he read the book and immediately bought an option on it. He described it to a possible backer as

> exactly the type of novel which would give me the best inspiration for my work – almost no action, but fascinating characters; very touching relationships between them; the basis for great acting performances; and an unexpressed, subtle, heartbreaking, innocent love story involving a little girl ... The action takes place in India, within the limits of a garden. It would not be an easy picture, but at the same time would not involve any insurmountable production problems.

However, like most ideas for films, this one did not at first seem to be going to happen.

Looking back, Rumer would sometimes say that 1946, the year she spent in London, was one of the best times in her life. When both children were at school, she was free in a way she had not been since Jane was born; her writing career had taken off again – after the success of *The River*, the *New Yorker* was pressing her to submit stories – and it appeared that she was making enough money to be able not just to support her family but to enjoy herself: 'That space of gaiety, even luxury, was what I needed.' She went several times to watch the filming of *Black Narcissus* and met the cast: Deborah Kerr was now playing Sister Clodagh, David Farrar was Mr Dean and the young Jean Simmons the seductive Kanchi. When the film came out in 1947 Rumer took her parents to the première, with mixed success. They were tremendously proud, but her father thought the film great nonsense: Powell and Pressburger had not filmed any of it in India, and had not been much concerned with authenticity so that some of the Indian characters wore the wrong clothes and behaved oddly, and the landscape, to anyone who knew Darjeeling and the mountains, was ravishing but unreal. Rumer came to feel that the film, although it stayed relatively close to her story, was not true to her intentions, and she would always react irritably when it was praised for its many admirable qualities. When *Enchantment*, the film version of a *A Fugue In Time*, was released in 1948 by RKO she hardly recognized it. If it was not for the money, she decided, she would just as soon not have her books turned into films.

Her new-found fame brought Rumer invitations to literary gatherings, which she now had the confidence, and the wardrobe, to accept. At first she was pleased to be taken seriously by other writers, but disillusion quickly set in. Dame Una Pope-Hennessy asked her to tea to meet Rose Macaulay, who admired *The River*, but although they told her they thought she should have won the Hawthornden Prize she felt the occasion, and others like it, was not really a success. She was probably right. Rumer was never at home in London intellectual circles. Her shyness, which never left her, made her seem stiff, and her old-fashioned good manners sometimes appeared prim and formal. It was only with the people closest to her that Rumer could relax enough to be her natural self, humorous and shrewd; she never found social occasions and small talk appealing. A basic lack of confidence, deriving partly from her temperament but also from her years of living a very different life in India, led her gradually to feel that literary London was not, after all, for her. 'And why did I think literary drinks parties would be different from the Calcutta ones from which I used to shrink? At which I always became what E. M. Forster called an "ice palace" – palace because, once again, shyness seemed arrogance?'

But she always felt at home with the Simons, either in London or at their country cottage in the Chilterns, James Haynes-Dixon was increasingly devoted, and in the holidays she was busy with the children, in Cornwall or in London. It was a struggle to work while they were all in the little mews house: she was looking after Simon again too, as he had been left at prep school when his parents returned to Calcutta. She employed helpers from agencies with names like Proxy Parents and Clean Doorsteps, with mixed success. However, Rumer often wove stories around her staff and especially treasured memories of Alfred, a sympathetic kleptomaniac, and a snobbish woman who despised the modest household until she realized that her employer Mrs Foster was Rumer Godden, the well-known writer: 'Now that I know who you are I will gladly wash up.'

By the end of the year Rumer had decided to leave London. There were several reasons: health was the one she preferred, and indeed she had suffered a series of chest infections for which she blamed the polluted London air. However, from her letters to Jon, there were other considerations: the need for more space for the children, and the familiar feeling that to write, she needed to lead a more solitary life. She gave up the mews house and talked of buying rather than renting a property. James Haynes-Dixon, who was now cropping up frequently in her letters, had recommended a house in Hampstead. The expense of London, and the fact that Rumer's tax affairs had been neglected so that she now owed large sums on her American earnings, also played a part. Like most writers, even successful ones, she was having to understand that it is hard to make a steady income from books, and that a down payment for film rights, such as she had received for *Black Narcissus*, is not as good as a percentage of the profits. Journalism did not really suit her; she found writing to order difficult and the results were somehow lifeless. Spencer Curtis Brown offered her work as a reader for his agency, but she knew it was wiser to decline. When in January 1947, through friends of Nancy's, she heard of a house to let on the edge of the Arundel estate in Sussex, she took Home Farm House as a temporary solution. The move, in that fiercest of post-war winters, reminded her of Kashmir; why, she wondered, did she have to make things so hard for herself? The answer was, partly, a restless perfectionism, a search for exactly the right place to live and work, which led to four more moves in five years, at considerable cost in emotional as well as material terms.

Rumer's new book was to be about a young dancer and her ballet teacher, and she had received permission from the Royal Ballet to attend classes at their school in Richmond Park. Meanwhile Jon's novel, *The House by the Sea*, was about to be published by Michael Joseph. Rumer's admiration for it was wholehearted:

> I am completely enthralled with your writing and not at all jealous though I have suitable twinges of envy and, sometimes, despair. Don't let's dissemble. It was ever thus: from our earliest beginnings it was always really you who were the mentor but I have the thrusting and pioneering spirit. You really could write the best all the time though you are not as skilled ... I see myself getting more and more precious and delicate ...

When Jon's book, an intense study of a lonely woman enthralled by a murderous intruder, was published in the autumn, it was much admired for its psychological insight and morbid, powerful atmosphere. It was, indeed, as her novels continued to be – she published ten in all over the next thirty years – much cooler in style and darker in content than Rumer's later books. Critics praised Jon Godden, and she made her mark as a novelist but she was never anything like as popular a writer as Rumer. After all, she had never wanted to compete in the market-place, and had little need to do so: she was married to a man who was able and happy to support her. The sisters remained close, and always helped each other with their books, but each came to feel that the other could have achieved more. To Rumer, Jon was held back by her erratic health and emotional vulnerability and her social obligations as the wife of a leading Calcutta businessman; she was bemused by her sister's refusal to promote herself in any way. To Jon, Rumer was increasingly to compromise her talent and lower her standards by writing too much too quickly, and by learning how to please rather than challenge her growing readership. Within their circle, it became the norm for relations and friends to remark, then, and for the next fifty years, that of course Jon was really the better writer. If Rumer minded, she never let it show: after all, no one admired Jon's work more or had done more to encourage and promote it than she had herself.

Meanwhile, Rumer had finished her novel about ballet, *A Candle for St Jude*, and found that once again she was drawn to write a book for children. *The Doll's House* had done well, and it remains a small classic, with its surprising miniature melodrama of love and murder among dolls; John Betjeman, to Rumer's enduring pleasure, was one of its admirers. There was something satisfying, she found, after the long haul of a novel, in a short and precisely focused piece of writing, as all her books for children are, with no description and no digressions. Nothing gave her more pleasure than to read fan letters from children; she had begun to receive a steady stream of letters from readers of all ages, and she tried to answer them all. Nothing annoyed her more, though, then and later, than the assumption that writing for children was easy, although she came to realize that to write for both adults and children was to court critical condescension. She gradually established a pattern that suited her, of alternating a full-length work with something for children. When *The Mousewife* was finished, she embarked on a new novel, *A Breath of Air*, a light-hearted reworking of *The Tempest*. There was never to be much of a gap for Rumer between books and she was usually well advanced with something new by the time the previous one appeared. This helped her to be philosophical when, as happened with *A Candle for St Jude*, the reviewers were lukewarm. Even those who liked it regarded it as slight, which she found painful. She was consoled that Jon thought it good.

Rumer's move from London had done nothing to deter James Haynes-Dixon, who was no longer just an occasional escort and dancing partner: he had begun to play an important part in her life. It was a new experience for Rumer, and a seductive one, to feel that a man longed to be allowed to look after her, to make her life easier, to protect her and spoil her. James would come to the country for a weekend bringing delicious food and drink, take her from her desk for long walks in the woods, let her work when she needed to and be there to help her relax when she had finished. She knew he was in love with her, and it worried her because she was not sure of her own feelings and felt strongly that she should probably never remarry. Also she knew from the start that it would be hard for him to fit in with her family.

For all his warmth and generosity there was something a little disconcerting to them about James's robust approach to life. Born in 1900 and thus seven years older than Rumer, his early life had been difficult and unhappy: his background was modest, and his father had been killed in the Boer War when he was very small. Maltreated by a violent stepfather, he left school at twelve and lied about his age to join the army in 1914. Between the wars he drove lorries and started his own transport and travel company. He had made money and had married, but the marriage failed and his one son had permanent health problems. When war broke out again he worked for the Ministry of Transport; when Rumer met him he had moved to the personnel department of the Central Office of Information, and lived in bachelor disorder in Dolphin Square. For all his achievements he remained something of a social outsider, and when he met Rumer's parents, it was clear that he and Arthur Godden had nothing in common. But he endeared himself to Mop, who recognized in him someone who truly loved her complicated daughter. Rose and Nancy did not take to him, but what mattered to Rumer was Jon's reaction. Jon had been used to being the emotional centre of Rumer's life, and the arrival on the scene of this forceful, determined man was calculated to displease her – and did. She never really saw the point of James, which was that with him Rumer felt unconditionally loved and cared for.

In the spring of 1948, Rumer's divorce from Laurence finally came through, on grounds of his desertion. She was given custody of the children, with Laurence allowed reasonable access to them; she did not ask for maintenance because, she always said, she knew that to do so would be pointless. Although the judge was kind, she described the hearing as 'dreadful to me beyond words'. She had refused all offers from her family and friends to accompany her to court: the Simons, she told her mother, had helped her to cope by distracting the children. Laurence eventually found work in the golfing world, and it was a relief to Rumer when in 1952 he married someone who shared his love of golf. She told Jon she hoped there was some money around and that she would like to think of him being happy at last.

By the end of 1948, Rumer was once again on the move. She decided to buy a house at Speen in Buckinghamshire, near the Simons. Before she had been there very long, news came that pushed her domestic and personal concerns to one side. Jean Renoir had not, after all, given up the idea of making a film based on *The River*.

CHAPTER TEN

Filming The River

1948–50

IN 1958, WHEN JEAN RENOIR was asked to name his favourite among the thirty eight films he had directed, he chose *The River*. When Rumer is asked which of the seven films based on her books she likes best, she always names *The River* without hesitation. Her collaboration with Renoir was something rare in the stormy annals of relations between writer and film-maker: it resulted in a beautiful and influential film, and a lasting friendship. Renoir recognized in *The River* a simple story with powerful undertones. He had been approached about *Black Narcissus*, and had considered it briefly. He was not familiar with Rumer's writing, but it did not matter to him that she was generally recognized as a novelist: as far as he was concerned she was just 'an English lady living in India'. But from the moment he read *The River* he wanted to turn it into a film. As for Rumer, she had never heard of Jean Renoir until he bought an option on her book in 1946; what mattered to her was that, from the first, he took her and *The River* seriously.

In 1948, when the project began to take shape, Jean Renoir was fifty-four and living in Hollywood. Born in Paris, he was the younger son of the painter Auguste Renoir; he grew up surrounded by artists and started out making ceramics, but by 1924 he had directed his first film. Much revered as a director, by 1948 he had reached a difficult point in his career; his move from France to the United States in 1940 had led to questions about his patriotism and to the suggestion, especially in Europe, that Hollywood had compromised his genius as a film-maker. His great pre-war films,

like *La Grande Illusion* (1937) and *La Règle du Jeu* (1939), were
certainly in a different class from the films he had made in
Hollywood during the war. After 1945, Renoir stayed on in
America, largely for personal reasons;. his second marriage, to Dido
Freire, a Brazilian who had worked with him for some years, was
not regarded as legal in France where his first wife was still living,
and although he disliked the studio system in Hollywood, he liked
the climate and the landscape: the orange groves and olive trees
reminded him of his father's property near Cannes in the South of
France. He was looking for the chance to make a different kind of
film in a different way, and he thought that *The River* could give it
to him.

He realized it would not be easy to find a backer. 'The studios
and independent producers don't at all share my enthusiasm,' he
wrote in 1947 to his nephew Claude Renoir, who was embarking
on a career as a cameraman. 'To tell the truth the best place to
make it would be in India. It's a simple and passionate subject,
almost all of it takes place outdoors . . .'

Renoir knew from the outset that the administrative and
technical problems of filming in India would be huge, but he did
not give up. Then, in 1948, an unlikely angel appeared on the
scene: Kenneth McEldowney, a successful Hollywood florist who
was married to Melvina Pumphrey, an experienced and energetic
film publicist. McEldowney had been stationed in India during the
war, and had acquired both useful connections and the ambition
to return there as a film producer. *The River* was suggested to him
as a vehicle, and although it did not at first appeal to him – it was
short on elephants and maharajahs, both of which he considered
essential ingredients for the kind of film he had in mind – he came
to an agreement with Renoir that they would explore the possibilities of a joint venture. By the end of 1948 the bones of a deal
had been worked out. McEldowney, having set up a company
called Oriental International Films, Inc., would acquire the rights
in *The River*, and the film would be shot in colour in India, using

American and Indian finance, during the winter of 1949–50. Elephants were not ruled out. McEldowney was keen for Renoir to make a preliminary trip to India during the 1948–9 winter, wrote Renoir, 'in order to meet some useful people, collect documentation for the script, and supervise the filming of a certain elephant round-up, an event which happens only every ten years and which would be incorporated in the picture'.

The collaboration between Rumer Godden and Jean Renoir did not start auspiciously: he wanted to enlist her help in adapting her book for what he knew would have to be 'a very delicate screenplay', but his first overture was rebuffed. In December 1948 he wrote to Forrest Judd, an associate of McEldowney who was to end up as assistant director, that he was unsure how to proceed. 'Finally I didn't write to Miss Godden. I still feel uncomfortable with her freezing wire, and I am afraid to say something which would harm instead of helping.' However, after Spencer Curtis Brown had impressed on Rumer that Renoir was 'simply the finest film director in the world', she was persuaded to thaw. When she learned that the Renoirs were on their way to India to meet McEldowney and look for locations and even perhaps to start casting, she wrote to Nancy in Calcutta to ask for her help with the preliminaries, while Spencer Curtis Brown started the prolonged and tricky process of settling terms. Between them they were determined that this film venture would be different. Rumer wanted *The River* to be treated with respect, and Spencer wanted to establish for her a really good deal.

Nancy Foster's help in Bengal was invaluable, as Kenneth McEldowney told Rumer in a long letter, adding that he especially appreciated her sister's efforts as his visit had coincided with the height of the social and racing season. On Rumer's advice, they were planning to take the Renoirs by train and river-boat to visit the old family home at Narayanganj – since Partition no longer in India but in East Pakistan – but he also agreed with her that it would certainly be more practical to shoot the film somewhere along the Hooghly close to Calcutta. At Nancy's suggestion they put an advertisement in the *Statesman*: 'Girls, Europeans, preferably English, aged 8–14, to appear in American Technicolor Motion Picture to be produced in Calcutta. No experience required. Director Jean Renoir.'

Hordes of little girls responded: one among them struck Renoir at once as a possible Harriet. 'She is an ugly duckling and that's not so bad.' Nancy greatly enjoyed her involvement with the film world although as she wrote to Rumer at the time, she thought they were all 'quite mad'; and she, like everyone who met him, found Jean Renoir irresistible. He never put on airs; he radiated an almost childlike enthusiasm and he was responsive to the point of impulsiveness. 'He can't be easy to work with as he gets wildly excited,' Nancy wrote to Rumer.

> ... he caused great consternation the other evening in the Great Eastern Hotel lounge which was packed with people. He came rushing in with a scarlet face and an enormous felt hat on the back of his head. 'Where is the Salvation Army? Where are the Christians of this world? Where are they, I say? We call ourselves Christians – Bah!!' All this to the astonished lounge in very broken English! It seems he had gone off on foot to see Kalighat [the important temple of Kali in central Calcutta] and what he saw so shocked him he went round pushing rupees into the hands of all the beggars, many of them dying.

Nancy evidently considered this very strange behaviour and had clearly never been near Kalighat: 'I believe it is ghastly there,' she added vaguely. She told Rumer how much the Renoirs wanted to meet her in England on their way back to California. Jean was 'strange to look at and at first you will think him most odd but wait until he stops feeling strained and gets going. She [his wife Dido] is a lamb but is frightened to meet you . . .'

India, which he had never visited before, had a profound effect on Renoir. He was struck by the juxtaposition of beauty and ugliness – he described Calcutta as 'a good copy of a London suburb including the fog and the smoke' – fascinated by its variety, and freed by his nationality from any imperial self-consciousness. He visited Bombay, Delhi and Benares as well as Calcutta, and met many Indians, including students and film enthusiasts whose knowledge and keenness to learn impressed him. He was introduced to film circles by a young Bengali who became one of his assistants on *The River*, Hari Das Gupta, who had studied in California before returning to India in 1947 and helping to set up the Calcutta Film Society. Renoir hoped to work with Indian technicians, as far as possible, and he shot tests with Indian cameramen and crew. In Calcutta, he was sought out by another young man who knew his work: Satyajit Ray was part of the Bengali intellectual élite. Then twenty-seven, an economics graduate from Calcutta University, he was working for a British advertising agency. He had also studied art at Shantiniketan, the university founded by Rabindranath Tagore, who had been a friend of his family. Ray called on Renoir one evening at the Great Eastern Hotel, to find the great director 'embarrassingly polite and modest'. For his part Renoir was surprised to find Ray 'very Anglo-Saxon, very correct'. When he told Ray how beautiful he found 'the charm and simplicity of primitive life' around the riverbanks, and how many dramatic stories he was hearing about the life of rural India, Ray told him that India

> was full of such stories which simply cried out for filming. 'And no doubt they are going to be made,' said Renoir . . . I said No, because the Indian director seems to find more inspiration in the slick artificiality of a Hollywood film than in the reality around him. 'Ah, the American film . . .' Renoir shook his head sadly, 'I know it's a bad influence.'

In his account of his first encounters with Renoir, written not long afterwards, Ray describes how Renoir attended a reception in his honour at the Calcutta Film Society and answered 'a barrage of questions ... with great ease and candour in his charming broken English'. He explained why he had chosen to film *The River*; Ray was not impressed.

> I had not read the novel, and had no idea what the story was about ... but after all the nightmarish versions and perversions of India perpetrated by Hollywood, I was looking forward with real eagerness to the prospect of a great director tackling the Indian scene. It was therefore an acute disappointment to hear Renoir declare that *The River* was being made expressly for an American audience, that it contained only one Indian character – a servant in a European household – and that we were not to expect much in the way of authentic India in it. Of course, the background would be authentic, since all the shooting was to be done on location in Calcutta. I couldn't help feeling that it was overdoing it a bit, coming all the way from California merely to get the topography right.

Even so, Ray escorted the Renoirs on several expeditions to look for locations in and around Calcutta, and was impressed at Jean's determination to get the details right. 'As he put it, you don't have to show many things in a film but you have to be very careful to show only the right things.' Ray soon realized that Renoir was longing for a complete change from 'the synthetic environment of Hollywood', and he knew that, whatever the result might be, filming *The River* in Calcutta would certainly provide it. At their last meeting on this first visit, Renoir also indicated that his own impressions of India would affect the script. He would sit down with Rumer Godden in London, he told Ray, and discuss the story. 'I may want to make some changes in it; add some new characters, maybe. Maybe an Indian family to show the contrast between their [the English] way of life and the Indians.' When they parted, Satyajit Ray felt, for all his misgivings, 'that there was any amount of creative vigour left in Renoir . . .' and that he would find what he was looking for in India.

Renoir and Rumer gave different versions of their first meeting.

As he remembered, it was over lunch at the Compleat Angler, a well-known riverside hotel and restaurant at Marlow in Buckinghamshire; she tells a more dramatic tale of how, to her alarm, the Renoirs expressed the wish to dine with her *en famille*, and how on James's advice she ordered smoked salmon from Harrods and pink champagne. After dinner, the Renoirs helped wash up, and Jean gave Jane and Paula a pound each before sinking to the floor to talk to Rumer about the film. Rumer was won over from the start. She was struck by his bulk: he was six foot tall, round and bald; 'his small shrewd eyes were hidden in rolls of fat which shook gently when he laughed; he had the most genial disarming face and voice . . .' The children thought he resembled Babar the elephant. Dido was very different, dark and slim, instinctively protective of her husband, but she and Rumer also took to each other. So successful were their first meetings that before the Renoirs left for California it was agreed that if all went well on the business side Rumer would stay with them in Hollywood during the summer to work on the script and then join them in India for the filming. Rumer always said that what really won her over to the idea of the film was that during his visit to Narayanganj Renoir had taken the trouble to spend the night in her old nursery.

After they returned to California the Renoirs and Rumer began an easy, affectionate correspondence. There were to be plenty of dramas and difficulties before *The River* was completed, but there was never trouble between Jean and Rumer. Predictably, there was much argument and negotiation between the film company and Rumer's agents over terms: as well as a lump sum for the rights, they were asking for a substantial salary for her while she worked on the film as well as all her expenses. As it turned out, McEldowney proved elusive as a source of funds and neither Rumer nor Renoir received what had been originally promised. But none of this affected their working relationship.

By the first week of June 1949, after a flurry of shopping for new clothes, Rumer was on her way by air to New York *en route* for Hollywood. Jon, who was in England that summer, agreed to look after Jane and Paula during their holidays; Giuliana, who had married a Swiss and was living in Zurich, came over to help. It was Rumer's first flight and her first visit to the United States, and she was making it in style. At forty-one, she was tasting some of the fruits of professional success, all the sweeter for it having taken more than ten years of hard work, loneliness and personal upheaval to achieve.

She noticed and relished every detail. The flight was luxurious, in a two-decker PanAm Stratocruiser complete with cocktail bar, dressing rooms and white-coated stewards serving dinner; Rumer drank champagne. Later, their seats were made into curtained bunks for the night. Unfortunately, the plane was delayed, and they arrived in New York after a bumpy flight – 'very hot and sticky and headachy'. However, for the first time Rumer found herself being treated as a valuable and distinguished author. Alan Collins, from Curtis Brown's New York office, met her with a limousine: 'I began to feel a little excited when I saw the negro porters putting my bags into his huge Mercury car,' she wrote to 'my dear family' at home. She was amazed by the 'tremendous pace' of the New York streets, the cars as long as battleships, the El (elevated railway) roaring, the steam rising from the subway vents and the crowds of foreign-looking people: 'One saw few Americans until one remembered that they were all Americans.' To her surprise, Collins lived in a small brownstone house that could have been in London. Edith Haggard, who had been handling her increasingly lucrative serial and magazine sales, came to call, and impressed Rumer with her combination of delicate prettiness and tough commercial sense. Rumer was now being published in America by Viking, and she had recently met their celebrated editor Ben Huebsch, the publisher of James Joyce and D. H. Lawrence, in London. She had taken to him immediately, and was pleased to be staying with him and his wife Alvilde in their large apartment on Central Park, 'utterly quiet, unpretentious and overflowing with books and music'. After this, Rumer regarded Ben Huebsch as a friend and one of her 'touchstones'. She spent three days in meetings with agents and publishers, all of whom sent her flowers and made much of her, and at night she was shown the sights. She went dancing, with gardenias pinned to her dress; she despatched parcels of sweets to her daughters. Then, dazzled and exhilarated, she flew on to Los Angeles to be met at the airport by the Renoirs and Kenneth McEldowney.

The Renoirs had only moved into their house on Leona Drive, where Rumer was to stay, since their return from Europe in April. It was in a cul-de-sac on what was then an empty hillside along Benedict Canyon and, by Hollywood standards, it was modest, a one-storey house with green shutters without a swimming-pool. The ground floor was open-plan, with the living room, dining room and kitchen opening on to a big terrace; the walls were covered with paintings by Auguste Renoir and his contemporaries. There was even a Cézanne in her bedroom, Rumer told Jon. (What she did not at first realize was that Dido had given up her own room to the visitor.) She was struck by the simplicity and informality of the Renoirs' way of life: they wore casual clothes (some of hers were far too elaborate) and Jean would often cook dinner on a spit over the fire. They liked the house to be open to the garden and the sun. After India, Rumer always avoided bright sunshine. She was amazed when, soon after she arrived, the bare hillside below the terrace was transformed almost overnight with plantings of olives, orange trees and white gardenia bushes. She liked to watch the humming-birds playing in the spray from the sprinklers. Although they avoided the celebrity circuit, in what Jean referred to as 'Tonsil Town', she met the celebrities who happened to be their friends: she recalled Charles Laughton in deplorable khaki shorts, the Stravinskys, Oona and Charlie Chaplin with their Irish butler and rambling house overrun with small children, and James and Pamela Mason who took their baby to parties in a carry-cot. At the MGM studios she had a cup of tea with Elizabeth Taylor and admired her astonishing eyelashes. One day in a dime store Rumer spotted Greta Garbo in a huge straw hat; when Dido introduced them, Garbo's reserve left her and they talked easily about the *River* script. Most flattering of all, and oddly appropriate, was the moment when Paulette Goddard, Chaplin's former wife who had been a close friend of the Renoirs since she appeared in *The Diary of a Chambermaid*, asked Rumer to help her write a speech she was to give to a gathering of veterans from the 14th Army who had fought in Burma. 'They are sending a bomber to fetch her,' Rumer told Jon. It was all a long way from her feelings of isolation and inadequacy in 1942 in Jinglam, listening to the news of the Japanese advance.

'Working with Jean was the best and richest period I've spent,' she told one of Renoir's biographers in 1990. It always amused her that he, among others in later years, cross-questioned her about her relationship with the great man, assuming that there must have been a romantic aspect to the friendship, a flirtation if not an affair. It was not in the least like that, she insisted. Their closeness was entirely to do with the work. From the first, Renoir told Rumer that she should not expect his film to be faithful to the plot or stick to the characters in her book, but he intended to be faithful to its spirit. 'We will put the book on the shelf,' he told her. 'Then we can keep the flavour while we re-create it in another medium.' They worked hard, shutting themselves away all day in the studio. 'Jean made me re-create ... the written book in visual terms, writing in shots; long-distance, close-up, middle...' He now wanted one of the central characters to be able to link Indian life and culture to the English family, so he and Rumer invented Melanie, a girl with an English father and an Indian mother. Bea, Harriet's elder sister, based on Jon, disappeared altogether. Rumer was relieved to learn that Renoir was determined to make *The River* as authentic as possible, 'with no Bengali peasant fieldworker or boatman singing or talking in English as they did in *Black Narcissus*.

Nowhere in the film of *The River* is there anything artificial that should be real . . .'

Although her relationship with Jean was entirely harmonious, Rumer soon realized that her presence in the household was not without drawbacks. Dido was not used to sharing so much of Jean's attention with anyone, and their friend Gabrielle, once Auguste Renoir's favourite model and Jean's nurse, who lived nearby as part of the family, took strongly against her. 'Où est la dame?' she would say suspiciously when she arrived at the house. Both Jean and Dido had tempers and enjoyed the occasional row; Rumer hated scenes, but learned that they soon blew over and never felt that Dido disliked her. 'Dido and I wrangled,' as she put it, 'half in amusement, half in truth.' Some of the Renoirs' friends were amused by the contrast between the large, ebullient, emotional Frenchman and the small, precise, reserved Englishwoman; one night after dinner Charlie Chaplin 'did an impromptu sketch of Jean and me working together,' wrote Rumer. 'It was hilarious . . .' A contemporary photograph shows Jean and Rumer working at a table on the terrace, a Renoir bust in the background. Jean's large stomach bulges over his trousers; he is wearing an open-necked shirt and looking rumpled. Rumer is at her most attractive, her dark hair short and brushed back, carefully made up, in a neat checked cotton frock and high-heeled white court shoes. They both look serious and absorbed.

By the end of July the script was done. 'I do feel very pleased as it was quite finished, polished and was read with great warmth by everyone; Jean himself was delighted and wants me to do a play with him in the spring from the French which I should like to do.' Jean's great friend Dudley Nichols, the script-writer, gave a farewell party for Rumer, with the Chaplins among the guests. She spent her last night in Hollywood at home with the Renoirs: 'They filled the house with flowers and we had a barbecue all on our own and champagne and a great deal of talk and emotion; it was perhaps the best evening of all as Jean told me so many of his plans and I felt I had lived up to their expectations.' She was right: Renoir was genuinely pleased with their collaboration and wanted it to continue. He wrote confidently to McEldowney, outlining the next steps. By early November, he hoped, he and Rumer would be in Calcutta.

> During the finishing of the sets and the completion of the organisation which we could personally oversee, I, with the help of Rumer, could adjust the script to the personalities of our cast, which would be more clear to us after the first rehearsals. We could then make any alterations in the script suggested by this personal contact with our cast ... our script is a great one and everybody who has read it is crazy about it, but even to this perfect script it is possible that Rumer's first acquaintance with the making of a picture and her reacquaintance with India will give her unexpected inspirations for certain scenes or maybe even for another picture.

He wrote in equally glowing terms to someone entirely unconnected with the project, Ingrid Bergman, then in Rome and under fire in the press over her affair with the director Roberto Rossellini: Jean was fond of Bergman and wanted to send her a gesture of support.

> I'm terribly happy to have the opportunity to do a good picture. I finished the script with the collaboration of the author of the book, Miss Rumer Godden. She is a magnificent writer, certainly one of the two or three great ones living in England now. I intend to continue collaborating with her. After the shooting of our picture, we will rewrite together a screenplay I did in French one year ago. If ever you feel the desire to say, in front of a camera, some good lines, sensitively carved in a delicate English, you just make a little sign and you join us.

After a brief stop in sweltering New York, where Rumer had further encouraging talks with Ben Huebsch about her work – to her immense pleasure he liked her new novel based on *The Tempest*, *A Breath of Air*, about which Spencer Curtis Brown had reservations, and told her never to forget that agents were only agents – Rumer flew on to New Hampshire, where it had been arranged for her to spend most of August at the Macdowell Colony working with Dorothy Heyward on a stage version of *A Candle for St Jude*. A writer's colony in the woods was a very different scene from Hollywood: her clapboard cottage reminded her of Sonamarg, and although she found some of her fellow colonists risible '. . . many intense women . . . saying all the things you thought were caricatures of poets and musicians . . .' she had to admit it was a good place to work and that she needed the peace and quiet. 'You can walk in the woods for miles without seeing a soul. I must say I begin to feel quietened down and soothed.' She admitted to Jon that her stay with the Renoirs had been exhausting: 'I have never had a more enthralling and interesting and adult time but it was a little too robust for me and I did not realize how tired I was . . .' Real life was beginning to reassert itself: she had just heard that Paula had fallen ill, which had upset various plans for the holidays. Maternal anxiety and guilt alternated in her letters with news of her adventures and successes. Jon, too, had been unwell, and there was a problem over unpaid bills. 'I ache to fly straight home . . . My poor Jon, I don't know what to say; everything one seems to do seems to have to be done at someone else's expense; I only hope I have the chance to make it up to you.'

There was something else to which she knew she must face up before she went back: James Haynes-Dixon had told her that unless she agreed to marry him when she returned he would not be able to carry on their relationship. Rumer was disinclined to marry again: 'I was quite happy as his mistress,' she would later say briskly. But when she contemplated life without him, without the support and help and love he gave her, she realized that she could not bear the prospect of losing him. It was also selfish, she reflected, to accept everything he offered her without giving him what he longed for in return. There is no mention of this dilemma in her letters from America, perhaps because she was afraid of how Jon would react, but while she was away she decided to accept him, despite her misgivings. Meanwhile, she hoped that the *St Jude* play would 'help with the family fortunes' – although working with Dorothy Heyward, 'delightful, little and dried-up and fragile', was not like working with Renoir. 'I have to grind my thumbs with impatience but I believe we shall make a play.'

Rumer flew back to London at the end of August 1949 and immediately took the children to Cornwall. After they returned to school she went back to Speen and spent the next few weeks preoccupied with *The River* script and preparations to leave again in late November for several months in Calcutta. There was further haggling with McEldowney over the terms of her contract, and where and how she could be paid to minimize tax, but in the letters she exchanged with Renoir after leaving California there is never any doubt about her commitment to the project. Even the censor – or Production Code Administration, as it was officially called – approved the draft script, while calling attention to some 'minor items', including 'the need for the greatest possible care in the selection and photographing of the dresses and costumes of your women. The Production Code makes it mandatory that the intimate parts of the body – specifically, the breasts of women – be fully covered at all times.' Even small children bathing in the river were not allowed to be naked, 'they should at least be wearing a loin cloth', and a scene where Harriet's mother tells her the facts of life was subjected to intense scrutiny. The words 'God' and 'slut' were not permitted.

But the main problem exercising Renoir and Rumer that autumn was the casting of the crucial part of Captain John, the wounded ex-soldier around whom the romantic themes of both the

novel and the film revolve. To satisfy the American backers and
audience, Captain John had to be an American and preferably,
despite Renoir's original notion of avoiding stars, with box-office
appeal. James Mason, James Stewart and Van Heflin were all
mentioned; for some time the front runner was Mel Ferrer. In the
end Renoir, with time running out, decided to opt for Thomas
Breen, a comparatively obscure young actor who, by an odd
chance, had himself lost a leg in the war. When Rumer saw
photographs of Breen, she was not impressed: she thought he
looked too young and stiff and unintelligent, 'like a football player';
she was also worried by various changes Renoir proposed in the
character of Captain John. He wrote back patiently and at length
to try to reassure her: it was a matter, he explained, of getting the
balance right between Captain John, the romantic hero, and the
confusingly named Cousin John, Melanie's father. He had rewrit-
ten part of their script, he told her, and hoped that she would
approve.

> In this little work that I'll submit to you in London, and which
> I ask you to consider as only a suggestion, I believe that I have
> found a way to have a strong development of Captain John's
> character without killing Cousin John ... there is only one
> thing which disturbs me and that is not to have found these
> things while I was with you because you would have improved
> them right away ...

He felt, he explained, that the right actor would often influence a
script for the better:

> I'm even very much inclined, in my work, to believe that the
> hand is the actor and the glove is the screenplay ... I'm for
> Tommy Breen because if as you say he has the face of a football
> player he also has the deep feeling of a Captain John. This I
> can vouch for ... I'm convinced that the American public will
> find such a born-to-be-strong boy more romantic when they

discover he is badly wounded than they would the classical
leading man . . .

He confessed that another advantage of Breen was that he
would be comparatively cheap. Although McEldowney was having
some success in attracting backing, including the support of two
Indian maharajahs (film rights in *The River* were eventually assigned
to His Highness Bhorajji, Maharaja Saheb of Gondal), Renoir
knew that the costs of the project were likely to rise once filming
in India began. 'Dear Rumer,' he concluded, 'I would so much like
to send you letters a little more idealistic. Alas, this work is terribly
down to earth and the making of a good picture depends too much
on practical questions.'

Rumer gave in on Breen, realizing that she had little choice.
Jean wrote to her with some relief:

> With all my love and confidence in *The River* as an inspiration
> for a film, I still had to find the little key that could make our
> picture widely accepted by an American public. I believe
> Tommy Breen is that key. He will take all our characters by
> the hand and bring them very close to the hearts of American
> audiences.

In London, Rumer was involved in the casting of flirtatious
Valerie, Harriet's older friend, and agreed that the striking young
red-haired actress Adrienne Corri would be right for the part. 'I'm
anxious to see your Valerie, which will change the script,' Renoir
wrote to Rumer on 25 October 1949. 'We are just at that point
when changes can be excellent and add those subtle changes that
make a picture really successful.' The Renoirs expected to see her
in London on their way to Paris and then in Calcutta early in
November. He sent his and Dido's love to Jane and Paula, adding,
'We are ready for our French conversations with Jane.'

Rumer knew that she had to be in India by early December to
work with Renoir on the final castings and revisions to the script
before shooting started at the end of the month, and she and James

had decided to get married before she left. Rumer always said that in James's opinion she married him to solve the problem of Jane and Paula's Christmas holidays, and certainly his plan to take them, and her mother, to Switzerland must have been a great help. Her second marriage took place quietly in a London register office on 26 November, with the Simons but none of her family present: Jon and Nancy were both in India, Rose was in France and her parents stayed in Cornwall. The Simons gave the couple a wedding lunch at Claridges, after which they then drove down to the country for a blessing in the local church, and supper at home by the fire. Within the week, Rumer was in India. She was away from England and her new husband for five months.

Her return to India in 1949 was in marked contrast to her departure just over four years earlier. Then, she had struggled on to a troop ship, with her ailing children, uncertain of her personal and professional future, on her way home to battered post-war Britain to face a new start. Now she was re-entering Calcutta at a film company's expense and a great director was about to turn the story of her Bengal childhood into a film.

It was an unlikely moment for a film crew to be arriving in Calcutta to make a film about the old days and the joys and sorrows of a middle-class British family. Although the transfer of power from Britain to India in August 1947 had been relatively peaceful in Calcutta itself, the city had witnessed appalling bloodshed during Muslim-Hindu riots the previous year; and Partition, which cut off Calcutta from part of its hinterland when East Bengal became part of Pakistan, led to a huge influx of desperate refugees. The fact that *The River* was resolutely unpolitical no doubt helped to make it acceptable: the Indian authorities were happy to have their country shown in a gentler light, and were ready to believe McEldowney when he urged them to regard *The River* as just the first of a possible series of Hollywood-based films made in India for the world market.

This was to be the first Technicolor film made in India, and

McEldowney negotiated a complex series of deals over the import-
ing of the latest cameras and equipment and the training of Indian
technicians. His principal Indian backer was now the magnificently
titled Prince Fateh Singji of Limbdi, inevitably nicknamed Fatty,
who drove around in a magnificent car and appeared to have
limitless confidence in the project. McEldowney also managed to
extract money from the British National Film Finance Corporation, on the grounds that the film was largely a Commonwealth
enterprise. In retrospect the film had an almost uncannily appropriate pedigree for its time and place: a Hollywood producer with
high-level Indian contacts, a French director with an international
reputation among artists and intellectuals, and an English writer
intimately connected with the Calcutta Anglo-Indian community.

Superficially, the circles Rumer knew best in Calcutta had
changed little, despite riots, massacres, Partition, refugees and self-
government. The long slow deterioration of the city's splendid
colonial buildings and gardens had hardly begun, and although the
tide of human misery was rising, it was still at the periphery, not
yet in the centre. Jon and Nancy were living with their successful
husbands in their attractive houses in the best part of the city,
surrounded by lovely gardens, looked after by troops of servants,
much preoccupied with their horses and dogs and the demands of
expatriate social life. For the well-placed box-wallahs, like Rumer's
two brothers-in-law and their friend Owain Jenkins, independence
did not lead to departure until they retired; it was business as usual
in Calcutta, where their experience was needed by both their
British employers and their new Indian rulers. After the war,
Jenkins resumed hunting, shooting and pigsticking, and even the
paperchases continued for a few more years. However, his distinguished ICS brother, who had risen to be Governor of the
Punjab, had returned to England after enduring the hideous
consequences there of Partition which, as he had predicted, had led
to violence and death on a massive scale.

At first, Rumer had hoped that during the filming she might be

able to live with Jon and Roland in Tollygunge, but she soon
discovered that it would not be a good idea to try to mix her family
life with the film world. She moved into the Great Eastern Hotel
in the city, where the Renoirs and most of the Europeans and
Americans in the crew were based. Renoir had managed to bring
two of his most trusted colleagues on to the team: his nephew,
Claude Renoir, was the cameraman, and Eugene Lourié the highly
experienced designer. For all the glamour and excitement, though,
Rumer had reservations: her anti-social side shrank from so much
group activity, and she never stopped feeling that she was neglecting
her real job, which was writing.

> The world of film was new to me [she wrote soon afterwards].
> I found it violently interesting and violently exhausting; I was
> immersed in it and my work. We lived in the polyglot
> atmosphere of Calcutta's Great Eastern Hotel; very far removed
> from any quiet nostalgia, the air hummed with all the schemes
> and discussions, conferences, quarrels, tensions, strains, that
> attended an emotional thing like picture making, especially one
> made in such difficult surroundings.

Not everyone regarded it as wise for the writer to be so closely
involved with the film:

> Producers and directors are exceedingly chary of the authors of
> the books they buy; an author is usually the greatest possible
> nuisance on the set, being liable to treat her work not as a
> working script but as the word of God; authors are also
> conceited, obsessive and ignorant of film; inexperience is
> hazardous, backers of films are not prepared to gamble, they
> like experienced script writers. All this I was told again and
> again and again.

She was lucky, she knew, to be under Renoir's wing.

Their first concern was to complete the cast. Renoir had settled
on Nora Swinburne and her husband Esmond Knight to play the
English parents; Knight had played the Rajah in *Black Narcissus*,

which made Rumer wince but otherwise she approved. The Irish actor Arthur Shields had been picked for Cousin John, and the one important purely Indian character, the family nurse, Nan, was to be an experienced Bengali actress, Suprova Mukerjee. Then there were the children. When Rumer met Patricia Walters, the thirteen-year-old English girl Renoir had picked for Harriet, she found her ugly-duckling quality touching and right. It was not Pat's nose but her teeth that were too big for conventional prettiness: Rumer wondered if they were not almost too prominent . . . The four other little girls in the family were also found among English families living in Calcutta, and innumerable small boys were looked at for the part of Bogey before Rumer and Renoir realized that her nephew Richard Foster, Nancy's younger son, would be perfect. Richard was six and already showing sign of a Bogey-like passion for animals, insects and reptiles. Renoir saw that he could make good use of Rumer's gift with children and she found herself taking charge of the preparation and coaching of Richard and the others.

There remained the most difficult part to cast, the half-Indian girl Melanie, added to the story as a link between East and West. None of the aspiring actresses of mixed race whom they saw seemed right. Then, over Christmas 1949, with time running out, Renoir decided to go to Benares and see a young woman, a student of Sanskrit and of Indian classical dance, of whom he had heard through a Swiss friend, Raymond Burnier. Rumer joined the Renoirs for a few days; it was her first visit to Benares, the holy city on the Ganges, and both the place and the people she met there made a lasting impression on her. Through Renoir, she was moving in progressive artistic circles where it was natural for Indians and Europeans to study and work together; this had never happened to Rumer before. Burnier and his musician friend Danielou were passionate Indophiles, living in Benares to study Hindu religion and culture; they had no time for the British Raj. Rumer remembers fighting back, telling them that her father had given his working life to India, but she knew that some of their criticism was justified. Many of the barriers between her and Indian culture that were the legacy of her background began, quietly, to come down as she observed how open Jean Renoir was to the spiritual side of India.

Rumer and Renoir saw Radha Sri Ram perform one evening at the Theosophical Society. At once, they knew they had found the girl who could play Melanie. The strength and precision of her dancing was a revelation to them and, although she was not exactly beautiful, Radha had a mesmerizing grace and a strong personality. Nevertheless, she was a curious choice in many ways, and she always looked back on the episode with some surprise. She had no European blood: she came from a Hindu Brahmin family, with progressive views, living in Madras, where her father was a leading Theosophist. Radha was a highly educated, serious-minded young woman in her late twenties, and although her background was comparatively liberal – 'my grandfather and father had broken caste and we had dropped many superstitions' – she retained many of the disciplined, ascetic attitudes of the traditional high-caste Hindu. It was the chance to demonstrate her skill and power as a dancer that drew her into the film, and her recognition that Renoir was 'a great man, and a gentleman'. She had had little contact with the conventional English scene in India, and had never heard of Rumer Godden: 'I had read the English classics at school but not much else.' She had never acted: 'Indian classical dance, in which I was trained, uses mime; it is narration, not impersonation. Acting as such was unknown to me.' As for the notion of conveying through Melanie the tensions of someone of mixed Indian and English blood, even half a century later she conveyed disinterest bordering on distaste for the whole idea: 'I could not have conceived of myself as Eurasian at that time,' she said firmly. 'It would have been almost impossible for me psychologically. I had had no contact at all with Eurasian families: not to be snooty, but most of them were people without culture, who wanted so badly to be British.' She recalled once waiting at Agra station with her father for a train in which they had reserved seats. When the guard showed them to their compartment some Eurasians inside started shouting, 'We won't have natives in here . . .' She said, 'Poor things. I don't have anything against them. In the Theosophical Society these barriers did not exist. I didn't take too much notice.' She was in two minds about being in the film at all: 'It was a difficult decision because I had been brought up in a very different way and I simply was not interested in a career in films. I went into it as a kind of experiment, a new experience. I nearly gave up more than once.' Renoir and Rumer were impressed by Radha's integrity and believed that to have her in the film could add to its depth and meaning. The McEldowneys were less taken with her: they were beginning to worry that the cast was short on glamour. It might help, they decided, if Radha would have her teeth fixed; she declined.

In deciding to use amateurs like Patricia Walters and Radha, and to film entirely in India, Jean Renoir knew that he was breaking new ground and that the process would be difficult. He was right: the logistical problems were daunting. Apart from the thirty or so Europeans, some three thousand Indians were involved in the filming, as technicians and extras, and most of them spoke little or no English. Conditions were taxing: although filming began in the cold weather, by late February in Calcutta it starts to get hot, and much of the shooting took place out of doors. Crowds gathered to watch everything they were doing, children and animals wandered across the set, changes of wind and tide hampered the river scenes, erratic power supplies disrupted the equipment. There were no facilities in India for processing the rushes, all of which had therefore to be sent back to England then returned to Calcutta before they could be screened in a local cinema. Kenneth McEldowney annoyed Renoir and Rumer by treating the screenings as a social occasion to impress his friends and backers. The Renoirs and Rumer were happy with Indian food but most of the other Europeans did not care for it, so two catering operations had to be set up. Everyone was afraid of being ill and Rumer found herself obliged to take over the supervision of the kitchens and lavatories at Barrackpore. Even so, Claude Renoir was seriously ill with typhoid for several weeks, while the senior soundman had to have an operation and a substitute had to be flown out from England. Renoir's willingness to wait for days to get the shot he wanted annoyed McEldowney as much as it impressed Rumer. Because he was so open to the discovery of India, he was endlessly willing to change and adapt the script to include new scenes; he always consulted Rumer, who almost always agreed to do what he wanted, but she found herself with many rewrites.

Adrienne Corri, the pretty red-headed eighteen-year-old who played Valerie, was soon causing trouble – as she remembered with some satisfaction. (Rumer remembered her, too – as a girl whose head was turned by her first experience of a Calcutta season, who could not resist the night-clubs and parties and stayed out too late to look fresh on the set the next day.) To Adrienne Corri, Rumer was altogether too prim and disapproving: 'I was very young,' she said. 'I had my eighteenth birthday during the filming. But I wasn't exactly one of the children, and I wasn't one of the grown-ups either, like Rumer and the Renoirs. My friends were the crew, and Gene Lourié, the designer, in particular. We went around a lot together.' She recalled being fascinated by 'the clash of cultures on the film, the way India influenced everyone involved in it. India changes your sense of time, your need to control everything; it breaks down Western ideas.' She was also amazed by what she saw of the conventional British side of Calcutta. 'It was not so long after independence, and there were still riots, and a feeling of danger not far away. I was staggered by the poverty and by the segregation, for example at the races. And at that Tollygunge country club. Indians were not allowed there, so we didn't go, Gene and the Indian crew and me. We met writers and poets, went out to the villages and to the markets looking for silks. I made wonderful dresses out of saris, which was much disapproved of by the boring Englishwomen in their Horrocks printed cotton frocks.' She remembered one day in Calcutta market seeing an Englishwoman shouting at the porters; when they seemed not to understand her she shouted louder and louder. 'Everyone was laughing at her behind her back.' Rumer struck her as 'a bit of a schoolmarm, and exceedingly English', with her 'little soft almost inaudible voice'. It struck Corri, however, that although Rumer sounded shy, she was a very strong character. 'Was she really shy, or just determined to make everyone listen hard? There was a steel core to her.'

As Adrienne remembered, Rumer's relationship with Renoir occasionally came under strain. The two women would sometimes share a car out to Barrackpore from the hotel, which Corri came to dread. 'Rumer would stop the car and cry and complain to me that Jean was ruining her book. Renoir was a divine man, but he was a great improviser; he would see something that moved him one day and decide to incorporate it. Rumer had to do endless rewriting, and she handed out new versions to us on sheets of pink and yellow paper. One wonderful time the ants got in overnight and ate the lot.' To the teenagers of 1950, some of the lines Rumer had given to Harriet, her younger self, were difficult to manage without giggles: Adrienne long relished the memory of the moment when Patricia Walters found herself unable to say to Captain John, of the cupboard where she hid her poems, 'I want to show you my secret hole.' Fortunately Renoir's English was not good enough to grasp the problem, so the girls asked the soundman to explain to Rumer. 'She came back rather red in the face and told us we all had very dirty minds, but she did change the line to "my secret place", which we could just about manage.'

Looking back, Adrienne Corri acknowledged that although she respected Rumer she did not much like her; no doubt the feeling was mutual. To Rumer, Adrienne was a wilful, spoiled girl whose antics were unhelpful to the picture. One day Adrienne asked Rumer what she would do if she was very rich; Rumer replied that she would have her hair done every day. The notion that Rumer

could ever have been romantically involved with Renoir made
Adrienne laugh; for one thing, Dido was always on guard, and for
another Rumer struck her as someone for whom sex would be 'too
messy, too uncontrolled'. As for Rumer's nephew, Richard Foster,
'He behaved so badly we all hoped the snake would get him. Renoir
was beside himself. Richard would stick his tongue out at the
camera and made them do take after take, but because he was
Rumer Godden's nephew we were stuck with him. We gave a party
when he was finally dead.'

Not surprisingly, Adrienne and Radha did not have much in
common. Radha, who chose to stay with relatives in Calcutta
rather than in the hotel, thought Adrienne, like most of the other
film people, superficial. Rumer she found 'a sympathetic and
sensitive person. She and Renoir understood that life did not
depend on glamour.'

A number of stories have been told about local antagonism and
threats of violence towards the film. Renoir and Rumer tried hard
to respect tradition and religious scruples; according to Rumer,
before filming began she had taken part in a ceremony in a pandal,
or shrine, specially built on the set to the goddess Sarasvati,
protector of artists, writers and musicians. One evening a technician
of the wrong caste was sent to remove a garland from the branches
of a sacred tree on the set, thus causing offence. Adrienne Corri
remembers that it had started out as an ordinary tree used in a
staged ceremony, after which somehow it became sacred. There
was almost a riot in consequence, but Renoir calmed the agitated
protesters and real trouble was avoided.

Rumer's account is, characteristically, more dramatic: she
describes the Indian crew forming a circle, being badly beaten up
and having sand thrown in their eyes by an angry crowd shouting
slogans, convinced that the foreigners were desecrating Hindu
shrines and insulting Hindu women. Renoir defused the situation
by inviting the protesters to sit down and ask any questions
they liked, and explaining to them exactly what was going on.

Considering the volatility of Indian crowds, and the nature of the whole enterprise, with its depictions of Hindu deities and festivals, its colonial setting and its touch of interracial romance, it is perhaps surprising that nothing more serious occurred.

Adrienne Corri's most alarming recollection was of seeing bodies floating in the river one day on the way to Barrackpore, after which they were all given armed guards to accompany them to and from the set. She was genuinely afraid one day when a crowd stopped her car and appeared to be about to attack her Sikh driver; then it transpired that they had recognized her from the filming and were simply asking questions.

Among the Indian technicians working on the film were several friends of Satyajit Ray, and he was a frequent visitor to the set. He had put off a planned visit to London to watch Renoir at work. He did not meet Rumer, and apparently his lukewarm opinion of the script did not change; he made one effective intervention, persuading Renoir that it would be unrealistic as well as sentimental to have Melanie, the half-Indian girl, marry the American hero, Captain John. What impressed Ray most was the way Renoir went about the filming, his single-mindedness and perfectionism, his insistence on authenticity, his choice of passages of Indian music for the soundtrack. Renoir's appreciation of the natural beauty of the people and places of India, shown with little or no artifice – he did not use filters or retouch the colour in the film, although he did allow Lourié to add green paint to trees and grass – confirmed Ray's growing belief in the possibility of making truthful films about Indian life. His biographers think he may have discussed with Renoir a film he wanted to make, based on a Bengali short story; this was *Pather Panchali*, the first of the now celebrated Apu trilogy. At all events, meeting Renoir and observing how he made *The River* was a formative experience for Ray: he learned from everything Renoir did, including his mistakes, and he never forgot the encouragement Renoir gave him. Renoir himself knew that some of his Indian admirers never lost their reservations about *The*

River, but he knew that it was the right vehicle for him at the time. 'I had to see India through the eyes of a Westerner,' he said later, 'if I didn't want to make some horrible mistakes ... It would have been very difficult to do anything else during my first contact with India.' He hoped there would be other Indian films, but there never were.

By the end of March 1950, filming was nearly over and Rumer was no longer needed. The Easter holidays were approaching; after a few days' rest with Jon she flew home to her children, her 'real work' and to start her new life as James Haynes-Dixon's wife.

Chapter Eleven

Houses and Writing

1950–61

'James and I are quite happy as long as we live in a desert island,' wrote Rumer to Jon, soon after her return, 'but that isn't possible and he has to learn.' The start of their married life was not easy: spring came late to the Chilterns in 1950 and the cold and the mud were depressing after the warmth and excitement Rumer had left behind in India. 'Never have I seen England look more uninviting ... the people look dirty, hopeless and ugly ...' Running a household was less congenial than ever, especially as she found a pile of work waiting for her: there were the proofs of *A Breath of Air* to correct, rewrites for the stage version of *A Candle for St Jude*, and before long she would be required for further work on *The River*. The cottage seemed too small with James in it, and Rumer knew that Jane and Paula, inevitably, had reservations about the arrival of a stepfather. When Jane was upset she became very quiet, but Paula, at twelve, had lost none of her capacity for dramatic scenes. James had a temper and, as Rumer always admitted, she had the sharp Godden tongue. She was as much preoccupied with her parents' problems and with Rose, who was now trying to build an independent life for herself in England.

James tried to adapt to the demands of her family, but he was accustomed to running his life in his own way and the strain was sometimes considerable. 'The adjustment to married life is a little difficult for us both,' wrote Rumer guardedly, 'but Jimmy is very dear and steady and good and has changed and mellowed. It is I who am not so good ... if only I could have a little whole time, say two hours daily, without interruptions . . .' James had kept his flat in Dolphin Square and would sometimes stay there during the week, which reduced the strain. Even so, 'several times in those first two years I found myself regretting that we, James and I, had not stayed as we were, he ever at hand, he to whom I could say, "I think we need an illicit weekend." Now it was not weekends – or visits, it was for always.' She and the children were not used to a dominating male presence, and some of his attempts to govern their lives caused trouble. 'I had not dreamed he would feel such a responsibility for us,' she was to write in her autobiography. 'I must have been blind, because what man worth respecting would have felt anything less?'

It was especially important for the success of Rumer's second marriage that James was 'worth respecting': it had been her early loss of respect for Laurence that had fatally undermined her relationship with him. She knew that James's background and his forthright manner struck some of her friends and relations as unfortunate; she also knew that he was entirely devoted to her interests. When she admitted, as she did from time to time to Jon in the early years, that the marriage might have been a mistake, she blamed herself as much as James.

> About the marriage I am in the position of the bridegroom at Hindu weddings who puts the lid back on the little pot when the bride takes it off, meaning that, whatever happens, he will keep things locked in his heart. I am, I own, at the moment not at all happy but hope it will get right slowly . . . he has little patience with the problems of Rose Mary and Paula for instance and then he can be abominable and I get nearly pulled in half . . . it is also that I have maybe a morbid dread of marriage and so on which makes me fly off in panic . . .

There were, of course, compensations. James, to his surprise, discovered the delights of owning a Peke: Silk became devoted to him, and it was not long before the household acquired three more

Peke puppies. Rumer redecorated the flat in Dolphin Square, and they would escape to London for the night to the theatre or ballet or an exhibition. James was knowledgeable about food and wine, and introduced Rumer to his favourite restaurants. At his suggestion she established a routine of getting up early and keeping the mornings free for writing; she also found good local help for domestic and secretarial chores. From now on, Rumer usually had someone to do the housework, cooking and to help her with typing and correspondence.

For several months after she returned, Rumer left Speen early in the morning for the Technicolor Studios at Elstree to view the rushes of *The River* before they went back to India. She kept in close touch with the Renoirs, who returned to California in May. 'It has been wonderful to me to see all the rushes and watch the film growing, and I do not at all feel severed from it,' Rumer wrote to Dido. 'All of the film that I have seen seems very beautiful . . .' She was especially impressed with Patricia Walters as Harriet, and with Radha; less so with Thomas Breen as Captain John. 'He seemed to me too much in command of himself, but perhaps this is a bit of Rumer Godden over-sensitivity . . .' She was sharp about Adrienne Corri, who, she thought, 'has worsened considerably, she looks a haggard old tart; what a silly child it is'. Renoir was happy with the film at this stage: 'Since I left France ten years ago I never worked so hard,' he told his agent and described *The River* as 'the first good one I did since I left . . .' The next stage was more difficult, as he struggled during the autumn and winter of 1950 to shape and finish the film. He realized that he would have to make drastic alterations to the opening and feared Rumer's disapproval. The solution he proposed, that there should be a voiceover commentary, worried Rumer considerably, but she was realistic enough to appreciate that it was up to him. They were both by now involved in acrimonious negotiations with Kenneth McEldowney over money, and Renoir was concerned about promotion and distribution; but, as he wrote to a friend, for all his drawbacks

'Kenny ... has unconsciously allowed us to make a film that we couldn't have done in the confines of a regular production.' Rumer's relations with the producers reached a point at which it was even suggested that she might take legal action to prevent the film being shown; sensibly she decided that such a course of action would be counter-productive.

On 1 September 1951 Rumer received a jubilant telegram from Renoir in Venice, where *The River* had its world première at the International Film Festival. 'River received enthusiastically by public last night applause cheers ovation ...' It was awarded the International Critics prize, jointly with films by Robert Bresson and Billy Wilder. That autumn *The River* was released by United Artists in America and France and was well received everywhere, especially in New York, where the *New York Times*' verdict was 'beautiful beyond words'. *Time* magazine called it 'a thoroughly unconventional movie and a very good one', *Newsweek* found it 'visually lovely and emotionally affecting', while *Vogue* simply said, '*The River* is a masterpiece'.

As always, it was Jon's approval that Rumer needed most. *The River* was given a grand opening in March 1952 at the New Empire Cinema in Calcutta, attended by Jawaharlal Nehru, the Indian Prime Minister; Nancy and Dick Foster were there, accompanying their small son, who as one of the child stars was chosen to greet the Prime Minister with a garland. Jon wrote an approving letter to Rumer, although she did not give the film unalloyed praise. Rumer wrote back,

> Yes, 'hand-made' is a good description of *The River*. You must remember that Jean was terribly hampered by his unprofessional actors and the fact that after cutting there was no possibility of any retake ... I feel so glad you liked and could admire it all. Jean's greatness comes out so strongly, doesn't it? I am glad Nancy had a little thrill and joy out of it ... No matter what are its faults I feel proud to have been concerned in it and could even forgive the despicable Kenny.

It opened in London the following month; Rumer attended the première, despite the lingering awkwardness of her dealings with McEldowney.

Adrienne Corri, who was in America to help promote *The River* in 1952, felt sure it had been the McEldowneys who ensured that *The River* received the exposure and promotion it needed. 'The finances really were a black hole,' she said, 'but Melvina did brilliant publicity. *The River* would have fizzled out in three weeks without them.' She gathered that the relationship between Melanie and Captain John had been cut to the minimum because American audiences were not considered to be ready for interracial romance; even so, American journalists asked her whether she had minded working with 'a coloured girl'. Radha was also in America at the time, staying with the Renoirs. She married Raymond Burnier from their house in Hollywood. The marriage did not last, and she went back to Madras to concentrate on her studies and to become director of the library at the Theosophical Society. For Radha, in later life, her part in *The River* seemed like a minor episode, enjoyable but not serious; nevertheless she sometimes attended screenings of the film, by then regarded as a classic, in London or Paris, as a guest of honour. At one of these, in the mid-1990s, she said that seeing it again reminded her how little Renoir had known of India and how 'he learned about India through the film; sometimes it showed'. Rumer Godden, she added, knew more but even so some details were wrong: a tree is called a peepul when it is obviously a banyan, for example. Asked whether Rumer had a true feeling for India, she said, after a long pause, 'If one can make a distinction, true feeling is not the same as deep insight. It is not easy for a person not born into a culture to understand it. The British lived in their own circles; their contact with Indians, no matter how sympathetic, was conditioned by that.'

Fifty years on, the film of *The River* is still much loved and admired (it was the Australian novelist Patrick White's favourite film) but also has its critics, especially in India. The two main components of the film – Rumer's autobiographical story and Renoir's discovery of Indian landscape and culture – sometimes fail to combine naturally, and there is inevitably something dated about the English family's idiom and accents. The voiceover in particular has awkward moments. But for all its occasional clumsiness, there is something timeless and moving about it, which explains why it remains a great achievement. Even a fierce contemporary Calcutta critic like Chidananda Das Gupta, who greatly dislikes what he calls 'the goody-goody colonial moorings' of Rumer's 'sentimental' story, and regrets that Renoir could not have spent more time in India and worked with a different script, has had to recognize that the film has great qualities. He concedes that it 'bore signals of the many things Renoir had talked to us about; among them the most important was his advice that for a national style to emerge the Indian filmmaker must look at the reality that surrounds him ... *The River* may have contributed critically to Ray's decision to make *Pather Panchali* his first film instead of, say, *The Prisoner of Zenda* for which he had written a script...' For all his hostility to the traces he discerns in the film of Hollywood's need for romance and of Anglo-Indian nostalgia for the old colonial days, Das Gupta acknowledges the film's importance. '*The River* occupies a permanent place at the fountain-head of India's new cinema. The history books will have to keep going back to it.'

To the English critic David Thompson, who had made a special study of Renoir and edited his letters, the film was significant for the way it seemed after a difficult period to 'revive Renoir's faith in himself and his work'. He wrote,

> Some have found reasons for taking *The River* lightly; it is a European's view of India; it has some moments close to tourist documentary; the Godden novel is focused on and was really written for teenagers; not all of the acting is assured or smooth. So maybe it could be better ... but the kindliness, the respect and the intuition are endless.

It is one of the films, he concludes, in which Renoir, comparatively late in his career, 'delivered a testimony as rich as *The Tempest* and *A Winter's Tale*, and as indelible as the late quartets of Beethoven. It was a sweeping return, and it established Renoir at a crucial time.'

Rumer remained as proud of her contribution to the film of *The River* as she was of anything else in her professional life, and with reason. It brought a new vision of India to the screen, and stimulated a long series of important films made there, both European and Indian. Working with Renoir taught her much, and she was always grateful to him. Through their collaboration, her simple account of an English childhood in an Indian setting became a work of art in another medium, poignant, timeless and full of universal truths.

The success of the film came at a time when not much else was going smoothly for Rumer: she was unsettled in both her private and her professional life. However, she continued to write: between 1950 and 1958 she published six books, while moving house three times, helping her parents to leave Cornwall, adjusting to married life with James and dealing with her daughters' adolescent upsets. Jane remembered what a relief it was to her and Paula when they were both sent finally to Rumer's old school, Moira House in Eastbourne, as boarders: 'We loved boarding-school; Mother was always moving.' It was equally a relief to Rumer to have them settled and happy, and under the eye of her old English teacher, Mona Swann, now one of her regular if not uncritical readers. Rumer continued to value Mona's opinions and advice on her writing; she never stopped feeling that her education had ended too soon and that there was much still to learn.

It was at this time, during the early 1950s, that Rumer began to move, tentatively at first, towards religious faith. Like the rest of her family, she had never been a churchgoer but spirituality had come to interest her, whether Christian or not; now she was beginning to feel the need for clarity of belief and a discipline to shape her ideas and behaviour. She was ready for guidance when she met two people who before long were to lead her into the Catholic Church. One was the priest of St James's Church at Princes Risborough, Father Diamond, who started to instruct her; the other was an elderly spinster, Miss Barnes, to whom she became close through their mutual friend Bob Philipps. When Bob and his wife Monica left England for Canada in the early 1950s they asked Rumer to look after Miss Barnes for them, and she did. Julia Barnes had worked all her life with Dr Barnardo's, and she was a woman of stringent standards and firm beliefs, a Catholic with a deep knowledge of religion and literature, especially poetry. She lived frugally and alone, surrounded by books in a tiny cottage not far from Speen, and she and Rumer fell into a close teacher–pupil relationship. They wrote to each other regularly, exchanged press cuttings and books, and Rumer visited her whenever she could, often bringing her a present of small luxuries, flowers or fruit. Julia Barnes's uncompromising, unworldly nature was important to Rumer at a time when she felt threatened by endless personal and material preoccupations.

In the summer of 1950 she and James had suddenly bought a nearby small-holding with seven acres of land. The cottage at Speen had been too small and noisy, and their aim was to live simply. 'We shall live on fruit and vegetables and our own eggs and chickens,' wrote Rumer, adding less rapturously, 'Jimmy says no more gin or London but we shall see ... I believe it will make a great difference to him.' For a while, the familiar exhilaration of a move lifted her spirits, although she did admit that the house was unattractive and needed a great deal of attention. Soon she started to worry about the expense and hard work involved. With the farm came four pigs, one about to give birth to a dozen more, thirty black hens and pullets, fourteen Aylesbury ducks, a Guernsey heifer calf and three hives of bees. James and a farm-hand called Ern took charge, while Rumer tried to work. The *St Jude* play had come to nothing when her collaborator collapsed with an alcohol-fuelled nervous breakdown, but after months of uneasy tinkering she had finally settled into writing a new novel based on her Kashmir journal. Her novel based on *The Tempest*, *A Breath of Air*, had been published to mediocre reviews, but sold nine thousand copies and was picked for the Book of the Month Club in America; Rumer was pleased for Ben Huebsch, who had convinced her it should be published despite Spencer Curtis Brown's reservations. Various film deals were in the air, although Rumer had decided against helping Jean Renoir with his new project, *Amphitryon*: she knew she needed a break from the film world if she was to settle into a new book.

White House Farm lasted just over a year. In her autobiography, Rumer paints the rural experiment in cheerful colours, making endearing stories out of pig-breeding and bee-keeping, although she does not conceal that she soon realized that farming life was not for her; but the reality was considerably bleaker. By the spring of 1952 both she and James were exhausted and their relationship was under severe strain. He had developed 'nervous indigestion . . . He says it is my fault and perhaps it is . . . For months now nothing has been done here and it is getting so out of repair,' she wrote to Jon. She convinced him that the answer was another move and when they found a house called Pollards, not far away, they bought it.

> The family will think I'm crazy for it is right in the middle of a village . . . but it seems to me a little safe easy place where one could be at rest but I do not know . . . I am so distrustful now and, rightly, everyone is distrustful of me . . . I have almost run out of money and we shall have to live quietly.

She had another large tax bill to pay. Evidently Jon wrote back a letter blaming James for their financial troubles; Rumer's defence of him tells much about how she had come to see herself and Jon in relation to men.

> No, it isn't fair to say he is a complete liability. Far from it; it is just that fierce people shouldn't live with tame ones . . . we

Rumer with Jane and Paula, Buckinghamshire 1949

On the set of *Black Narcissus*, with David Farrar (top), Deborah Kerr
(second from right) and Jean Simmons (front), 1946

Filming *The River* with Jean Renoir and Rumer's nephew,
Richard Foster, 1950

On the set of *The Greengage Summer*, 1960, with Susannah York, Jane Asher,
Elizabeth Deare and Richard Williams

With her second husband, James Haynes-Dixon, 1960s

Dame Felicitas Corrigan, 1987

In Scotland, 1980s

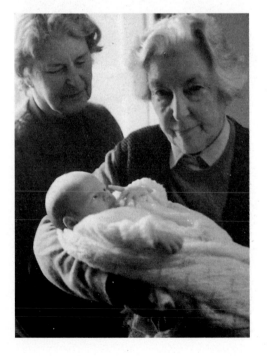

With Rose and
great-grandaughter
Victoria, 1989

Filming with the BBC, Narayanganj 1994 *(Brian McDairmant)*

With Mrs Monisha
Chaudhuri, Calcutta 1994
(Brian McDairmant)

Rumer Godden at ninety

are so sharp and strong and though we fascinate them we wear them out . . . James is a great help to me in very many ways . . . in fact no one will ever know what he is to me, and for that I have to accept the rest. Remember, too, he pours out his all for me and I am very difficult as you know. It is a great wrench for him to forsake his dream but no one man could do all he has been trying to do.

Jon herself was not happy at this time, struggling with a book, hating Calcutta life and undergoing a rough patch in her own marriage. The bond between the sisters strengthened in times of trouble, and the Godden women were always inclined to close ranks against men. Jon had evidently been hearing about Rumer and James's tensions from their mother: 'Don't believe all Moppy says,' wrote Rumer. 'It is not as hard for me as all that. You must remember she has never understood about husbands.' James wrote to Rumer's mother around this time, a letter that Rumer kept. 'Believe me, it isn't always so very bad as it seems to you. We do have fun, we do have happiness. The second year is always the worst I have heard . . . Jacob served fourteen years: I have only twelve more to go.' 'It did not take another twelve years,' was Rumer's comment. 'Soon our boat seemed to enter calmer waters – though, being ourselves, there were patches of storm – and we grew content.' The James she knew and valued was 'knowledgeable, tolerant, gentle, even tender'. As the years went on, she came to rely on him more and more.

Rumer looked back on Pollards as the happiest of all her homes. Her daughters liked it. Paula, at fourteen, was turning out to have the family passion for animals and acquired her first pony; she was still a volatile, slender, accident-prone child, with a disconcerting blue gaze, but she was doing better at school. Jane, now seventeen, was very pretty, with her coppery hair and sweet expression. They had all made friends with the family of Edmund Rubbra, the composer, who lived nearby; Dominic Rubbra developed a teenage passion for Jane, which Rumer thought touching but Jane found tiresome. Rumer's friendship with her Darjeeling friends, the Majumdars, resumed when Agnes Majumdar's daughter Tara came to England with her own daughters, Joya and Sita, who were much the same age as Jane and Paula. They all visited Pollards, and when Joya and Sita were left at English schools Rumer helped to look after them in the holidays. Joya especially grew close to Rumer who came to consider her 'my Indian daughter'.

The girls and James gradually grew used to each other: he enjoyed giving them treats and they grasped how much he loved their mother. Their father played no part in their lives but they kept in touch with their Foster grandparents; Jane was already thinking, perhaps under her doctor grandfather's influence, that she would like to be a nurse. Neither was particularly academic, which did not much trouble Rumer, and nor were they especially bookish, which did a little. It was hard for her to accept that, like many writers' children, they had grown up with a certain resistance, even resentment, towards the occupation that took so much of their mother's time and attention. Both her writing and her daughters were central to Rumer's life, but for her, as for every woman who tries to combine writing and running a family, the strain and the penalties were unavoidable. Jane and Paula knew from the cradle, as did everyone around Rumer, that her writing conditioned their lives – where and how they lived, the hours the household kept, their travels and holidays. 'If it didn't suit the writing, we didn't do it,' was how Jane put it, looking back. She also admitted that many times in their childhood they wished that Rumer Godden the writer was not their mother; they would probably always have settled for Peggie Foster. Like all children, they wanted an ordinary, cosy, available mother for whom they were the centre of the universe, and Rumer was never that.

After initial uncertainties, Rumer's parents settled down in the cottage she had found for them close to Pollards. Her father, who did not become easier as he grew older, disliked the move to a small house in a village and made his feelings all too clear: Grace Cottage,

Lacey Green, was rechristened Disgrace Cottage, Lousy Green, and Arthur frequently sank into dark and angry moods, which Rumer and her mother found hard to bear. All the daughters wanted to do their best for their parents but for some years after the war Rumer was the only one of the four living in England: Nancy and Jon continued to live in India and Rose, too, after doing a secretarial course, went back to Calcutta for a while. Whenever possible, Rumer would take her mother to London for an outing to the theatre or some shopping, and she also began to subsidize her parents financially. Over the years, much of Rumer's income from her writing went on supporting anyone in her immediate family who needed help. She was naturally generous towards anyone she loved, and although she was often worried about money, as soon as she had any she looked for ways to spend it. James, who liked to live well and have beautiful things around him, did not discourage her.

By the summer of 1952 Rumer had finished her Kashmir novel, *Kingfishers Catch Fire*. In her autobiography she mentions it only as one of two books she wrote at Pollards but was not pleased with. At the time, she did not seem emotionally disturbed at having to relive the experience and write about it, although she was not sure that it worked as fiction. 'Has making it a novel spoilt it? Should I have left it as an autobiography? Is it all silly, impossible, trivial?' she wondered. Jon cabled to reassure her. Perhaps it was only after *Kingfishers Catch Fire* was published that Rumer realized just how much of herself she had exposed through Sophie, the well-meaning young woman who brings trouble on herself and those around her. Her Author's Note at the front of the book shows that she did not want her readers to realize how close it was to the facts: 'This book is written out of experience, not of any special experience, but compounded of three years' living, thinking and perhaps dreaming in Kashmir.' One thing is clear: if she wrote *Kingfishers* partly as an act of exorcism, to enable her to forget what had happened to her in 1944, she failed. The episode remained on her mind, buried for years at a time but unresolved and still capable of causing her pain. And as she grew older she felt that the recurrent digestive problems that bothered her could be ascribed to it.

What upset her considerably at the time was Spencer Curtis Brown's reaction to the book. He was already annoyed with her for turning down a film offer for *A Candle for St Jude* because she disliked the film company concerned and for having insisted, with James's encouragement, on asking for more money than they were prepared to pay; now he was evidently not impressed with *Kingfishers*. She copied out the key paragraph in his letter: 'I read the book over the weekend and I think it will do very well. All the people who use your phrase "I do as I must" for "I do as I wish" will be delighted with your leading character, and I believe that the sale might be considerable for that reason.'

This was the second novel in a row that Spencer had not cared for, and it was not surprising that Rumer was beginning to feel that perhaps it was time she found a different agent. It was uncomfortable to be made to feel that she was falling short of his expectations and turning out a lesser writer than he had hoped. There was another reason why their relationship was deteriorating, which was the one Rumer chose later on to remember more clearly. Once they were married, James's wish to help and protect Rumer in all aspects of her life came to include her dealings with her agents and publishers. He felt that it was no bad thing for someone with wide experience of the business and public-relations world to keep an eye on the deals being done on her behalf, and he took to making specific suggestions and questioning financial and other arrangements.

Spencer Curtis Brown did not take kindly to this interference: he had been fond of Rumer and protective towards her himself for nearly twenty years, and James's attitude provoked an explosive mixture of personal and professional jealousy. It was at a dinner at the Ritz in London, Rumer recalled, that it all came to a head and the two men ended up throwing punches at each other. After this, by mutual agreement, Spencer withdrew from the day-to-day handling of Rumer's affairs, although they managed to remain friends. She stayed with the agency, where by the late 1950s her career was in the hands of Graham Watson, a younger and gentler character, who in time became a good friend. Rumer needed to bring her agents and publishers into a magic circle around her; indeed, as her success grew she seemed to need the loyalty and affection of her professional supporters all the more. In 1949 she had left Michael Joseph and moved to Macmillan, who remained her publishers for the next half-century; Alan Maclean, who took over from Rache Lovat Dickson as her editor in the early 1960s, became the adviser and friend she valued most of all.

Kingfishers Catch Fire was published in 1953. In England, after a slow start, it received some excellent reviews; the *Daily Telegraph* called it a 'haunting tale . . . the whole book burns with the beauty and poetry of a matchless landscape, but the human side of it is wry, delicate and true'. Most concentrated on the descriptions of Kashmir and Rumer's skill at writing about children; the *John O'London's* critic noticed something more: 'a touch of the sinister which at times raises her book to a point where it is not unreasonable to compare it with that other classic of Anglo-Indian misunderstanding, Mr Forster's *Passage to India*'. It was well received in America, also, where it, too, was a Book of the Month Club selection. Over the next few years several film options were taken, but Rumer maintained she could never face the thought of a film version. In 1961, Jean Renoir was approached by David Selznick to direct it, with Selznick's wife Jennifer Jones as Sophie: 'I expressed several times my love for this novel and my confidence in it as a vehicle for the screen,' Jean wrote to Rumer, adding, 'How wonderful it would be to collaborate with you again.' The idea went no further.

For the dwindling number of those who remember Kashmir in the old days, or the still smaller handful who can recall the old scandal there in 1944, it retains a peculiar power. Like *Black*

Narcissus it can be read as a subtle delineation of a late-imperial mood of mingled affection, fear and regret. By the time it came out, the Kashmir Rumer had known had gone for ever, fought over after Partition between India and Pakistan, destined to become a steadily more dangerous source of tension and violence between the two.

The other novel written at Pollards was very different. *An Episode of Sparrows* was set in post-war London and inspired, Rumer always said, by the arrival of some fierce Belgravia neighbours at her mews cottage to tell her that she had filled her windowboxes with stolen earth. The story of Loveday, the spirited Cockney child with a passion for a garden, is told with all Rumer's narrative dexterity and her unfailing insight into the minds and hearts of awkward little girls; but it illustrates how her writing could become almost too fluent and charming. There were to be more of such books, contemporary fairy tales with children as heroes, that pleased her increasingly wide readership but were too insubstantial to do her literary reputation much good. *An Episode of Sparrows* came out in 1956, as did a short biography of Hans Christian Andersen, which she was asked to write for a series published by Knopf, the distinguished New York publishing house. She was reluctant at first to take it on, but could not afford to turn it down; although she rather enjoyed the research – which she took seriously, visiting Denmark with James and her daughters and consulting Andersen experts – she was never really at home writing non-fiction, unless it contained a strong personal element. Some of her comments on Andersen's stories provide clues to her own approach to writing for children: she admired their 'perfection of form ... each story has the essence of a poem' and their 'extraordinary swiftness ... so that they are over almost before we have had time to take them in and we have had the magical feeling of flying'. She also defends Andersen against a charge sometimes made of her: 'People call him sentimental; in a way he was, but in the first meaning of the word, which is not "excess of feeling" but an abounding in feeling and reflection.' She recognized his darker side, which she knew was an important ingredient in the best children's books. Rumer always deplored the idea that books for children, even very young ones, should be relentlessly cheerful – 'perhaps the reason why these books are so lifeless is that living things have shadows'. Her study of Hans Christian Andersen is sympathetic and respectful, a tribute from one professional to another. 'It is not a happy thing to be a writer,' one chapter began. 'It may sound an easy life but it is not.'

Her own writing for children, which at first she had thought was a genre she should resist, came to give her more and more satisfaction. Asked why, she would explain that she had always been fascinated by the miniature, ever since as a child in India she had been sent as a present a tiny doll in a matchbox. She enjoyed reducing a story or a drama to its essentials and telling it in few words. She never lost her capacity to see events and emotions from the child's point of view: 'I sometimes think I never quite grew up,' she would say. She took a keen interest in the choice of illustrators for her books, often selecting unknown young artists because she liked their work and wanted to help them. Her standing in the world of children's literature grew: between 1951 and 1972 she published thirteen books for children, including several small classics like *Impunity Jane*, *The Fairy Doll*, *The Story of Holly and Ivy*, and *Miss Happiness and Miss Flower*.

During the 1960s and 1970s she worked with Marni Hodgkin, an American editor who took over the children's list at Macmillan, whose acumen and stringency Rumer greatly respected. Marni found Rumer always professional and ready to listen to criticism: 'The books would arrive perfectly formed; sometimes they would strike me as over-sweet, and I would say so. She never took offence, although by the time I met her she was already a *grande dame* at Macmillan and had to be dealt with as such. Luckily we got on, and I also got on well with James.' Marni felt that, behind his boisterous manner, James was very shrewd and that he understood

Rumer. 'He would tease her sometimes, and look at her in a faintly satirical way. He played a role he thought pleased her, and he knew how she liked to be cherished.'

Prompted, perhaps, by watching her own daughters grow up, Rumer's next novel was rooted in her memories of the family visit to France in the summer of 1924, and the troubling, dangerous, formative experiences she and Jon shared in the Hôtel des Violettes. *The Greengage Summer* is, with *The River*, her most delicate and touching exploration of the themes that moved and inspired her most deeply: emotional growing pains and the potent mixture of guilt and pleasure that accompanies the discovery of sex. To help her remember and re-create the background for her story, she and James revisited northern France. Over the next decade, they were to travel often to Europe, to Switzerland, France and especially Italy, which James knew well. They would usually drive: James loved planning their journeys and introducing Rumer to the good hotels and restaurants he enjoyed; some of their happiest times were spent travelling, when she was free from writing and family responsibilities, although often a journey was connected with an idea for an article, a story or a new book. Sometimes they travelled with one of the girls: Rumer badly wanted Jane and Paula to be exposed to some foreign culture and sophistication. 'She wanted them to have what she had not had, even if it was not really what they wanted,' said their Indian friend Joya.

When Jane left school in 1953, she went to Paris for a year to study French and art at the Sorbonne before starting her nursing training at the Middlesex Hospital. Two years later Paula was sent to a finishing school in Switzerland, which she did not much care for; after a further spell learning to cook, and a brief attempt at drama school as a stage manager, she found work at a riding school in Devon. Paula was determined, and Rumer came to appreciate that it was wise to let her follow her own course. She became a successful professional rider, trainer and breeder of horses. In their different ways Rumer's daughters had high standards, as she had.

To some of their friends, it seemed clear that although Jane was always the more biddable of the two and the closest to her mother, it was Paula who was most like her in her passionate determination to live her own life. Jane and Rumer were brought closer by Jane's decision, in 1956, to become a Catholic. She was received at Farm Street in London by Archbishop Roberts, formerly Bishop of Bombay and another of Rumer's spiritual mentors, who became a family friend. The following year he received Rumer. Her religion was to become more and more important to her, but for some time complete membership of the church, for which she longed, was impossible: both she and James were divorced, with spouses still living, so she was not allowed to take communion at Mass. She was consoled by Father Diamond, who taught her that in such cases, though physical communion was prohibited, spiritual communion could certainly occur. In the light of her conversion she came deeply to regret the mistakes of her past, especially her divorce; but the Catholic Church's strictness on such matters also appealed to her. Forty years later, she said, 'Catholicism suits me because I like the way everything is clear and concise. You'll always be forgiven, but you must know the rules.' Rumer believed in discipline and accepted the rules, but also she never forgot the respect for other religions that her father had taught her as a child, as expressed by Krishna in the *Baghavadgita*: 'The god Krishna says: However men approach me, even so do I welcome them, for the path men take from every side leads to me.' To her family, apart from Jane (and Paula, who converted some years later), Rumer's decision to become a Catholic was hard to understand. They were all sceptical, even Jon, and it was a measure of the importance of her new-found faith that Rumer could accept Jon's disapproval.

By the time *The Greengage Summer* was published in 1958 Rumer and James were living in London. The decision to leave Pollards was prompted, Rumer recalled, by her instinct that it would be better for Jane to have a family base in London while she did her training and found her feet socially rather than for her to have the use of Dolphin Square where there would be too many opportunities for unsupervised parties with unsuitable friends. Rumer remembered her own 'giddy, silly' youth, and she remembered, too, how what seemed like harmless fun could have serious consequences: like all parents, she did not want her children to repeat her mistakes. James agreed with her that it was important for the girls to have 'a background'; their finances had improved, and they were both finding travelling between London and Whiteleaf increasingly tiresome. When Rumer saw an advertisement one day in *The Times* for a large flat in an historic seventeenth-century house in Highgate she took it. They sold Pollards equally quickly to the Simons.

The Old Hall was imposing and elegant, a mark of Rumer's growing success and earning power and of her and James's confidence in each other and in their future. Rumer loved its literary associations with Francis Bacon and Dickens, the beauty of its huge garden and views across London, and the fine, large rooms with oak panelling and elaborate plasterwork ceilings. She greatly enjoyed finding the right Persian carpets and aquamarine silk curtains, and filling the rooms with flowers from Covent Garden. The house was divided into six apartments, but Rumer and James had the main entrance, the large hall and the splendid drawing room, with its open fireplace, overlooking the garden. Rumer worked in the White Study next door; there was a separate flat downstairs for the girls. Margaret Rutherford, the much loved and eccentric actress, and her husband lived in one of the flats upstairs and Rumer acquired some vintage Rutherford stories – she once helped Margaret to entertain a chimpanzee for tea. She admired the actress's capacity for hard work, and would sometimes invite her in for a reviving whisky when she came home after a performance.

Rumer remembered the Old Hall as a good place to work. It was during her time there that she began a habit that would last for the rest of her life. On each New Years' Eve she would go to her desk after dinner to start a new piece of work with a new pad of paper and a new pen. She found an exceptional secretary and assistant in Celia Dale, herself a writer and critic who was put in touch with Rumer by Curtis Brown, their mutual agent. Celia remembered that it was, in fact, James who hired her: he appeared to run all Rumer's professional affairs. She soon saw that, underneath his sometimes brash and off-putting exterior, James was a kind and affectionate man: 'He really was a rough diamond, but he had a heart of gold.' She became very fond of him, especially after her own husband died suddenly and James found her soon afterwards weeping into her typewriter: he gave her a comforting hug and a mug of Bovril laced with sherry. She found Rumer composed and charming, always professional and 'a very private person . . . There was steel underneath.' As well as typing Rumer's manuscripts, Celia helped her with the considerable work involved in a series of poetry readings Rumer organized, with the theatre director John Carroll, at Kenwood House on Hampstead Heath. In 1957 Rumer and James set up a small group they named the Company of Nine, a reference to the nine muses. The group, which operated for six years, included Carroll, the publisher Erica Marx, the poet Christopher Hassall, the writer Pamela Frankau, and Rumer's friend Jean Primrose, an artist who illustrated several of her children's books. It put on poetry readings at Foyle's bookshop and the Arts Theatre Club as well as at Kenwood, and also gave readings for children in schools and libraries. For the first time Rumer was finding that certain aspects of the public side of literary life appealed to her. She was briefly involved with PEN, but their meetings bored her. More satisfactorily, she accepted an invitation to join a Book Society panel, helping to choose novels to recommend to members. She always recalled the excitement of reading and recommending *Memento Mori*, an early novel by Muriel Spark.

After *The Greengage Summer* appeared in 1958, to excellent reviews, Rumer produced two books for children, *Mouse House* and

The Story of Holly and Ivy, before settling down to write *China Court*, a romantic family saga set in an old house in Cornwall, much influenced by Darrynane and her love for the Cornish landscape. Like *A Fugue In Time*, it was technically adroit in the way it mixed the generations, and it pleased her American readers in particular, with its somewhat far-fetched portrait of a young American woman finding her place in a traditional English family.

Meanwhile, her own family was on the move again. After Rumer moved to London, her father's discontent with Grace Cottage deepened and it became clear that her mother's life would not be worth living until they found somewhere to his liking with more space. Rumer and James looked at several houses before they found Lydd House at Aldington in Kent, a pretty, substantial house in several acres with an adjacent cottage. With Rumer's help, her parents bought the house and she and James kept the cottage, planning to use it for weekends. But it was not long before the cottage was needed for Jon, whose marriage to Roland, uneasy for several years, came to an abrupt end. In 1957 Jon had returned to England, after spending most of her adult life in Calcutta where, despite her problems and discontents, she had been cushioned by money and servants and protected from reality by the lingering privileges of belonging to the Calcutta social élite. Rumer, who had earlier advised her sister to try to make her marriage work if she possibly could, realized that readjustment to life in England would be hard. She knew that Jon, now fifty-two, was 'spoiled in every sense . . . She had not dealt with money, only spent it.' The divorce left her badly off: she wanted to be near her parents but could not live with them, so Lydd Cottage was the obvious answer. She lived there for the rest of her life.

In 1958, when she was twenty-three, Jane married a young officer in the Royal Artillery, Anthony Murray Flutter. It was a large, formal wedding at St James's, Spanish Place, in London, with the reception held in a marquee in the Old Hall gardens. Celia Dale remembers how pleased Rumer was that her elder daughter was happy and settled with an eminently suitable man. Jane had known Anthony for about two years; he was handsome, ebullient, energetic, and also a Catholic convert. Jane was soon pregnant with their first child, Mark, born in 1959, in Wales where they were stationed. She went on to have three more children, all girls, and Rumer found that being a grandmother suited her exceptionally well.

In 1960 James retired from the Central Office of Information, and he and Rumer moved yet again. It seems that he had not quite given up the idea of a country life: Little Douce Grove, in East Sussex, eight miles from Rye, was very different from the run-down farmhouse in the Chilterns. It was a substantial property, with forty-six acres, three cottages and a chapel; the house itself had been converted from a large farmhouse and two oast-houses. The Haynes-Dixons embarked on an ambitious and expensive pro-gramme of alteration and modernization. This house was to be the fulfilment of the dream James had abandoned nearly ten years earlier, although Rumer missed London and sometimes felt uneasy at the way they were accumulating responsibilities and possessions. It was not just the expense that bothered her, for she was approaching the peak of her earning power: *The Greengage Summer* was being filmed with two budding young actresses, Susannah York and Jane Asher, in the parts based on Jon and Rumer. Jane Asher still recalls how strongly she identified with the part and how true she felt it was to the emotions of her own early adolescence. Rumer enjoyed advising on the film, which was directed by Lewis Gilbert and made largely on location in France. Meanwhile American sales were strong. The frugal, ascetic side of Rumer, which longed for simplicity, had been dormant, but in 1961 a new friendship reminded her of the appeal of a different way of life, and brought her in touch with a place and a tradition that enthralled her.

CHAPTER TWELVE

Stanbrook and Brede

1961–9

STANBROOK ABBEY, at Callow End in Worcestershire, had been an enclosed community of Benedictine nuns since 1838. Founded in France in 1625, by Dame Gertrude More, the great-great-granddaughter of Sir Thomas More, the order arrived in England after the French revolution; by the late nineteenth century Stanbrook was a substantial and respected establishment, with its fine dark red complex of high Victorian Gothic buildings and its tradition of excellence in music and scholarship. Although in 1961 the nuns lived an enclosed life, based on the strict Benedictine rule of prayer, silence and contact with the outside world only through a grille in the parlour, they were also dedicated to helping those in need, and their prayers and advice were constantly sought. In 1961, when her daughter Jane was pregnant, problems developed that worried Rumer badly. Through a Catholic friend she learned about the Stanbrook nuns and wrote to the Abbess to ask them to pray for Jane and her baby. When Elizabeth Rumer Murray Flutter was born safely, on 19 July 1961, her grandmother wrote again, saying that although she had been introduced to the Abbess as Rumer Godden, 'this week I am far more importantly the mother of Jane Murray Flutter, for whom you and your community have prayed with such steadfast kindness. Almost immediately the toxaemia that threatened disappeared . . .' She asked if she and James might visit Stanbrook on their way to Wales to see the new baby.

When they arrived, they were shown into one of the parlours where the nun who greeted them from behind the grille was Dame

Felicitas Corrigan, a shrewd, humorous woman of about Rumer's age and herself a writer, scholar and musician of distinction. She had been offering prayers for Jane and she was the obvious choice from the community to meet a well-known novelist, as she was regularly in touch with academics and writers and had published, in 1956, a much-praised book based on the correspondence of a former abbess, Dame Laurentia McLachlan, with Sydney Cockerell and George Bernard Shaw. Stanbrook had a famous library and its own printing press; Rumer had found the Stanbrook translation of a medieval Book of Hours useful in *China Court*. She had also admired a Stanbrook edition of poems by Siegfried Sassoon, himself a correspondent and friend of Dame Felicitas, and bought a copy for Ben Huebsch, Sassoon's American publisher. When she said how much she would like to meet Sassoon, Dame Felicitas said she would write to him to suggest it. When she wrote to thank her, Rumer called their first meeting 'a wonderful experience', and sent a generous donation to help the community build a new cloister. From then on Stanbrook became part of Rumer's life and Dame Felicitas, in particular, one of her most valued friends. Through her, Rumer was able to share a powerful spiritual and intellectual tradition, which she came to admire greatly. In Dame Felicitas she found another mentor, someone who could teach her about her faith and guide her through spiritual difficulties, although her new friend was refreshingly averse to too much intensity about religion. Their relationship was one of mutual liking and respect; they grew to trust and feel protective towards each other. Both were strong women with high standards, more vulnerable than they appeared. Dame Felicitas, struck at first by Rumer's elegance and worldliness, soon saw through what she later described as 'the shy, reserved possibly arrogant appearance . . .' while Rumer came to realize that the life of a contemplative nun was not all serenity and holiness. 'She knows what is behind my armour,' said Dame Felicitas of Rumer after more than thirty years of friendship; Rumer could have said the same of her.

Within a few months of their first meeting, they were writing to each other about their work and their preoccupations, about poetry, books and music. When Dame Felicitas had to go to hospital, Rumer went to see her and observed that she was unable to eat the food; she went straight to Fortnum and Mason and arranged for tempting meals to be delivered. It gave Rumer and James great pleasure to send the whole Stanbrook community treats from time to time: they would arrange deliveries of fruit and cheese at Christmas or a special fish for the Easter feast after Lent. Through letters and visits, Rumer gradually became familiar with Stanbrook's religious and domestic routines, the ceaseless round of prayer, work and correspondence that constituted convent life. She began to gain an unusual insight into the way the community functioned, how the nuns related to each other and to the outside world.

Meanwhile, after nearly three years of extensive work on the house and garden, Little Douce Grove was finished. James planted a rose garden, Paula started a riding school in the stables and Rumer found an excellent secretary in Peggy Bell and a most satisfactory new cook in Mrs Manders, with whom she was to produce a book based on favourite recipes. She was still going regularly to London for meetings of the Arts Council poetry panel which she had been asked to join in 1959; she relished being part of a new initiative to promote the reading and publishing of poetry and having poets she admired, like Stevie Smith and William Plomer, as colleagues. She embarked, with James's help, on a series of poetry readings in schools in Kent and around the country, selected by her and read by young actors. Her poetry activities took time and energy, but even so by the beginning of 1963 she had a new novel ready. *The Battle of the Villa Fiorita* was set in a villa on the shores of Lake Garda where she and James had spent a summer holiday. Rumer maintained that this book had been prompted by a distaste for novels in which children whose parents separate are invariably presented as the helpless, passive victims of events; she had decided to write a story in which the children fight back. Around this simple but original premise she produced a subtle, quietly subversive book, in which the gentle English Fanny, and her film-director lover, Rob, find that for all their deep love for each other they are no match for Fanny's children, in particular for her youngest daughter, Caddie, another of Rumer's awkward, determined, plain but lovable small girls. By the time she wrote it, her own troubles with Jane and Paula over James had receded, but that experience and the guilt she felt over her failed marriage to Laurence, especially since her conversion, helped to tip the moral balance of the book against the lovers. She also had both Miss Barnes's and Dame Felicitas's scrutiny to consider. She was still sending all her work to Jon, who wrote to her with her usual directness, calling the book

> the mixture as before; children, a spot of Catholicism, animals, flowers, houses, a little sentimentality and piety, all exquisitely written and perfectly done as only you can do it. But if this is a typical Rumer Godden it is a vintage one ... A lightweight novel about a very serious problem ... I feel sure that it should be a great success, and will be, except perhaps with the critics, as usual ... It is a very clever and subtle book, and intensely feminine.

She also tackled Rumer, not for the first time, on her idiosyncratic punctuation, on which a series of editors had battled with her in vain: 'Why do you have a comma at the beginning of a clause and not at the end? It isn't grammar or sense.'

Ben Huebsch also expressed qualified praise: 'I'm sure it will be your most successful (commercially) book,' he wrote to her in January 1963. 'I am less sure that it is your best ... but it didn't have to be that to give me some delightful hours and a fresh sense of your magic.' After nearly thirty years as a novelist, Rumer had herself begun to wonder if she was in danger of repeating herself and to cast around for a new direction, but before *The Battle of the*

Villa Fiorita was published, she found herself homeless overnight. In early March 1963, while she and James were out at dinner in Rye, leaving Paula and a friend in the house, a pan of oil left on the stove caught fire and Little Douce Grove was reduced to a shell. The girls rescued the dogs and horses, some of the carpets, a few special treasures and the proofs of the new book, but everything else, including many of Rumer's manuscripts and papers, was destroyed.

The blow, Rumer always said, was worse for James than for her. The shock and the aftermath of the disaster made him ill, and she felt that he never quite got over it. The financial loss was considerable and the disruption was immense; they were negotiating with the insurance company for months. Rumer always rose to a crisis, and her work remained her anchor. She and James moved into a local hotel; she finished the proofs of *Fiorita* and began to think about her next book.

Her connection with Stanbrook had given her an idea for a novel about a community of enclosed nuns. Dame Felicitas, she always said, planted the seed by remarking how much she wished that, for once, someone would write a realistic book about the religious life; Rumer, who had come to feel, as she learned more about Stanbrook, how ill-informed and over-dramatic her earlier novel about nuns, *Black Narcissus*, had been, now made up her mind to do just that.

She and James decided not to look for another country house but to move into the old town of Rye. In the ten years they spent there together after 1963 they lived first in a rented house before moving to the fine old Hartshorn House; in 1968, they took on the tenancy of the dignified and historic Lamb House, once the home of Henry James, from the National Trust. Lamb House had also been the home of E. F. Benson and Montgomery Hyde, so it was a house with a considerable writing tradition. Although few traces of Henry James were left, Rumer used his writing room and rather enjoyed showing visitors round. She was asked one day if she knew Rumer Godden; 'All too well,' was her reply.

When *The Battle of the Villa Fiorita* came out later in 1963 it did especially well in America, where it was taken by the Book of the Month Club and extracted by the *Reader's Digest*. Serial rights were sold to the *Saturday Evening Post*, and Rumer used the money to set up a trust for Jon. Viking paid forty-five thousand dollars in advance and the first print run was for fifty thousand copies. Film rights were quickly sold for a hundred thousand dollars, and it was shot the following year, with Rossano Brazzi and Maureen O'Hara. In England, Macmillan sold twenty thousand copies, despite what Alan Maclean referred to as 'bad luck' with the reviews. Several papers ignored the book altogether and one or two were unflattering.

From the early 1960s, it began to be apparent that while Rumer's readership was solid and her earnings at their peak, her critical reputation in England was in decline. She was increasingly regarded as a popular rather than a literary novelist, but as she had never really felt she belonged in intellectual circles she could afford to pay little attention to whether she was fashionable or not while her sales proved that her readers were loyal. She was beginning to have confidence in her own judgement, and the substantial sales, also in 1963, of *Prayers from the Ark*, a group of unpretentious poems in which birds and animals speak to God, written by a Frenchwoman attached to a Benedictine Abbey south of Paris and translated by Rumer, proved her point. Rumer continued to write poetry herself but, although she sometimes sent a poem to Jon or to a trusted friend like Ben Huebsch or Miss Barnes, had long given up any serious idea of having her poems published; the success of *Prayers from the Ark*, which was published with delicate illustrations by her friend Jean Primrose in time for Christmas, gave her particular pleasure. She sent the impoverished author, Carmen Bernos de Gasztold, and her community in France, the bulk of the proceeds.

Rumer's novel of convent life, *In This House of Brede*, was her longest and most complex book, and she always said it took her five years to write. She was determined that it should be as accurate as she could make it, and she immersed herself in detailed research into Benedictine history and tradition, liturgy and music; with Dame Felicitas's support, she gained permission from the Abbess of Stanbrook to make regular visits, observe all the services and ceremonies and talk to many of the nuns. It was agreed that the text should be submitted to the Abbess for approval before publication. She did not want to make the identification between her fictional abbey and Stanbrook exact, so she altered the geography and the architecture, taking the name and setting of Brede from the countryside around Little Douce Grove and Rye; she visited other Benedictine communities, but Stanbrook and Dame Felicitas were always central to the enterprise. James supported her loyally but some of the other people who mattered most to her were lukewarm about the project, not least her sceptical sisters. If her publishers had doubts they kept them to themselves, for Rumer's recent commercial success enabled her to write whatever she wanted. Ben Huebsch, though, found it hard to understand both Rumer's conversion and why she was now determined to write a book about the religious life. As she recalls, when he asked her why she had chosen the subject, 'My writing self, which is the more truthful, answered: Because nuns are dramatic. Theirs is the greatest love story in the world.' She had agreed with the Abbess that she would not use any of the Stanbrook nuns' personal histories in her book, but what she learned from them gave her imagination plenty of material. She had worried that they might find it hard to be open about their problems and feelings with an outsider; in the event, she found nearly all of them more than ready to talk, and her main problem became how to avoid inadvertently revealing to one nun what she had heard from another. They came to trust her to a remarkable extent. Asked what made her decide to allow Rumer such unprecedented access the then Abbess, Dame Elizabeth, simply said: 'She was the kind of person one did trust.'

During the years she spent working on *Brede*, and as she reached her sixties, Rumer was more productive and energetic than ever. Between 1964 and 1969 she published three children's books, *Mrs Manders' Cookbook*, a collection of short stories and, in 1966, *Two Under the Indian Sun*, the evocative account written jointly with Jon of their childhood in Narayanganj. In 1964 she had been back to India for the first time since 1950: Nancy's husband, whose career had flourished and who had become chairman of ICI in India, was approaching retirement and Nancy had been urging Rumer to visit them before it was too late. The Fosters had a large house in Delhi as well as one in Calcutta, and Rumer went there first. It was spring, the best season in Delhi and, as she told Dame Felicitas in a long letter, for once the journey had nothing to do with work. 'This coming to India is a rest, a holiday, which is perhaps why I feel a bit lost . . .' Dame Felicitas, it seems, had been worried about her doing too much, but Rumer was reassuring. 'India, remember, is my natural habitat and Delhi is at the moment so lovely.' The house was splendid, there were twelve servants and Nancy had made a wonderful garden, 'all the English flowers muddled with cascades of orange creepers, bougainvillaeas, jessamine, plumbago, morning glory and fountains playing for refreshment'. For the first time Rumer saw some of the glories of Rajasthan, the palaces of Jodhpur, Jaisalmer and Udaipur. Nancy and Dick had many Indian friends in high places, including Muchu Chaudhuri whom Nancy and Rumer had known since their Darjeeling days. He had made an outstanding career in the Army and by 1964 had risen to commander-in-chief. He helped to arrange their journeys and ensured that they were received in style wherever they went. Rumer also visited Calcutta, where she attended Mass with Mother Teresa's community; she then travelled south to Cochin and the famous game reserve at Periyah where she stayed on an island in the lake, got up at dawn to watch the elephants and had an alarming encounter with a poisonous spider in her bedroom; she would probably have been disappointed if her trip had been quite without drama. Everywhere, she was looked after and entertained in the grand traditional style, but Rumer was well aware of how much India had changed since 1950. 'I must say the new Indian India is, to me, far more interesting than the old,' she wrote to Dame Felicitas, 'and it is good to see the friendliness everywhere . . . I always hated the manners of most English here.' She attended Mass in Delhi at the Aspostolic Internuncio's chapel; she wished that Nancy, whose kindness and efficiency impressed her hugely, could share her faith. 'Why is someone so good and sweet without it?' she wondered, and sent Dame Felicitas a poem she had written about Mary and Martha.

By the mid 1960s, although Jane and Anthony were living in Cyprus with the Army, Rumer's family was otherwise within easy reach of Rye. Paula was running a riding school and livery stables at Udimore. Rose, after some years' working in Calcutta, was back in England; she had not remarried, and had moved into Lydd House to look after the Goddens who, by now both well into their eighties, needed her help and companionship. When Nancy and Dick Foster left India in 1965, they bought a handsome house, Simnells, not far away. The four daughters were thus nearby in 1966 when their father died, at eighty-nine, followed soon afterwards by their mother. Rumer had hoped that after many years of devotion to an increasingly difficult husband Mop would have a little time left. She arranged a ninetieth birthday dinner in Rye for her mother with all her children, not long before she died. Both the Goddens were cremated and their ashes placed in the church-yard at Aldington. Rose inherited most of their property and Jon was left a share, but Rumer and Nancy had agreed to take only small keepsakes from their parents' estate. Rumer always wrote a detailed weekly letter to Jane while she lived abroad, usually on Sunday, her lifelong letter-writing day. She sent Jane a calm factual account of her grandmother's last hours, how the daughters covered her with her favourite Kashmiri shawl and watched by her coffin. After the funeral, Rumer admitted, she felt exhausted and could not stop crying. James had looked after her with loving understanding, and she told Jane she knew she was lucky to have him to lean on at such a time. Dame Felicitas helped her, too, and Rumer was able to spend a few quiet days at Stanbrook where she had already arranged to attend the ceremony, known as the Solemn Profession, when a novice becomes a nun. By this time Rumer had herself been accepted as an oblate, one of a small group of lay people attached to the Stanbrook community, who say prayers at times coinciding with the offices at Stanbrook and are entitled to wear beneath their clothes the symbolic scapular – black and white tabs on a black ribbon – indicating allegiance to St Benedict.

Despite Rumer's fears James appeared to have recovered after the shock of the fire faded and they were established in Rye. He especially liked Lamb House, where he made another rose garden and supervised the rebuilding of the kitchen and dining room, and where he wrote *Home Made Trousers*, an account of his painful childhood, which Macmillan published in 1968. Meanwhile, he was more involved than ever with Rumer's professional affairs, and they travelled together a good deal especially, during the later 1960s, in the United States. Her American agents, publishers and her public treated her as the literary *grande dame* she had undoubtedly become. There were always baskets of flowers in her hotel room, cars and escorts to take her wherever she had to go, lunches and dinner parties at the best places, respectful interviews with reporters; for several years she toured the country on the lecture circuit, talking to clubs, schools and colleges about writing. For all her shyness, there was a strong performing streak in Rumer: she had been back to Mona Swann for coaching as a public speaker, and with her talk typed out for her to fall back on, and James in support, she found herself capable of facing and holding large audiences although she was always agonizingly nervous beforehand. She needed good amplification, as her voice was naturally light and high, and sometimes she needed to stand on a box to see over the lectern, but she became an effective and entertaining speaker.

It was James who first proposed the lecture tours and contacted a leading agency, W. Colston Leigh Inc., of New York, Chicago and San Francisco. 'The Celebrated Best-Selling Author— A Delightful Platform Personality,' they proclaimed in a leaflet. Rumer worked out talks on a range of subjects including India, Talent, Hans Christian Andersen, Writing for Children (subtitled 'Just a Little Story Anyone Can Write') and one on women poets, with a title taken from Sappho, 'I Cannot Mind My Wheel'. On this last, the leaflet announced, 'She poses the question of why a woman poet is so rare and why her life is apt to be a war with domesticity.'

While she was in America as well as talking to her publishers and addressing her public, Rumer would usually manage a few days' relaxation with James. One year they went to New Mexico, but their favourite part of the continent was New England, especially in the autumn, where they would retreat to a comfortable hotel and walk in the woods. Rumer loved Emily Dickinson's poetry and they visited her home at Amherst; in 1968 she produced an edition of Dickinson's poems for young people. They liked New England so much that they even toyed briefly with the idea of moving to Connecticut or Massachusetts. They had become close friends of Orville and Lilias Prescott, who lived in Connecticut and with whom they would usually stay a few days; Prescott was for many years the lead reviewer for the *New York Times* and a staunch admirer of Rumer's work. She had learned over the years not to set too much store by the opinions of critics, but she was intensely proud when Prescott included her in a book in praise of his favourite writers. After Ben Huebsch died, aged eighty-nine, on a visit to London in 1965, it was Bill Prescott's good opinion she valued most in America.

By the middle of 1968 *In This House of Brede* was in its final stages, and Rumer was ready to submit it for approval to the Abbess of Stanbrook; it had been agreed that a panel of Dame Felicitas and two other nuns would read it. On 5 May, as she sent the text to Dame Felicitas, Rumer wrote to the Abbess:

> If she thinks the book possible, I shall, if I may, come to Stanbrook and go through it with her as, even if there are no major falsities, there are bound to be many minor mistakes. The difficulty has been that to make a story there has to be conflict and drama, which should both be alien to the life of a contemplative nun.

The verdict was favourable, and on 19 June the Abbess wrote to Rumer to tell her that Dame Felicitas was 'happy about the book and thinks it first rate. This of course does not surprise me but it does please me very much . . . knowing the spirit in which you have worked at it and written it I am sure it will do much good, with God's blessings on it.'

Brede did seem to be blessed: everyone who read it before publication was impressed by it. A hint of amazement is sometimes discernible behind the compliments: against the odds, Rumer had written a respectful book about nuns that was also likely to be a commercial success. Her agent, Graham Watson, told her it was a triumph; Macmillan were delighted, and Alan Williams, the editorial director of Viking, wrote from New York to tell Rumer he found the book 'absolutely extraordinary . . . I would have been incredulous had anyone told me how terribly involved with and concerned for a community of Benedictine nuns I could become . . .' Rumer herself was genuinely surprised that the response was so strong: she had prepared herself for the book to have a limited appeal, especially in America. Again, it was a Book of the Month Club main choice and taken by the *Reader's Digest*. 'That's what we Yankees call hitting the jackpot,' as Viking's chairman Tom Guinzberg wrote to Rumer, and offered an advance of a hundred and fifty thousand dollars. James was deep in consultation with Graham Watson about the best way to minimize tax; eventually it was agreed that the money could be paid in annual instalments for ten years. He had been in negotiation the year before with Bookers trying to make a deal for Rumer similar to the arrangements the company had made for Agatha Christie and Ian Fleming, but it had fallen through; now, Rumer Productions Ltd was set up. Rumer had always intended that Stanbrook should benefit from any financial success the book might have; now she asked Viking to send them five thousand dollars. In due course Stanbrook became part owners of the copyright in *Brede*.

By the time the book was published, in the autumn of 1969. Jane and her family were back from Cyprus and living near Dumfries in lowland Scotland. Anthony had left the Army and was setting up in business there, and Jane was beginning to build the kind of settled country-based family life she had always wanted. Rumer followed her four grandchildren's progress – by this time Mark and Elizabeth had two younger sisters, Emma and Charlotte – with the keenest interest and loved to have them to stay at Rye; it gave her great pleasure that summer to take Jane to Stanbrook. There was a flurry when an unguarded interview Rumer gave to the *Sunday Express* led to a dramatic story about how Jane and Elizabeth's lives had been saved by the prayers of the Stanbrook nuns; Jane, who had long ago come to terms with her mother's renown as a writer, nevertheless preferred that such matters should remain private, and Rumer was apologetic. The article prompted a spate of letters from people in trouble, both to her and to Stanbrook, and she realized that the book would lead to many more. Eventually the Abbey produced a leaflet for her to send to correspondents who wanted to know about the community and what it stood for. When the book was published, it was indeed a major popular success, selling better than any of Rumer's recent books and appearing on the bestseller lists; Rumer spent a month in America on a publicity tour, during which she spoke at the Library of Congress in Washington and inaugurated an annual lecture on children's literature in Baltimore. She was careful, though, in interviews not to name the pregnant girl whose plight had first sent her to Stanbrook Abbey.

Of all the praise she received for *In This House of Brede*, it was perhaps Jon's that was the most unexpected. She wrote to Rumer that she found it 'a stupendous achievement ... real, true and authentic'. She added that she liked 'the austere parts' best. Rumer's skill at conveying, in simple terms, the power of religious conviction and the beauty of the Benedictine rule and ritual is impressive, and the book is structurally her most ambitious. It covers nearly twenty years and deals with some two dozen major characters, most of whom are never shown outside their enclosed Abbey. At the centre of the story is the worldly, successful civil servant, Philippa Talbot, a widow in her forties whose only child, when the book opens and she enters the Abbey, is long dead. Through and around Philippa, Rumer constructs a sequence of interlocking stories of how women of very different backgrounds and temperaments decide to become nuns and what difficulties and triumphs ensue. Although nothing very sensational happens, there is plenty of emotional drama: a revered Abbess turns out to have mismanaged the finances, a senior nun becomes too attached to a gifted novice, Philippa's spiritual development stalls when a newcomer turns out to be linked with her painful past. The nuns are shown to be as capable as any other group of malice, envy and ambition, but they are also shown as dedicated, compassionate, shrewd and, above all, serious about their relationship with God. *In This House of Brede* succeeds because Rumer believed deeply in the truth and importance both of what the nuns were doing and what she was doing in writing about them. There is no doubt that the book reached many people on a level deeper than entertainment: letters poured in, to Rumer and to Stanbrook, many from readers in search of help, a number from potential or actual nuns. The letters kept coming for years: nearly twenty years after *Brede* was first published Dame Felicitas sent one on to Rumer from a young woman living in America, who wrote:

I was raised a Protestant though we attended church seldom. At sixteen years of age, I read a book of which you may have heard. The title is In This House of Brede by Rumer Godden ... My attraction to the Catholic faith was initiated by that book. Though the story was based on fictitious characters and events I knew that the spirituality described was genuine.

She became a Catholic and later an oblate attached to a Benedictine community. 'The Sisters are an embodiment of Christ's ideals. I felt I had come home.'

Dame Felicitas wrote to Rumer: 'If or when you feel despondent over your work, remember letters like these and take heart. You can say to Our Lord: "These are the children I have borne for You – May we all alike reach everlasting life and see your Face."'

CHAPTER THIRTEEN

Moving On

1970–93

WELL BEFORE *In This House of Brede* was published, Rumer was busy with her next two books. She was not happy unless she was writing something: the idea of taking a break had little appeal to her. It was also important, she knew, to take full advantage of her earning power: her income was more than healthy but they did not live frugally at Lamb House, and her strong sense of family responsibility involved her in helping all those she cared about. Large sums went into backing Paula's riding establishment, and she made trusts by assigning rights from different books in favour of Jane and Anthony and their children, as well as for her parents, Rose and Jon. James had his civil service pension but little else, and he had his disabled son to support: it was Rumer's income from her writing that enabled them to live as they both wished, and pay the staff they needed to run Lamb House, entertain, and to travel in style. Rumer paid little attention to how her finances worked; James had taken charge from the beginning and she trusted him and her agents to do what was best. Graham Watson recalled trying to suggest around this time that it might be prudent to look towards a time when Rumer might need the income she was giving away, but to no avail: James's main concern was to reduce her tax burden, which they succeeded in doing, and meanwhile she was more productive than ever.

In 1970 she published *The Raphael Bible*, her selection of frescoes from the Vatican alongside the appropriate texts, wrote a lively account of the filming of the Frederick Ashton ballet based

on Beatrix Potter's stories (*The Tale of the Tales*, 1971) and agreed
to a further collaboration with Jon. The success of *Two Under the
Indian Sun* led to a proposal for another joint book about India.
Nora Smallwood, who had published several of Jon's novels at
Chatto and Windus, asked them to write the text to accompany a
set of striking black and white photographs by the photographer
Stella Snead. Jon would drive over from Aldington to work on the
complex project at Lamb House, and the sisters spread out the
pictures on the breakfast-room table where they stayed for months.
It proved a demanding job: the photographs ranged the length and
breadth of India and were often unexpected, with semi-abstract
images of shadows on stone, ripples of water or sand, and studies
of goats or cows. Jon provided most of the research, and it was
Rumer who found herself trying to give a mass of scholarly material
a shape without either narrative or characters; between them they
made it work, using the stages of a man's life as a structure,
interspersed with passages on Indian culture and religion. They
included descriptions of markets, weddings, food (including some
recipes), festivals and funerals. Sheila Bonnerjee, whom Rumer had
first met with the Simons in Calcutta, had remained a friend of
Jon's; she had married the geologist John Auden, brother of the
poet, was living in London, and contributed delicate traditional
Bengali designs to punctuate the sections. In their introduction,
Rumer and Jon called *Shiva's Pigeons* 'a conglomeration of
glimpses', an attempt not to summarize or analyse but to evoke
India's vast complexity. 'Stella's camera can only tell what it has
seen,' they wrote, 'and we can only try to interpret our pooled
experience: what we have seen, heard, touched, smelled and tasted
since our babyhood days, learned since – there was so much to
learn – and always remembered because, like the pigeons, our
spirits haunt the places we have loved.' The handsome, idiosyncratic
book, with a cover photograph of a huge stone lingam carved with
Shiva's face, come out in 1972.

In 1971 Paula, now thirty-three, married Barry Kenilworth,

whom she had first met through her riding school. The wedding was in Rye, and the reception was held at Lamb House; Rumer was happy for her younger daughter, who had not lacked admirers including brother officers of Anthony's, but had seemed disinclined to commit herself. Barry was tall and good-looking, keen on the outdoors, a good horseman and a first-class sailor, who had worked in Australia and Canada before taking a job with a firm selling agricultural machinery. Not long after they were married they decided to try farming in Scotland close to Jane and Anthony, but after six years of struggling to be self-sufficient gave up and moved down to the Isle of Wight.

Subsequently, a certain distance grew, over the years, between the Kenilworths and the rest of the family. The sisters were always on affectionate terms, and Paula would visit her mother from time to time or meet her in London; but she and Barry preferred to avoid anything connected with Rumer's writing life. Rumer noticed this, and could not understand why it should be so; to onlookers, it seemed likely to relate to Paula's stormy childhood and the persistence of mixed feelings about her mother's success as a writer, which had both deprived her of attention yet had also provided her with many advantages. Paula's strength of character equalled her mother's: she would not conform to anyone's expectations. In Barry Kenilworth, she had chosen someone equally determined to protect their independence, who resisted from the first any attempt by anyone, most of all Rumer or James, to influence their way of life. Paula and Barry were not to have children and Jane's busy home in Scotland became the natural setting for family gatherings. Jane loved to bring her friends and relations together, and Anthony gave her his full support while managing to build a relaxed, teasing relationship with his mother-in-law.

In 1972, a book that Rumer wrote for teenagers, *The Diddakoi*, won the Whitbread Prize in the children's book category. *The Diddakoi*, the only book for which Rumer has received a major award, is a short novel with many quintessential Rumer Godden qualities, in which a small gypsy girl battles ignorance and prejudice in an English village. To write it, Rumer did careful research into gypsy life; after reading *Gypsies, Diddikois and Other Travellers* she contacted Norman Dodds, the author, to ask his advice: 'Please don't think I am trying to write a romantic gypsy novel,' she wrote, and told him that she had been interested in the subject since her encounters with the nomadic goat children who had picked herbs for her in Kashmir. He agreed to make sure her account of gypsy ways was accurate. A courageous child under attack, the cruelty of conformists towards outsiders, the abuse of power by the strong, the resilience of the weak were all recurrent themes for Rumer and *The Diddakoi* used them to great effect. Kingsley Amis, who with Antonia Fraser and George Malcolm Thomson judged the Whitbread children's entries that year, called the book 'a rich, exciting, funny, touching, modern story with its roots deep in the world of the fairy tale'. Rumer was pleased, especially when she received a letter of congratulation from Harold Macmillan, although she did not herself feel that the book was her best work, and she was annoyed when Viking insisted on publishing it on the adult list. The letter she wrote them gives a glimpse of how vulnerable she could still feel.

> What is acceptable in a children's book, a certain obviousness of plot, a more 'surface' telling, condemns an adult novel, as the epithets 'a sweet little tale', 'frankly sentimental' confirm. I wonder that you cannot see how damaging these remarks may be when it comes to future novels.

In fact, as even admirers of her work concede, she often did come dangerously close to sentimentality, just as she often skirted round the edge of sexual menace. Her genius lay in drawing back at the last moment, cutting the sweetness with a sharp note and never making ugly sexual possibilities explicit. *The Diddakoi* did well, was translated into nine languages and, in 1974, as *Kizzy*, made a fine series for BBC children's television.

However, in the early 1970s Rumer's increasing anxiety about her husband's health overshadowed all else. James had blood pressure problems, which led to fainting and dizzy spells; eventually he was discovered to have diabetes, and his diet and alcohol intake were restricted. He had always enjoyed a drink, and by this time both he and Rumer were used to the regular consumption of what sometimes struck their friends and family as rather too substantial drinks. Now, Rumer had to take a bottle of Coca-Cola with them on outings in case James needed a sudden intake of sugar. Their travels were curtailed: he was advised not to drive, but did not like to be driven. They tried to carry on as normally as possible, but James went on to develop arterial disease, which affected him mentally as well as physically and the semi-public side of life at Lamb House became difficult. His behaviour became erratic: he would sometimes lash out wildly at those around him or become incoherent. James, who had always been so strong and vigorous, and who for nearly thirty years had supported Rumer, now needed protection himself. Rumer, who for all her dependence on him had often struck their friends as the dominant partner, took control.

Another move seemed imperative and she found a suitable house nearby, but nothing could be done to arrest James's decline. By the late summer of 1973 he was in hospital in Hastings. On 10 October 1973 he fell into a coma and died. 'I do not want to be consoled, ever,' wrote Rumer afterwards. She knew she had lost someone for whom she was the centre of the universe, who had understood what she was really like and who had truly loved her. There is some truth in the saying that in every relationship there is always one who loves and one who lets him or herself be loved, and with Rumer and James there is no doubt that James was the former. Twenty years on, in talking about their marriage, Rumer would speak of how much James loved her, not of how much she loved him. It was perhaps natural for someone of her reticence to say so, though it was also what everyone close to them thought; but she never ceased to miss him and always spoke of him with affection, tenderness and respect. She once said that it became her habit to give herself a present on her birthday, so that she had something to distract her from missing James, who had always loved celebrations and a chance to delight her.

When it became clear, as it did in the aftermath of James's death, that he had left their financial affairs in considerable disarray, Rumer did not blame him. His various schemes had reduced her income, and he had allowed their expenses to mount, apparently without thinking of the consequences. This she put down to the panic into which he had fallen after the Little Douce Grove fire, the insecurity he had carried with him from his grim childhood, the ravages of his last long illness, and herself for her inattention. For a time, the situation did not seem too alarming: she was still earning well, especially in America, and she had no intention of slowing down – she knew well enough that the answer to her unhappiness was to work more, not less, and her own health, apart from recurrent stomach trouble, was good. Her most immediate preoccupation was where to live: she did not want to leave Rye, but she knew she could not continue in Lamb House, and she disliked the house she had bought as a refuge for James. When a house in Mermaid Street that she had always admired came on the market, she bought it, and found herself with three Rye properties on her hands at the same time. She solved the problem with comparative ease but not without considerable expense: the new house needed, as usual, rearranging and redecorating to meet her standards, so she stayed on in Lamb House while the work was carried out. Meanwhile she sold the other property to a doctor, and agreed with Graham and Dorothy Watson that they would take over the remainder of the lease on Lamb House when she moved out. Lamb House without James was sad: Rumer's family looked after her as best they could, although Jon's health was failing. Rumer found her Pekinese a great comfort.

While struggling with her changed circumstances Rumer was distracted by a particularly tricky negotiation over the filming of *In This House of Brede*. When the question of a film had first come up in 1969, Rumer had been against it. As she wrote to Graham Watson: 'Solecisms might slip through, the nuns be offended and hurt; this is something I just could not bear. Even if the film made a great deal of money for me, and perhaps for them, I would not care to take the risk.' By 1970, she had changed her mind, having been assured by her agents that she would have the right of veto on any screenplay and would be 'closely involved' with the making of any film. A deal was done and a draft script was prepared by an experienced Hollywood screenwriter, James Costigan. Rumer had been scrupulous about consulting the Abbess of Stanbrook, who had given permission for the project on the understanding that Rumer would oversee it. The Abbess was especially concerned that there should not be too many 'dramatic highlights' and that the relationship between the senior nun and the novice should remain, as in the book, to do with 'love, but not lesbianism'. It was not until the summer of 1974 that the draft script reached Rumer. She was not pleased: she sent back several pages of detailed notes and a long, firm letter. Costigan, she conceded, had done a good job of compressing and structuring her long and complex story, and there was 'nowhere anything that could possibly offend in the sense of being obnoxious. Yet, the result is far from what I hoped, indeed expected . . . I hope you will forgive me if this letter and notes are outspoken.'

For a start she disliked the new title. 'I earnestly hope you will reconsider *A Lark in the Morning* . . . it has echoes of *The Song of Bernadette* and gives the sentimental image we wanted, at all costs, to avoid.' She also found the dialogue unfortunate:

Mr Costigan has made the nuns speak in places no nun would;
quite apart from a sort of schoolgirlishness ('awfully', 'jolly', in
any case, are out of date), which is far from these extremely
mature and cultivated women, there is an uncharitableness
which I don't think any religious would allow, no matter what
she felt ... I could not show this script to the Abbess as it
stands.

She had hoped, she wrote, that the film, like the book, would be
the story of a great religious house, not

simply to tell the story of one woman who chooses to become
a nun ... What I should like to do would be to rewrite the
dialogue – if necessary on the same construction – but
contriving to make the situations more believable, working
with the script-writer or, preferably, the director, as I did with
Jean Renoir. [The writer] is obviously out of his depth ... I
understood that the script-writer would come here to discuss
his or her script with me; that the director would visit an
Abbey with me, talk to the nuns and so sense the atmosphere
and flavour ... Is this to be so? I would co-operate in any way
you wished.

To their credit, the producer and script-writer did not flinch
and, in due course, Costigan arrived to work on the script with
Rumer and to visit Stanbrook. As Rumer recalled, it was an epic
encounter. They drove down to Stanbrook in a large hire car, while
he and the director, George Schaefer, tried to convince her of the
merits of the script. The nuns greeted the extracts read to them
with gales of laughter; Costigan, according to Rumer, soon decided
to repair to the Lygon Arms, the best hotel nearby, for dinner,
several drinks and a belligerent and inconclusive meeting on the
script in Rumer's suite. Early the next day Rumer took a taxi to
Stanbrook for Mass, and sent a note to Dame Felicitas. When
Costigan arrived for what was intended to be a courtesy call on the
way to the airport and a flight back to Hollywood, he was asked if
he would allow 'one of the more literary nuns' to have a brief word

about the community's concerns. 'He went in like a lamb to the slaughter,' said Rumer, with glee. When he emerged, his tone had changed. 'That nun! She's a born dramatist! I've learned so much!' Eventually, a script was agreed. 'It was still pretty ghastly,' said Rumer, twenty years later, 'but better than it was.'

The film was made, with Stanbrook's full co-operation, and came out in 1975 under the book's original title. Although it had an impressive cast, with Diana Rigg as Dame Philippa, stylishly downing three double whiskies in the pub before advancing on the Abbey to embark on the religious life, it has not worn well. Rumer did not care for it, and omits it both from her autobiography and her *Who's Who* entry. Some of the Stanbrook community remember it more positively, and recall that it was a help in educating people about the realities of monastic life; and Rumer made sure that the Abbey received a large proportion of her earnings from the project.

The year after James's death saw Rumer making another visit to India. For the first time in her life no member of her family was living there. Once again she stayed in Delhi, as her purpose was to gather material for a novel set in the diplomatic quarter about the daughter of a United Nations official who falls in love with an Indian student working as a gardener. *The Peacock Spring*, which was published in 1975, had been sparked off, she wrote later, by a scandal she recalled from her Calcutta dancing-school days when one of her teenage girl pupils fainted in class. It was rumoured that her parents had left her alone at home and that she had become pregnant by one of the servants. Rumer added to the story a beautiful, hot-tempered Eurasian governess with a fat old mother; both of them owed much to the Narayanganj nursery and to her memories of pre-war Calcutta, while the sophisticated Delhi setting was taken from her earlier stay with Dick and Nancy. The scenes in Benares, where the young couple take refuge, go back to her time there in 1949 with Jean Renoir. Rumer was still in touch with the Renoirs; until he died in 1979 they would exchange affectionate letters. *The Peacock Spring* was not written as a book for teenagers but its most enthusiastic readers were, and remain, adolescent girls. It is Rumer's most sexually explicit book, with its love scenes between the Indian student and the English girl in a hut in the garden, and its graphic description of the blood running down her legs when she miscarries the baby she has fought her father to keep. It reads as if Rumer had tired of being thought romantic and restrained, and had realized that in the mid-1970s she could write directly about experiences she had previously kept veiled.

In 1977, Rumer celebrated her seventieth year by writing her forty-third book and deciding to move house for the twelfth time since her return from India in 1945. The book was *The Butterfly Lions*, a beautifully illustrated account of the Pekinese in history, legend and art in which Rumer deftly combined research from the Royal Archives at Windsor and the court of the last Empress of China with stories of her own dogs, and of the breeders and trainers she had known and admired. The move to Scotland in 1978 was perhaps the most sensible of Rumer's many moves, although some of her friends thought it a risk, both personally and professionally, for her to retreat so far from her own territory and make her life so close to her children. Rumer herself knew that the move would have drawbacks, and she was always to pine a little for London, where over the last twenty years she had finally begun to feel at home and appreciated, but, as she told Celia Dale at a seventieth birthday party given for her by her publishers, Macmillan, she had decided, with old age looming, that it was wise to make the move while she was still active and before she became too dependent on her friends. One of her favourite sayings was: 'You can be a nuisance to your family; you mustn't be a nuisance to your friends.' In 1978 Rumer moved into a converted stable block alongside Jane and Anthony's Old Manse. There was to be one more move, when she followed them to a similar arrangement not far away, in 1986.

There was no question, however, of Rumer regarding the move to Scotland as a form of retirement, still less as the moment when she could stop driving herself and others in pursuit of the next book. She simply adapted herself to her new base and expected those around her to follow suit. It was beginning to be apparent by this time that her finances had not recovered from the confusion following James's death, and over the next few years her sales, and thus her earnings, fell off noticeably, which she found hard to accept and was determined to remedy. It was a time when novels like Rumer's were in a critical and commercial shadow; long disregarded by the fashionable and avant garde, her books were too gentle and well-mannered for a mass readership fed by blockbusters of the Jackie Collins or Harold Robbins variety. But she was not going to give up: during her seventies she wrote eight more books. Three were novels, one drawn from each of her three main sources of material and inspiration: the religious life, pre-war India and the ballet. Rumer's inventiveness never flagged but by this time she was inclined to reach into her past for an idea that she could fill out either with research or from memory. *Five for Sorrow, Ten for Joy* (1979) was a novel about an order of French Catholic nuns, the Dominican Sisters of Bethany, who worked with prisoners and prostitutes. To write the story of Zizi, a child who grows up in a brothel, and the madam turned nun who tries to help her, Rumer spent six months improving her French; she then enlisted Dorothy Watson to go with her to France to visit courts, prisons and the back-streets of Paris. Rumer was not above a little string-pulling to get what she wanted: the British Ambassador in Paris was asked to pass on a letter to the French justice minister from Harold Macmillan, who vouched for Rumer as 'a person of the highest probity and discretion', who would be willing to submit her book for approval before publication. Dorothy Watson, observing Rumer at work, was impressed with her stamina and determination. They attended a murder trial, visited the women's prison at Rennes and were driven round the roughest quarters of Paris in the small hours; Rumer then went to stay in the convent at Fontenailles where many of the postulants were ex-prisoners. Two of the Sisters of Bethany were her special advisers. One, Sister Imelda, was Scottish by birth and a friend of Dame Felicitas Corrigan. The other, Sister Jean-Dominique, eventually came to stay with Rumer in Scotland to go through the text with her before publication. She found the book 'a truthful reflection of our life and work', and enjoyed taking the Pekes for walks, sharing family dinners with Jane and Anthony, and the early-morning tea Rumer would bring her in bed. 'Such a luxury for a poor little Sister of Bethany!' As she had with Stanbrook, Rumer made sure that in return for their help the Sisters of Bethany benefited financially from the book. She also took an interest in the small, impoverished community that the order had set up in north London. When she found they could not afford to furnish their chapel, she undertook to do it by persuading 'everyone who had benefited from my writing' to help. Her family, agents and publishers all found themselves making contributions. Once Rumer had decided to do something, it usually got done. The book attracted some excellent reviews; the *Financial Times* called it 'a very readable and dramatic story of manipulation, violence, double-dealing and redemption', while Auberon Waugh in the *Evening Standard* said it was 'a first-class story, with a nice and unusual plot'.

Her next two books had an Indian background. *Gulbadan, Portrait of a Rose Princess at the Mughal Court* (1980) was, again, a beautifully illustrated book telling the story of Princess Rosebody, the youngest daughter of the first Moghul emperor in the sixteenth century. This time Rumer found a young Indian writer, Shahrukh Husain, married to an English academic, to help with the research. Shahrukh, who had been told that Rumer could be a demanding employer, was struck on their first meeting by how small and elegant she was, and by her quiet, low voice; she had been expecting someone more obviously formidable, but she soon discovered Rumer's perfectionism and strength of character. The book lacks the liveliness of *The Butterfly Lions*, perhaps because Rumer had no personal knowledge of the subject, but it is full of scholarly detail. Shahrukh became very fond of Rumer: she asked her to be godmother to her small son, introduced her to her parents and would often consult her on emotional matters, finding her wise and non-judgemental.

The Dark Horse (1981) was set in the Calcutta of the 1930s and based on a true story about a temperamental racehorse and a charitable order of nuns. It was written with an ease and verve sometimes lacking in Rumer's later fiction. It brought her in touch again, after many years, with Owain Jenkins, now knighted and living in retirement in Sussex. He had thought of writing the story himself, but in the end he relinquished it to Rumer and they shared the profits. Nancy, too, was called in to help – with descriptions of the glamorous pre-war racing world and the running of a racing stable. Macmillan decided that sales might be boosted if they presented the book in an overtly popular style; by now Rumer was regarded very much as a *grande dame* by the younger Macmillan employees, one of whom remembers that there was some anxiety about whether she would take to the new approach or consider it undignified. Rumer thought it an excellent idea, and co-operated fully.

In 1984, after a long period of slowly deteriorating health, Jon died at the age of seventy-eight. In her last years, she had seemed to Rumer to have become calmer and easier than the often difficult, emotionally volatile Jon she had always been; but to the end she never lost her power over her sisters. Rumer felt her loss too deeply to write or speak of it, beyond expressing her love and admiration for her elder sister, whom she described as 'a very big person; a great person, in her way'. She always denied that there had been any competition or jealousy between them, and accepted that within the family Jon would always be regarded as the more talented writer. Apart from her daughters, Jon had been the most important person in Rumer's life, and at her funeral, Rumer spoke of her sister's 'fierce proud spirit, always completely original' and her 'unerring love of truth and beauty'. She read a passage the sisters had found in one of Jon's scrapbooks: 'All the beautiful time is yours for always, because it is life that takes away, changes and spoils so often – not death, for death is the warden, not the thief, of our treasures.'

Although nothing could fill the gap left by Jon's death, Rumer's bond with Nancy and Rose remained strong. Nancy's husband had died suddenly in 1973; her son Richard, inspired so he always said by Renoir and *The River*, was a successful maker of wild-life films based in Belize, while Simon, who remained devoted to the aunt who had helped to bring him up, became a successful businessman. After living abroad for some years he eventually settled in London with his second wife. Nancy stayed on at Simnells, sharing it at weekends with Simon and his family; she made regular visits to Scotland and Rumer would go south to stay with her once or twice a year. Rose decided in 1991 that she too would move up to Scotland to be near Rumer and the Murray Flutter clan. When the three sisters, now all advancing into old age, were together, they would tease each other and squabble like schoolgirls, but there was no missing their loyalty to each other. Neither Nancy nor Rose could understand, as the years went by, why Rumer felt compelled to go on working so hard, or why her work had to dominate her life; pride in her fame and achievements was tempered by irritation at the demands her writing made on her, and they were not slow to grumble when, as they saw it, she played with the facts of their shared past to make a better story. It was bad enough, they felt, when she did so as fiction, but before long she turned to more direct self-revelation. Between 1981 and 1984 Rumer published three more children's books and a short novel about the ballet, *Thursday's Children*, but by 1985 she was preoccupied with her autobiography.

A Time to Dance, No Time to Weep, Rumer's account of her life up to 1945, was published to coincide with her eightieth birthday in December 1987; the second volume, *A House With Four Rooms*, which she ended with her move to Scotland, came out in 1989. Like all the best autobiographies, it was eccentric in form and selective in content: Rumer described it as 'this curious ragbag . . . snippets of diaries, letters, memories . . .' She had mixed feelings about writing it at all: she had already drawn so much from her life in her fiction that the process of retelling it as cold fact was unnerving. She was also disinclined to explore episodes over which she had long preferred to draw a veil, in particular the failure of her first marriage and the circumstances in which she had left Kashmir. For Rumer, as for many accomplished story-tellers, the boundary between reality and imagination was never fixed: over the years she had shaped many of the most significant moments of her life into stories, both consciously and unconsciously, and she was not enthusiastic about exposing herself or others to scrutiny. But with her sales and reputation flagging, she was assured by her advisers that an autobiography would succeed, and she approached the task with her usual professionalism and determination. She made full use of the notebooks, diaries and letters she still had in her archives; much had been lost in the Little Douce Grove fire, but with Jane's help she sorted through what remained. She allowed herself to mine her own writing freely, so that the line between fact and fiction became more blurred than ever. She worried over how to describe the financial crisis of 1941 and the deterioration of her relationship with Laurence. He had died in 1977, and although in later years Jane had kept in touch with him, and was on affectionate terms with his widow, she and her mother avoided the subject. Rumer did not want to pin down on paper the saga of his financial irresponsibility and its aftermath, nor the sequence of events that took her to Kashmir and the decision to seek a divorce. When she sent the first draft of her autobiography to Alan Maclean, who although he had left Macmillan in 1980 remained a close friend and her 'touchstone', Laurence was barely mentioned. He persuaded her that her first marriage, and how it ended, could not be left out, but she was still uneasy, and wrote to Mollie Kaye, with whom she had remained in occasional contact over the years, to ask if she thought it would be in poor taste to

rake up old scandals. Mollie Kaye took a robust line: Rumer had
been badly treated and had every right to show Laurence in a dim
light.

When the book came out, some people were surprised at the
extent to which Rumer had written about painful personal matters.
Those who had known her only since she returned from India, as
the successful writer, composed, formal and in full control of
herself and her life, were astonished to learn of her long years of
emotional uncertainty, effort and anxiety. To some, including her
own family, she had gone too far: they disliked the way in which
she had exposed herself and them, and they sometimes questioned
the accuracy of her recollections. Rumer tried to defuse their
criticisms by expressing in her acknowledgements her gratitude to
her friends and family 'for their corroboration – or non-corrobora-
tion – of events; to the latter I must point out that this is a book
of my memories, not theirs, and I have checked as carefully as I
could'. Nancy and Rose grumbled, but they raised no serious
objections to what she had written; on the other hand, her son-in-
law, Barry Kenilworth, made it known that he preferred not to be
mentioned in the book at all. A photograph of Paula on her
wedding day therefore omits the bridegroom, whose name does not
appear in the text.

The interest aroused by her autobiography, which was widely
and favourably reviewed, reassured Rumer that she had been right
to do it. But she was not pleased when before publication she was
asked by the publicity department of Viking, her American
publishers for forty years, to fill in a questionnaire that began:
'What makes you think your books are different from anyone
else's?' The books sold respectably in both England and America
but more important was the revival of interest in her work that
came in their wake. Sales of her backlist picked up, particularly in
England, and after 1987 her publishers brought six of her novels
back into print in a bright new paperback edition. In 1989 she
published a last, posthumous collaboration with Jon: *Indian Dust*

was a collection of their short stories and poems, all set in India, including some they had worked on together nearly fifty years earlier. Rumer's stories showed how keenly she could observe cruelty and squalor; her description of a day in the New Market in Calcutta in 'Mercy, Pity, Peace and Love' is one of the strongest pieces she ever wrote.

In 1991, at the age of eighty-four, she published a new novel, *Coromandel Sea Change*. This was another book she said had been 'vouchsafed'; she woke one night with the story virtually formed in her mind. Set on the coast of the Bay of Bengal, the action takes place in and around a hotel based on the one at Gopalpur, where she had stayed with Laurence and the children in 1941, where Wing had chased the waves along the beach and the hotel donkey had wandered in and out of the bungalows. The hotel staff, especially its Eurasian owner, the strong and lovable Auntie Sanni, were characters drawn from Rumer's earliest memories. The novel also drew on her recollections of her honeymoon at Puri for its protagonists, the receptive English girl Mary and her stiff, inhibited husband, Blaise. Mary's relationship with the handsome dark-skinned Krishnan, part aspiring politician, part god, takes the story away from realism towards myth. Suddenly, Rumer was receiving critical acclaim for the first time in years: a new generation of reviewers was reading her work with fresh eyes. Lucy Hughes-Hallett in the *Independent on Sunday* called her prose 'as simple and luminous as the fantasy it elaborates'. Kate Saunders in the *Evening Standard* simply stated: 'The miracle of this book is Godden's genius for story-telling.' *Coromandel Sea Change* was submitted for the Booker Prize, and would have won, his biographer Margaret Drabble tells us, if the chairman of the judges, Angus Wilson, had had his way.

By the early 1990s, Rumer had arrived at a point where she was admired as much for her long and varied life as for her writing. She had never much enjoyed personal publicity, but she knew it was part of the job of being a writer and had, over the years, undertaken many interviews, spoken often on radio, and occasionally appeared on television. She was not particularly pleased to be found of interest as a character rather than as a writer; she much preferred talking about her work to talking about herself, and she was determined to go on working as long as she could. When people asked her when she intended to give up writing, her response was 'Not until it gives me up.' In her mid-eighties, she was a small but formidable presence, with her large head and prominent nose, hooded eyes and soft, precise voice. She always dressed carefully, in trousers with a long cardigan over a blouse during the day and usually changing, perhaps into black trousers with an embroidered tunic top, in the evening. She had never liked her looks, and the signs of old age did not help, but she knew what suited her and wore rich dark colours in good fabrics. Her surroundings mattered too: the single-storey house converted for her from outbuildings alongside Jane and Anthony's home was full of the colours she had always preferred, pale blue, deep red and a little pink, with the sitting room kept formal and free from clutter, looking out into a small rose garden by a fast-flowing river. Her favourite Persian rug, in pinks, creams and turquoise, hung in the hall. Her study was both pretty and functional; she worked at a table facing bookshelves containing dictionaries and anthologies; a room at the far end of the house made an efficient office, with filing cabinets for her papers and correspondence and cupboards containing copies of all her books, including paperbacks and foreign editions. By this time she had been published in seventeen languages. She avoided looking at her own books: once they were finished she did not really want to see them again. 'They give me indigestion,' she remarked, wincing. Since Rumer's move to Scotland, Jane and Anthony had taken on much of the administration of her affairs. Rumer still relied on professional typists for her books, and had secretarial help for a couple of days a week. She liked to make friends with the people who helped her. Always, before she sent a new book to her publishers, she would read it aloud to a friend or a relation. Her purpose, she always said, was not so much to obtain her audience's view of the book, as to hear for herself whether the rhythm and balance of the prose were right. She discouraged comment and interruption.

Although her house was self-contained, with its own front door, it was linked to Jane's kitchen by a garden room full of plants and straw hats and they would often have lunch together. Rumer was determined from the start to leave Jane and Anthony alone in the evenings, so she would have supper on a trolley in her sitting room, even if it was provided by Jane. Cooking appealed less and less to Rumer; she preferred simple food, and had to be careful about her digestive problems, which did not improve as she grew older. She kept to a strict routine, revolving around prayer, work and her animals. Throughout most of her eighties she had two Pekinese, as well as a large fluffy cat called Cameo. They all needed grooming, as well as feeding and walks, and she enjoyed brushing the dogs; 'It's therapeutic: you can think while you do it,' she said.

Her days began around seven with prayer and reading, after which she would feed the animals, have a light breakfast and get down to work around nine. She would work until midday, when she would take the dogs for a short walk, then have a drink – invariably gin and tonic – before lunch. After lunch she would rest, reappearing around four to attend to the animals before going back to her study for correspondence and paperwork. Dinner would be preceded by another drink or two, always whisky and usually Famous Grouse, and afterwards she would often settle down for another spell of writing. She also liked to watch concerts or serials on television and listen to classical music, opera in particular, or go to the cinema in Dumfries. She also went regularly to Mass. From time to time her family, or her doctor, would suggest that her alcohol intake was on the high side for her age and physique, but Rumer paid no attention.

Several times a year she would go to London on the train, usually for something connected with her work. If possible she would stay with Simon in Victoria; there were several restaurants nearby that she had known for years and where she liked to entertain. She would always try to see Joya, now married to a doctor and living in Putney, or visit Shahrukh and her children. As she grew older and needed an arm to lean on or someone to help her find taxis and cope with her luggage, the grandchildren would be called in: she was proud of her tall, intellectually inclined grandson Mark, who had studied military history and worked as a curator in the Armoury at the Tower of London, and her granddaughters were all spirited, pretty young women who appreciated her even if they seldom read her books. When Rumer was eighty, Jane collected reminiscences and tributes in an album for her. Her eldest granddaughter, Elizabeth, who was then twenty-six, wrote that when asked who was the most interesting person she had ever met she had replied unhesitatingly: 'My grandmother'. She continued her regular visits to America until well into her late eighties, taking one of her daughters or a granddaughter with her for support. In New York she would stay at the Cosmopolitan Club, for professional women, and do the rounds of her publishing world under the friendly auspices of Marilyn Marlow, her agent, visit the Prescotts in Connecticut and give the occasional interview or talk.

Every summer it became her habit to go with Rose to Glyndebourne, with Alan Maclean and his wife Robin, usually combined with a visit to Nancy. In 1992, when she was eighty-five, she decided to write a novel, *Pippa Passes*, about a ballet company on a visit to Venice, which required a research trip; she took an old family friend, Peggy McKeever, as companion and assistant. They kept to a demanding schedule, carefully planned in advance, and Peggy was impressed by Rumer's application to detail and the way in which she questioned waiters and gondoliers about their hours and conditions. In April 1993 she took part in a memorial poetry reading at Kenwood in honour of her friend John Carroll: her reading was perfectly timed and her performance poised and confident. In October that year she spoke on behalf of the writers in front of five hundred guests at a party given by her publishers to celebrate their 150th anniversary. Her realism and humour were at their most effective; acknowledging that during her forty-two years as a Macmillan author there had been one or two battles, she added, 'I am happy to say I won most of them.' In the same year, she was awarded the OBE; her pleasure and pride were only slightly marred by the coincidence that the other writer honoured, Muriel Spark, was made a Dame. For Rumer, it was a reminder that she was still considered a popular rather than a literary success. Some of her friends and family felt that her years of public-spirited work for children's literature and the appreciation of poetry deserved better.

CHAPTER FOURTEEN

Back to India

1994

IN THE EARLY SUMMER OF 1994, Rumer was approached by the BBC with a proposal. *Bookmark* wanted to make a documentary about her life in India and the books she had set there, and asked if she would travel back with a film-crew to the places she had known best. Rumer hesitated, but not for long: she knew that such a film could only stimulate fresh interest in her work; it was flattering to be asked; and the performer in her rose to the occasion. She was a little unnerved at the thought of the physical strain of several weeks on the road in India, but when her doctor told her that there was no reason why she should not go, and *Bookmark* suggested that Jane should accompany her, she agreed on one condition: they had to understand, she told the director, Sharon Maguire, that it was quite out of the question for her to go to Kashmir. The authorities would not permit it; she would not be safe. It was almost fifty years since she had driven over the border from Kashmir into British India, but she was convinced that there might still be legal proceedings outstanding against her. In her autobiography she had written: 'I shall not forget the almost unbearable relief when we passed the Border Post – I ached from head to foot with the tension of that drive ... I cannot go back to Kashmir.'

Bookmark, however, felt that the Kashmir episode was the dramatic climax to the story of Rumer's India years and that without taking her there they could not make the film. They promised her that they would use all their influence to ensure her safety; the BBC's experienced correspondent in Srinagar, Yusuf Jameel, reported no sign that the authorities would take any interest in her return. A Kashmiri researcher set to work: there appeared to be no records of police and court proceedings in what even in 1944 had been a minor matter involving unproven accusations and no deaths or serious injuries; most records in such cases were destroyed after twenty years. At that, Rumer gave in – but she secured a promise that she would not be asked to revisit either Dove House or the village of Bren. There, she felt sure, would be people who even after fifty years would remember the trouble and disgrace she had brought on them; Kashmiris have long memories, she explained, and a tradition of vengeance handed down through generations.

She made one or two other requests. She would need to rest every afternoon, on her doctor's advice; and as she did not relish the thought of India's public facilities she asked for a portable lavatory to be provided for emergencies. Her other request was for an adequate supply of Famous Grouse, as she did not trust Indian-made whisky; Indian gin would suffice at lunch-time. With these details agreed, she embarked on the necessary injections and, with Jane's help, organizing a suitable wardrobe. It would be her first trip to India since 1974; Jane had never been back since leaving in 1945 at the age of nine. Rumer knew it would be a significant journey for Jane to share with her and she did not want Paula to feel left out; she offered to take her too, but Paula declined. Some of those close to her felt the whole idea was crazy and were full of foreboding about the likely effect on her health. When Giuliana, their former nanny and now a family friend of long standing, living in Switzerland, heard that the trip was to include Kashmir she was horrified: she could recall all too well what had happened to Rumer there in 1944.

The journey was planned to start in early October, when it would not be too cold in Kashmir nor, it was hoped, too hot everywhere else. The plan was to go first to Srinagar, then to Dhaka

in Bangladesh to film at Narayanganj, then back to Calcutta and
on to Puri on the Orissa coast. Because of the need to allow for
travel and days off, and Rumer's afternoon rests, the schedule
stretched over a full month. The political situation in Kashmir was,
as always, volatile. After a bad moment in July when an English
schoolboy was kidnapped while walking with his parents in
Kashmir, an uneasy calm descended when he was freed; a preliminary trip to Srinagar in August by Sharon Maguire and her assistant
Adrienne Solley was reassuring. They were especially captivated by
the beauty of Dal lake and Sonamarg, and made arrangements for
the party to stay in an old-established group of houseboats at Nasin
Bagh. For the rest of the trip the group, consisting of Sharon and
Adrienne, the cameraman Brian McDairmant, his assistant Mike
Carling, Fraser Barber, the soundman, and myself as consultant,
would stay in the best hotels, including the old Grand Hotel in
Calcutta, now the Oberoi Grand. The last weeks of preparation
were made more interesting by a sudden outbreak of plague in
Central India. Panic set in all over the country as tourists cancelled
their plans and airlines set up precautionary measures; the BBC
assured us that they were adding the right antibiotics to their
medical kit. Rumer, who knew that there are always hazards and
often false alarms in India, remained calm. Once she had decided
to do the film, her resolve did not flicker.

The party flew overnight to Delhi in the first week of October.
When we assembled at Heathrow with some forty-five pieces of
baggage, Rumer met the cameraman for the first time and
apologized to him for being so old and ugly a subject. From the
start she established a friendly, humorous relationship with the
crew, and they soon came to respect her stamina and stoical
acceptance of long hours and discomfort. We changed planes in
the early morning and flew straight on to Srinagar, where Rumer's
return to Kashmir was marked by a medical examination in a
makeshift tent by stern young women doctors, who checked the
party for fever and swollen glands. Then it was on by car to Mr

Butt's Claremont Houseboats, fifteen minutes out of Srinagar looking across the lake to the mountains behind the gardens of Shalimar and Nishat. It was a golden autumn morning, with the garden by the water full of bright flowers, and Rumer was greeted effusively by the ebullient Mr Butt, whose father had run the houseboats before him, and his amiably old-fashioned staff, who carried cases and handed Rumer down steps and across the grass under the tall chenar trees with experienced courtesy. After the long, tiring journey she appeared unruffled and at home: 'You must remember it is normal for me to be in India,' she said, and retired to her room at the far end of the largest houseboat for a short rest.

The houseboat was a riot of carved wood, brocade and chintz, with heavy dark furniture, stout armchairs, lace mats and vases of brilliant pink and purple dahlias. A dignified elderly houseboy, Ahmed, was in charge: he especially liked waiting on Rumer, running her bath and preparing her trays of tea and hot-water bottles. She was far more relaxed with the staff than any of the rest of the party, who were self-conscious about being waited on. Meals were prepared in the separate cookhouse in the garden and served by Ahmed, who was not best pleased when, one after another, we decided against the meat and chicken dishes on offer and chose omelettes, rice, dahl and vegetables. As alcohol is prohibited in Kashmir, discretion had to be observed when pouring drinks, so we kept the bottles in a box and helped ourselves. The back of the houseboat was open, and a good place to sit, on a cushioned bench amid the carved birds and peonies, to watch the light change over the lake, the women collecting weed from small boats, and the turquoise kingfishers diving from a nearby post. At dawn we were all woken by the sound of prayers from the great Hazratbal mosque nearby, repository of a hair from Muhammad's beard.

Mr Butt's establishment was very nearly exactly as Kashmir had always been, but to Rumer there were disturbing differences all around. The lake, which had been clear, was clouded and clogged with weed; Srinagar was filthy and battered, empty of visitors, with armed soldiers and sandbags on most corners and an atmosphere of suppressed violence. There was a curfew each evening at sunset; any vehicle that coincided at any time with an Army convoy had to pull off the road; and when Jane suggested a walk along the lake we were advised against it. Instead, on our rest day before filming began, we decided to take a boat across the lake to look at the Moghul gardens. Several shikaras were moored at the Claremont, their canopies gaily painted with names like *Happy Days* and *Bubbles*. Rumer decided to come with us, and we sped quietly into the afternoon sun reclining on cushions with the sky reflected in the water. She had wanted to go to Shalimar, but when we neared the other side of the lake the boatman told us we were heading for Nishat as Shalimar was closed for restoration. Rumer became alarmed: 'I can't go to Nishat,' she said. She felt that it was too close to Bren and that some of the gardeners there might recognize her; she had drawn a map for Sharon indicating the places she would not visit, and Nishat was one of them. Jane reassured her, and she did not insist, but it was clearly worrying for her, as she slowly climbed the terraces among the late roses under the chenar trees where she had so often picnicked when her daughters were small. The terraced garden of Nishat is still beautiful but the watercourses are broken and there is a melancholy air of neglect about the place.

The next few days were spent filming Rumer in and around Srinagar and on Dal lake; she agreed to everything, including another visit to Nishat. She got up before dawn, to Ahmed's alarm, to be filmed floating in a shikara among lotus blossoms. As the season was over, paper lotuses had been brought from London to be scattered on the water, and it was immediately obvious to Rumer and Jane that the pretty pink flowers were not the correct size or shape and were, in fact, water-lilies. To enhance the romantic image Rumer was asked to wear a large straw hat and to drape a flowered red shawl round her shoulders; she disliked this garment, which featured frequently, but wore it dutifully. She sat for hours, being towed in wide circles, a hot-water bottle under her coat. One evening we were late coming back to the houseboat, having been filming in the sunset, and were called over by a patrol boat to explain ourselves. By this time several of us, including Rumer, had been keeping out the cold with sips of whisky from paper cups; they were rapidly emptied overboard, to Rumer's disgust: 'Why waste good whisky for a lot of soldiers?'

It was cold enough at night for the stoves to be lit, and after dinner Rumer would sit discussing the script with Sharon. There were some arguments: they had rather different ideas about what the script was for. To Sharon, it was a basic structure around which she intended to tell the story through interviews and images. Rumer regarded it as a text to be agreed and then performed. Naturally Sharon also hoped that in interviews Rumer would open up on such topics as her troubled state of mind before the move to Dove House and her feelings about Laurence, but Rumer was not keen to be drawn on personal matters although she realized that they could not be left out altogether. Listening to their discussions, it became clearer than ever that Rumer saw the events of her life as dramatic material to be shaped and edited rather than as facts to be clarified. When Sharon wanted to use some of her letters to Jon, perhaps showing a page on the screen while Rumer read a few lines aloud, Rumer could hardly bear it, not because of the content, but because she did not like the words. She tried to persuade Sharon to let her rewrite the material; the idea was dropped.

With unfailing composure she was filmed in a grubby TB ward of the Mission Hospital where she had suffered from paratyphoid and jaundice, in a boat with Jane on the Jhelum in central Srinagar and in a village similar to Bren where she sat with a group of children in the square and taught them to count in English. 'They remind me of my goat children,' she said, with pleasure. Everywhere, a large and curious crowd would gather. In the village, an elderly man said, as he watched, 'Personally I much preferred life here when we were under the British yoke.'

One afternoon, while Rumer rested, Jane and I decided to take a taxi and visit Dove House. What had once been a small house by itself on a hillside was now a medium-sized suburban villa with a concrete car-parking area. The orchards were still there, and the view over the lake, but the hill was dotted with new houses and Dove House itself had been extended and modernized in raw new wood. The old wooden house was clearly discernible inside its modern carapace and Rumer's writing room was still recognizable at the top of the stairs.

Then we went to call on the one man unearthed by the BBC researchers who could recollect the drama that had brought Rumer's life at Dove House to an end. Mr Shah was a tall, affable lawyer in his early sixties, and he was still living in the house on the edge of Bren below Dove House where he had grown up. His father had been a government official and one of the leading members of the local community, and Mr Shah well remembered hearing him talk about the case. As a small boy, he had been one of a group of curious children who were fascinated by the English family living up the hill. They would climb trees or peer through the bushes to see what was going on, and sometimes watched the family eating. 'It looked very strange,' he said. 'Why were they not eating with their hands?' He and Jane contemplated each other over the spiced tea and biscuits, served at a table in his large garden. 'I was the little boy looking over the garden wall,' he said. 'And I was the little girl inside,' said Jane.

To the local people it had seemed odd that the English memsahib was living there alone with only her children and the servants: 'Nobody knew exactly what she was doing; I knew only this year that she was a great writer.' He did remember that she had the reputation of being good to work for, unlike her friend Mrs Hopman, whose temper earned her the title of Hot Memsahib; Rumer had been known to take care of her servants. This was partly why Mr Shah remained convinced that what had happened at Dove House had been some kind of accident, not a deliberate act intended to harm anyone. 'What could be the motive?' he asked. He also maintained that no trace of poison had ever been found. 'It was not a poison, that was shown by chemical tests. There was glass, but perhaps that was from crushed light-bulbs used against rats – maybe it fell into the food,' he said. Rumer's servants, he explained, were well known in the neighbourhood; the only trouble in the household was a certain rivalry between them 'over who should be nearer to the lady'. So could the wish to influence their employer have been behind an attempt to drug her, if not to poison her? Mr Shah was adamant: 'There was no poison. What happened was not intentional, there was no motive and there was no evidence. And when the case was brought, the lady did not turn up.' The two servants, he added, had been arrested, held for six weeks, then given bail, then allowed home. The case had lapsed; that had been the end of it. No defamation case had ever been brought. The affair had caused much bad feeling in the village. 'It was upsetting for the whole area. It is still a small place; then, there were very few houses. Everyone knew about it.' Jane took him up on one point: the key servant in the case, Siddika, had not been a local man, she pointed out. And what about the letter from his former employer in Gulmarg, saying that he had done something similar before? Mr Shah did not reply. To the suggestion that perhaps the true story would never be known, and that the episode at Dove House in July 1944 would remain a mystery, his response was unequivocal: 'No,' he said. 'There was no mystery. There was no evidence that it was a deliberate act.'

As we drove back round the lake in the early evening, with the farmers threshing wheat and bringing in the cows – Rumer's 'cow-dust time' – stopping to let some trucks full of armed Indian soldiers go by, Jane was in a passion of indignation. 'Mother was quite right. It's all just a whitewash,' she said. To her it was obvious that the medical-test results had been fudged and that, as her mother had always said, the Kashmiri authorities' main concern was to conceal the truth for fear of damaging the tourist trade.

Certainly, for someone looking back fifty years to a time when he was a small boy, Mr Shah had a strikingly clear grasp of the details of the case; he talked as if he had been able to refresh his memory from the records that everyone had assured us could no longer exist. One thing was clear, though: such records were not available to us in Srinagar in 1994. And there the matter must rest; another unresolved incident, a small area of darkness where the English and the Indian version of events can never coincide.

The next day, Rumer and Jane were filmed in Mr Butt's sunny garden eating rice and dahl and reliving the moment when Jane, aged nine, found the glass in her mouth. Ahmed carried the food across the lawn; in the bushes, a group of local children played the part of Mr Shah and his friends. Rumer knew that Jane and I had been to see Dove House, but we never discussed our tea with Mr Shah.

It had always been part of the *Bookmark* plan to take Rumer out of Srinagar up to Sonamarg, the scene of several summer camps and the place where she went to recover after leaving Dove House. Sharon had been put in touch on her first visit with someone else who had known Rumer and her family when he was a small boy: Amah, the son of Jobara – the pony man who had helped Rumer and her sisters with several camps and treks – was living nearby and ready to meet her. For a while the expedition was in jeopardy: the weather turned unexpectedly cold, snow fell in the mountains, and at Sonamarg the tourist bungalows, where we had been assured the party could stay in reasonable comfort, turned out to have been unused for years and were thought to be too cold and broken down to be wise for Rumer. When Sharon explained the problem to Rumer, though, she found her subject determined that the plan should go ahead and quite prepared for a little discomfort: why not buy a number of pherans, Rumer suggested, the long woollen overgarments the Kashmiris live in during the winter, and a supply of kangris, small clay pots, to fill with coals? Mr Butt's team, well used to organizing treks, would provide everything else. It was becoming more and more apparent that Rumer, at rising eighty-seven, was made of sterner stuff than the rest of the party. When the soundman complained that at night their houseboat was invaded by rats and he could not sleep, Rumer was neither surprised nor sympathetic: 'We had swarms of rats at Dove House,' she remarked. 'They used to arrive with the bakriwars.' Of course we should go to the mountains; she particularly wanted to see Sonamarg again.

It was a long drive up bad roads, but the Sind river was aquamarine and glistening and the walnut harvest had begun. We climbed steadily towards the snowy peaks; the air was cold and clean. A few miles from our destination, we were stopped by a small group at the edge of a shabby village. Amah, a small man with a wrinkled face, was waiting with the leading villagers to receive his honoured guest and escort her himself to Sonamarg. Rumer was helped out of the car and led, with Jane, into the middle of the throng to be given the traditional welcome of eggs and tea. Amah and his father's old employer looked at each other with undisguised amazement and affection; they spoke a little through an interpreter, enquiring about each other's families. Later, over an elaborate picnic lunch at Sonamarg, Rumer presented him with a heavy cream Arran jersey bought in Scotland. Amah became a constant presence, hovering as close to Rumer as he could get. They were filmed together on the windy mountainside beneath the hut where, he said, his father had taken the memsahib when she was so ill after losing her baby; and they re-enacted the start of her flight from Kashmir, with Amah waving goodbye as the cream Ambassador car drove slowly away. When the time came to say another real goodbye, Rumer said: 'I don't want to lose him,' and Amah's eyes were filled with tears.

After a fairly uncomfortable night, made tolerable by whisky and the portable stoves brought by Mr Butt's team, the party set off back down the valley. The trip took six hours instead of four, as we coincided with a military supply convoy, and it was dark by the time we reached home. As we were struggling out of the cars a loud explosion came from the road we had just left, followed by shots and shouting. All the lights went out and we were hurried into our houseboats where we had hot baths, prepared by Ahmed, in candlelight. Later we learned that a small bomb had been thrown at the military post nearby. It was an insignificant incident by local standards but we were glad we were not still on the road; lorries roared by for most of the night. Our drivers and interpreters were all used to helping journalists reporting the Kashmir troubles and were veterans of violent incidents and kidnaps; they, like all the Kashmiris we met, longed for an independent Kashmir. Rumer's links with the colonial past amused them. The old man in the village was not the only Kashmiri who told us that things had only got worse since independence, and no one appeared to blame the British for the confusion they had left behind in 1947.

For all its beauty, it was a relief to leave Srinagar, after endless searches and more medical checks. Rumer's collapsible stick was taken to pieces three times, and Jane's sewing kit was confiscated. The only emotion Rumer expressed as she left Kashmir was sadness at the destruction and decay of what had been such a beautiful place, but Jane was sure that the return had put to rest fears and anxieties that had tormented her mother for fifty years. She had been back and faced them, and nothing terrible had happened. There was a sense that unfinished business had been settled at last.

After a night in Delhi the group was supposed to fly via Calcutta straight on to Dhaka, but plague precautions had given Bangladesh the kind of chance it relished to cause India trouble, and all Calcutta–Dhaka flights were cancelled. The party was therefore obliged to spend a night in Calcutta and make the journey by road, which meant a dawn start, a near eleven-hour drive and a long wait for baggage and medical checks at the border. It was hot and uncomfortable, especially at the border town, where there was no scope to bring out the portable lavatory, which all the women had found a comfort, and officials tried to confiscate the lunchboxes supplied by the Calcutta hotel and to spray valuable cameras with sticky disinfectant. Rumer remained good-tempered, which was more than could be said for the cameraman. As dusk fell we reached one of the river crossings outside Dhaka and Rumer found herself being loaded on to a grimy, rickety ferry crammed with trucks and travellers. The sky was dark gold, a crescent moon was rising and the stars were coming out; she looked at the scene with satisfaction. 'It is a long time since I saw my river,' she observed.

The week in Dhaka, however, put her under great physical and emotional strain. Each morning after breakfast she would set off by car for Narayanganj; the twelve-mile journey was through streets so congested that it usually took an hour. Women and children were breaking stones by the edge of the road but when Jane deplored the sight, Rumer was brisk. 'You always say how terrible, but there are so many terrible things.' The car was air-conditioned, but there was no protection for Rumer during the filming, which was all outside and continued until after midday in temperatures of over ninety degrees. The base of operations was a large comfortable house on the river not far from the Goddens' home; it belonged to a prosperous and generous Bangladeshi family, who knew Rumer by reputation and agreed to let *Bookmark* use their grounds and their adjacent jute mill. They also gave her a cool room where she could rest before setting off back to the hotel for a late lunch. For two days she was filmed in a small boat on the river, sitting in a cane chair under a parasol amid bales of jute. The river is wide and busy, and Rumer and the boat seemed small and fragile, bobbing in the wash of large cargo boats a long way from shore. Sharon and the crew argued about whether it was too risky; Sharon won. For the first time Rumer was critical of some of the background details, comparing *Bookmark* unfavourably with Jean Renoir and his passion for accuracy. When two little girls appeared in frilly white lace and buttoned boots to play her and Jon as children in the garden, she could hardly bear it: 'Please, please,' she said, 'not those boots.'

Finally the day came when she was to be filmed going back to her childhood home. Again, Sharon was keen to capture her first reactions, and although we had driven past the entrance several times and glimpsed the house over the wall, Rumer had not been near it since 1945. Leaning on Jane's arm in the burning heat, with a microphone round her neck, she walked slowly up the path in front of the camera and a large crowd of people who had gathered, as usual, to watch. The house still stands on its own in a large open space that had once been the Goddens' well-kept garden, with its tennis court and rose-bushes and the big cork tree, surrounded by canna lilies, where Rumer used to hide her poems. The tree has long gone, like the tennis court and the vegetable patch and all the flowers. The house itself has been for some years the headquarters of the local water authority, with offices in the main rooms and living quarters for employees everywhere else; it is decayed and grimy, with broken pediment and cracked steps, but it is otherwise little altered. Rumer sat on the verandah where her mother's plants used to stand and submitted to Sharon's questions; her voice was even smaller than usual and she looked frail and worn. Perhaps, she admitted, it had been a mistake to come back; now, her memories of the house as it used to be would be overlaid by images of dirt and destruction. She had hoped to be able to go up on the roof again, where she used to fly her kite, and look down across the bazaar and the river; but the stairs were rotten and she was persuaded not to try. She did walk to the corner of the house to look at her old nursery; young men peered out of the upstairs windows, festooned with their washing, to watch her.

Back in Calcutta, with two weeks still to go, Rumer's health began to cause concern. Apart from being exhausted she had almost lost her voice, her eyes were inflamed, she could eat almost nothing and she was unsteady on her feet. Nevertheless, she managed an early-morning walk down a ramshackle street near the New Market and a short sequence in the old South Park Street cemetery among the elaborate tombs and touching inscriptions; she was relieved, she told Jane, that the crew did not insist on taking her to the cemetery where her first child was buried. The Grand Hotel, where long ago she had held dancing classes in the ballroom, was familiar territory, and very comfortable; one evening she entertained Monisha Chaudhuri to dinner in the Chinese restaurant. Monisha, beautiful as ever in a dull gold sari, had become a little vague, and she and Rumer did not find it easy to hear each other; but their pleasure in seeing each other again was evident.

Two days were spent at the Tollygunge Club, scene of so many of Laurence Foster's golfing triumphs; his name appears regularly on the boards recording sporting occasions of the 1930s. Tollygunge is not as perfectly manicured as it used to be, but it is still an oasis in the Calcutta sprawl, with its green lawns, swimming-pool, air-conditioned restaurant and comfortable lounges. Rumer was filmed having drinks and talking to Bob Wright, the club secretary and last of the expatriate old guard, who had met her during the filming of *The River*; he told louche stories about the old days, which did not amuse her, but his patience with the disruption of filming and his eagerness to please her were endearing. One evening the crew set up a party at the club, partly to evoke the old days and partly to form the background for a scene from *The Lady and the Unicorn*; a pretty Eurasian had been persuaded to play a B girl, one of those regarded in the 1930s as good enough to amuse young Englishmen but not to marry them, and a suitably fresh-faced young expatriate businessman had been provided as a dancing partner. They danced decorously to 1930s tunes while Rumer sat on a sofa with Monisha nursing a large whisky. The room was full of acrid smoke from braziers ordered by the cameraman to soften the look of the scene; everyone's eyes watered and it was ferociously hot, as no fans could be turned on because of the soundtrack.

Rumer was glad to leave Calcutta: she had never liked it much and now she said she liked it even less. A young reporter from the *Calcutta Telegraph* appeared to interview her; he had clearly never heard of her, but they did their best. 'City of Joy's Lost Charm Saddens British Authoress', said the headline the next day. 'Squalor and mouldiness have swallowed much of the old-world charm that she so fondly remembers.' Next day we flew out for the final few days in Orissa, where we were to stay in the best hotel in Bhubaneshwar, to the disappointment of Rumer and Jane who had been hoping for an old-fashioned seaside hotel at Puri or Gopalpur. Rumer seemed a little better out of the stifling Calcutta heat, but it was clear now that will-power was keeping her going. The crew had become more and more concerned and protective, providing arms for her to lean on, chairs for her to sit on, and occasionally simply lifting her from place to place to spare her legs: her feet and ankles had swollen badly in the heat. Three final sequences were required: one on the beach near Puri, one in a train, and one, the most important, at the Sun Temple at Konarak, where Rumer was at last to see the buildings she had missed on her honeymoon in 1934.

On the beach, in a haze of heat, Rumer walked along the sand while a handsome young Indian in a wet lunghi, the evocation of her hero Krishnan in *Coromandel Sea Change*, splashed among the waves. 'Mother hates beaches,' said Jane, watching. 'She hates holidays. She never really had a holiday.' At the mighty Surya Temple, while the sun beat down and the tourist guides steered their victims to the most graphic depictions of sexual intercourse, Rumer explained the Hindu reverence for the phallus in front of a huge, magnificent carving of the sun god's chariot wheel. Afterwards, we picnicked in the shade while a pale cow tried to steal our dry cheese sandwiches and Rumer sipped gin and lemonade from a flask. Small boys tried to interest the crew in suggestive souvenirs.

On the last day, Rumer waited for several hours on the local railway platform at six in the morning for a train so that she could be filmed looking out of the window. When at last the shot was done, she was so exhausted that two of the crew carried her, protesting vigorously but secretly pleased, over the foot-bridge and into the car. That night at a farewell dinner by the hotel swimming-pool she toasted the crew and told them how much she had admired their perfectionism and care, and how she knew that if she had been a sensible old lady she would never have agreed to the journey and how glad she was that she had never been sensible in her life.

One evening in Kashmir Jane said that before they left Scotland her mother had told her that all her affairs were in order and that if she were to die in India she did not want to be taken home for burial; an Indian cremation would suffice. The subject of death had also arisen in Sonamarg over the Famous Grouse after dinner: Rumer had told the company that she intended when she died that there should be fireworks, and that she liked the idea of her ashes being taken into the night sky on a giant rocket. 'You are all invited,' she said. She survived her Indian journey in October 1994, although she did not afterwards quite recover her health and energies and some of those who loved her continued to feel that she should never have gone, but she herself had no regrets. The film was finished in Scotland before Christmas, and on New Year's Eve 1994, Rumer Godden began her next novel.

Afterword

1995–7

BETWEEN 1995 AND 1997, as Rumer approached her ninetieth birthday, the inevitable ailments of old age, in particular
difficulty in walking and increasing deafness, irritated her but were
not allowed to dominate her life. With Jane's loving support, she
kept to her usual routine, built around regular working hours. As
well as writing a new novel in which she returned to the Indian
seaside hotel and some of the characters in *Coromandel Sea Change*,
she also completed two anthologies: *Cockcrow to Starlight*, poems
for a child's day, and a personal selection of religious poetry,
A Pocket Book of Spiritual Poems. In 1996 she published two
children's books whose origins lay in her own childhood, one
about a Bengali girl's Diwali, *Premlata and the Festival of Lights*,
and the other called *The Little Chair*, built around a treasure that
had been in the family for six generations and stood in her own
hall. She still made occasional visits south, to London, to Glyndebourne with Rose, to the Macleans in Wiltshire or to her sister
Nancy in Kent.

The new novel was based on a true story Rumer had spotted in
the newspapers, about a stolen statue of Shiva; she made a special
journey to the British Museum to consult an expert in Indian
bronzes, who to her delight turned out himself to have been
involved in the case.

In November 1995 she flew to New York for ten days,
determined to keep up her American publishing contacts and to
see her friends. She spent a weekend in Connecticut with the

Prescotts, and managed a visit to her favourite New York art gallery, the Frick.

When the Indian novel was finished, Rumer immediately started to plan a new children's book, about a unicorn. Although there was little need for concern about her income, which since the late 1980s had been consistently impressive, she felt she had to keep working. 'I have my living to earn,' she was overheard to say one day, when her doctor suggested that she could now afford to have a rest. 'I have to think of my old age.'

The *Bookmark* film, first shown in March 1995, prompted a new wave of interest in her life and letters flooded in from friends and admirers, all of which Rumer attended to diligently. In January 1996 the programme was shown again, to coincide with a well-received two-part adaptation for television of her novel *The Peacock Spring*. *The River* was also shown on television, along with a documentary on Jean Renoir, in which Rumer took part; less to her liking, *Black Narcissus* was revived in a London cinema. There was interest from America in adapting *In This House of Brede* for television, and prolonged negotiations over a film version of *The Dark Horse*. Rumer considered all such offers carefully, and was quick to turn down any script that took liberties with her stories.

In 1996 she took part, for the second time, in *Desert Island Discs*. Her choices mixed Indian music with 1930s dance tunes, and opera. In 1975 she had told Roy Plomley that her luxury would be her four-poster bed. This time, she announced that she would like a widow's cruse (an inexhaustible supply) of good Scotch whisky. As her ninetieth birthday approached, a stream of interviewers and researchers travelled to Scotland to talk to her; she was kind and professional with them all, but deplored the time she lost from her work.

In mid-November 1997, Rumer fell in her bedroom in Scotland and broke her hip. She was thus in hospital when on 21 November her twenty-first novel, *Cromartie v. the God Shiva Acting Through the Government of India*, was published, heralded by a glowing review from a fashionable young critic, Philip Hensher, praising her long writing career and remarkable gifts, calling her 'one of our best and most captivating novelists ...' and the book 'a witty, delectable miniature, studded with charming character portraits and yet affecting the reader with strange currents of feeling and troubling moments of deep thought.' Macmillan had organized a 90th birthday celebration for her in London, and Jane had arranged a family gathering. Rumer was back at home by early December, but the aftermath of the hip injury prevented her trip to London; the family party, however, was a great success. As well as her sisters Nancy and Rose, Simon Foster and Paula and Barry Kenilworth, all four grandchildren were there and all seven great-grandchildren, who helped Rumer blow out the candles on her cake. The week of her birthday was also marked by a visit from some of her American publishing friends, an avalanche of flowers, presents and cards, several pre-recorded press and radio interviews, and new radio dramatizations of *Black Narcissus* and her children's book *The Dragon of Og*.

To some of her circle, the new novel had a poignant, almost valedictory quality. In it she not only returned once more to the Indian settings and characters she had written about over more than sixty years, but she seemed, with great simplicity, to have distilled some of her deepest beliefs about art and love and the human need for a spiritual dimension without which life is meaningless. As 1997 drew to a close, Rumer's health was fragile but her will-power was still strong. She struggled on her zimmer frame to her study whenever she could, writing her thank-you letters and dealing with her professional correspondence. She was not to be deflected from her firm intention to see New Year, 1998, in as usual, seated at her desk at midnight, pen in hand.

During 1998, although Rumer's health was poor, she managed to write the first draft of a book for children set in Cornwall about a unicorn, and to celebrate the publication of this biography at a family dinner in Scotland. In the summer, she summoned her agent to inform him that her next book would be an account of her time in Hollywood with Jean Renoir in 1949; she asked Shahrukh Husain to start work on the research. But if her will remained strong, her energies were flagging; by the autumn it was clear that she needed to return to the nursing home in Dumfries.

By the first week of November, though, she was well enough to be sitting up in bed discussing the Booker prize and making plans to return home. So, although it was not unexpected, it was nevertheless a shock when she died, in the early hours of Sunday, 8 November. She had left clear instructions: a Requiem Mass for family and close friends was held nearby. She had specified white flowers for the Chapel, and ordered that good (underlined) champagne should be served afterwards.

She also asked that her ashes should be buried with her second husband, James Haynes-Dixon, in Rye. Her daughters arranged a memorial service at the small church of St Anthony of Padua in Watchbell Street where she had often worshipped during the Rye years; it was held on 10 December 1998, which would have been Rumer Godden's 91st birthday. Alan Maclean, Rumer's friend and editor, gave the address, and reminded us of a passage in her autobiography telling how she would sometimes visit the church at lunchtime when it was empty. As he suggested, we carried away with us the image of her small, upright figure sitting in a pew, accompanied by a Pekinese and the church cat.

Note on Sources

Unless otherwise indicated, all correspondence quoted, whether personal or professional, comes from Rumer Godden's own archives, which also contain her surviving notebooks and journals. Comments from her about her life are taken either from interviews with the author or from her autobiography.

Chapter 1 is based largely on *Two Under the Indian Sun*, written with Jon Godden (Chatto and Windus, 1966). In Chapter 3, quotations from the late Sir Owain Jenkins are taken from his book *Merchant Prince*, published by BACSA (British Association for Cemeteries in South Asia) in 1987. Details of the Bonnerjee, Majumdar and Chaudhuri families come from a privately printed family memoir, *Pramila*, by Agnes Janaki Penelope Majumdar, edited by Muchu Chaudhuri and kindly lent to me by Mrs Sheila Auden.

In Chapters 4 and 5, quotations from Margaret Martyn are from *Married to the Raj* (BACSA, 1992). In Chapters 10 and 11, quotations from Jean Renoir's letters are taken from *Jean Renoir, Letters*, edited by David Thompson and Lorraine LoBianco (Faber and Faber, 1994). For my account of the filming of *The River*, I have also used *Jean Renoir, A Life in Pictures* by Celia Bertin (Johns Hopkins University Press, 1991), *Jean Renoir*, a biography by Ronald Bergan (Bloomsbury, 1992), and *Satyajit Ray* by Andrew Robinson (André Deutsch, 1989). In writing about Stanbrook Abbey and the friendship between Rumer Godden and Dame Felicitas Corrigan, I have used the latter's two books, *Friends of a Lifetime* (John Murray, 1985) and *Benedictine Tapestry* (Barton, Longman and Todd, 1991).

The following books were also useful:

Plain Tales from the Raj, ed. Charles Allen, André Deutsch, 1975

Indian Art, Roy C. Craven, Thames and Hudson, 1993

A House by the Hooghly, Eugenie Fraser, Corgi, 1991

E.M. Forster, vols I and II, P. N. Furbank, Secker and Warburg, 1977, 1978

Vignettes of India, Percival Griffiths, The Spartan Press, 1985

A History of the Joint Steamer Companies, Percival Griffiths, Inchcape, 1979

Merchants of the Raj, Stephanie Jones, Macmillan, 1992

Calcutta, Geoffrey Moorhouse, Weidenfeld and Nicolson, 1983

The Stones of Empire, Jan Morris, Penguin, 1994

The Last Days of the Raj, Trevor Royle, John Murray, 1997

A History of India, Percival Spear, Penguin, 1990

Calcutta Through British Eyes, ed. Laura Sykes, Oxford University Press, 1992

Acknowledgements

This biography was made possible by the co-operation and help I received from the outset from Rumer Godden herself. She talked to me about her life and work, gave me access to her personal and professional papers, introduced me to her family, friends and colleagues, and told me to be sure to talk to people who did not like her as well as to those who did. She read and commented on the text, but did not ask for any veto. Above all, therefore, I must thank my subject for her generosity and her patience.

I am also greatly indebted to Rumer Godden's elder daughter Jane, and to her son-in-law Anthony Murray Flutter, who have put up with repeated demands on their time and hospitality with great kindness and equanimity. Jane's advice and help have been invaluable. Rumer Godden's younger daughter, Paula Kenilworth, preferred not to talk to me about her mother. Rumer Godden's two surviving sisters, Nancy (Lady Foster) and Rose (Mrs Smith), despite misgivings, shared their memories with me, as did her cousin Betty Godden, her nephew Simon Foster and her grandson Mark Murray Flutter.

Rumer Godden's friends, acquaintances and colleagues were also generous with their help, in particular Mrs Sheila Auden, Anthony Bent, Mrs Radha Bernier, Stuart Connolly, Adrienne Corri, Dame Felicitas Corrigan, Gwenda David, Mrs Anila Graham, Lady Hamilton (M. M. Kaye), Lady (Marni) Hodgkin, Mrs Hazel Hyde-Clarke, Shahrukh Husain, Mrs Lenore Johnstone, Alan and Robin Maclean, Joya Nicholas, Mrs Celia (Dale) Ramsay, Lady (Jimmy) Simon, Graham and Dorothy Watson and Mrs Joan White. Her agent Mike Shaw and her publisher Suzanne Baboneau were also helpful.

For my researches in India and Bangladesh, I am especially grateful to Peter Leggatt of the Goodricke Group, who helped me to arrange my visits to Dhaka, Narayanganj, Calcutta and Darjeeling. Without Sharon MacGuire, Adrienne Solley and the resources of the BBC my visit to Kashmir would hardly have been possible. My thanks also go to Mr Abu Subhan of Duncan Brothers, and Mahavir Pati and his mother, Mrs Pati, of the Kumudini Trust in Narayanganj. I was also greatly assisted by the late Mrs Monisha Chaudhuri, Mrs M. R. Das, Chidananda Das Gupta, Mr and Mrs Bunny Gupta, Miss Nandita Gupta, Mrs Samina Mahmood, Mrs Aloka Mitra, Biresh Paul, Sudeshna Roy, Mrs Romola Sinha, Ravi Singh, Pearson Surita and Bob Wright.

I am indebted to Marilyn Marlow of Curtis Brown, New York, and the following American friends and colleagues of Rumer Godden for their help and hospitality: Ann Beneduce, the late Edith Haggard, Emilie Jacobson, Mrs Elizabeth Riley, the late Orville Prescott and Lilias Prescott, Jean Primrose and Alan Williams.

Finally, I was given invaluable support in various ways by Xandra Bingley, Gill Coleridge, Michael Davie, Bernard Gadney, Fay and Reg Gadney, Adam and Caroline Raphael, Sally Sampson, Caroline and John Sandwich and Nora Sayre. Milly Jenkins and Rani Singh gave me efficient help with research. Georgina Morley and Catherine Whitaker at Macmillan were consistently responsive; Hazel Orme's meticulous editing and personal knowledge of the subject were very useful.

List of Rumer Godden's Books

FICTION

Chinese Puzzle, Peter Davies, 1935
The Lady and the Unicorn, Peter Davies, 1937
Black Narcissus, Peter Davies, 1939
Gypsy, Gypsy, Peter Davies, 1940
Breakfast with the Nikolides, Peter Davies, 1942
A Fugue In Time, Michael Joseph, 1945
The River, Michael Joseph, 1946
A Candle for St Jude, Michael Joseph, 1948
A Breath of Air, Michael Joseph, 1950
Kingfishers Catch Fire, Macmillan, 1953
An Episode of Sparrows, Macmillan, 1956
Mooltiki: Stories and Poems, Macmillan, 1957
The Greengage Summer, Macmillan, 1958
China Court, Macmillan, 1961
The Battle of the Villa Fiorita, Macmillan, 1963
Swans and Turtles: Stories, Macmillan, 1968
In This House of Brede, Macmillan, 1969
The Peacock Spring, Macmillan, 1975
Five for Sorrow, Ten for Joy, Macmillan, 1979
The Dark Horse, Macmillan, 1981
Indian Dust: Stories, with Jon Godden, Macmillan, 1989
Coromandel Sea Change, Macmillan, 1991

Pippa Passes, Macmillan, 1994
Cromartie v. the God Shiva Acting Through the Government of India,
   Macmillan, 1997

CHILDREN'S FICTION

The Doll's House, Michael Joseph, 1947
The Mousewife, Macmillan, 1951
Impunity Jane, Macmillan, 1955
The Fairy Doll, Macmillan, 1956
Mouse House, Macmillan, 1958
The Story of Holly and Ivy, Macmillan, 1958
Candy Floss, Macmillan, 1960
Miss Happiness and Miss Flower, Macmillan, 1961
Little Plum, Macmillan, 1963
Home is the Sailor, Macmillan, 1964
The Kitchen Madonna, Macmillan, 1967
Operation Sippacik, Macmillan, 1969
The Old Woman who Lived in a Vinegar Bottle, Macmillan, 1972
The Diddakoi, Macmillan, 1972
Mr McFadden's Hallowe'en, Macmillan, 1975
The Rocking Horse Secret, Macmillan, 1977
A Kindle of Kittens, Macmillan, 1978
The Dragon of Og, Macmillan, 1981
Four Dolls, Macmillan, 1983
The Valiant Chatti-Maker, Macmillan, 1983
Thursday's Children, Macmillan, 1984
Fu-Dog, McRae, 1989
Listen to the Nightingale, Macmillan, 1992
Great Grandfather's House, Macmillan, 1993
The Little Chair, Hodder, 1996
Premlata and the Festival of Lights, Macmillan, 1996

POETRY AND ANTHOLOGIES

In Noah's Ark, Michael Joseph, 1949
Prayers from the Ark (translation), Macmillan, 1963
Round the Year, Round the Day, Round the World, Poetry Programmes
    for Classroom or Library, Macmillan, 1966
The Beasts' Choir (translation), Macmillan, 1967
A Letter to the World (ed.), Poems for Young People by Emily
    Dickinson, Bodley Head, 1968
Cockcrow to Starlight (anthology for children), Macmillan, 1996
A Pocket Book of Spiritual Poems, Hodder, 1996

NON-FICTION

Rungli-Rungliot, Peter Davies, 1943
Bengal Journey, Longmans Green, 1945
Hans Christian Andersen, Hutchinson, 1955
St Jerome and the Lion, Macmillan, 1961
Two Under the Indian Sun, with Jon Godden, Macmillan, 1966
Mrs Manders' Cookbook (ed.), Macmillan, 1968
The Raphael Bible, Macmillan, 1970
The Tale of the Tales, Frederick Warne, 1971
Shiva's Pigeons, with Jon Godden, Chatto and Windus, 1972
The Butterfly Lions, Macmillan, 1977
Gulbadan, Macmillan, 1980
A Time to Dance, No Time to Weep, Macmillan, 1987
A House With Four Rooms, Macmillan, 1989

Index

Abdul (nursery bearer), 13, 23–4, 25

Aenid Ballon School, 58

Ahmed (houseboy), 295, 296, 300, 302

Amah (bearer), 170, 300–1

Amis, Kingsley, 274

Amritsar massacre, 36

Andersen, Hans Christian, 248–9

Arberry, Helen, 164, 165–70, 175, 176–7

Arts Council, 258

Arts Theatre Club, 253

Asher, Jane, 255

Ashton, Frederick, 271

Assam, 4, 6–7, 38, 50, 66

Auden, John, 272

Austen, Jane, 155

Azad Ali (butler), 10, 13

Bacon, Francis, 252

Ballon, Aenid, 58, 62

Balmer Lawrie, 44

Barber, Fraser, 294

Barnes, Julia, 241, 259, 261

Barrie, J.M., 74

Baughan, Nigel, 39, 44, 72

Bell, Peggy, 258

Benares, 226–7, 279

Bengal Club, Calcutta, 53, 80

Benson, E.F., 260

Bent, Anthony, 38, 193

Bergman, Ingrid, 218

Bernos de Gasztold, Carmen, 261

Blomfield, John, 38

Bonnerjee, Bharat, 60

Bonnerjee, Minnie, 60

Bonnerjee, Nelly, 47

Bonnerjee, Protab, 60

Bonnerjee, Sheila, 60, 272

Bonnerjee, Susie, 47

Bonnerjee, Womesh Chandra, 47

Bonnerjee family, 47–8, 59–60, 62, 79

Book Society, 253

Bookers, 268

Bookmark (BBC), 292–307

Bourillon, Phyllis, 62, 63, 78, 104

Brahmaputra River Steam Navigation Company, 9

Brazzi, Rossano, 261

Breen, Thomas, 221–2, 236

Bresson, Robert, 237

British National Film Finance Corporation, 224

Bromfield, Louis, 96

Brown, Tigger Ramsay, 49–50
Burnier, Raymond, 226, 238
Butt, Mr, 294–5, 300–1

Calcutta, 50–67, 76–85, 183–6,
  223–31, 263–4, 302–3
Calcutta Film Society, 211
Calcutta Light Horse, 3
Calcutta Telegraph, 306
Cardew, Michael, 98
Carling, Mike, 294
Carroll, John, 253, 290
Cézanne, Paul, 215
Chamberlain, Neville, 96
Chaplin, Charlie, 56, 215, 217
Chaplin, Oona, 215, 217
Chatto and Windus, 272
Chaudhuri, Amiya, 47–8
Chaudhuri, Hem, 77
Chaudhuri, Milly (*née* Bonnerjee),
  47, 48
Chaudhuri, Monisha, *see* Sen
Chaudhuri, Muchu, 263
Chaudhuri family, 47–8, 60, 62,
  63
Chekhov, Anton, 39, 87
Chelmsford, Frederick Thesiger,
  Lord, 36
Chisholm, Anne, 294, 298
Christie, Agatha, 268
Churchill, Winston, 100
City of Canterbury, SS, 44–5
Clay, Surgeon Captain, 167–8
Clutterbuck, Sir Peter, 169
Cockerell, Sydney, 257
Collins, Alan, 194, 214
Company of Nine, 253
Connolly, Stuart, 64–5

Convent of the Presentation,
  128–30
Corri, Adrienne, 222, 229–32,
  236, 238
Corrigan, Dame Felicitas:
  friendship with Rumer, 256–9,
  263, 264, 265; *In This House of
  Brede*, 260, 262, 267, 269–70,
  278
Costigan, James, 277–9
Cosway, Richard, 5
Curtis Brown: Rumer's first
  publications, 73; Rumer's
  London visit, 74; *Black
  Narcissus*, 86; advice, 97; Jon's
  work, 97, 160, 172; Rumer's
  New York visit, 214; Dale
  connection, 252
Curtis Brown, Spencer:
  relationship with Rumer, 74,
  98, 153, 203, 246–7; *Black
  Narcissus*, 89, 95; *Gypsy, Gypsy*,
  100; advice on publishers, 160,
  161; on Godden style, 194; film
  negotiations, 209; *Breath of Air*,
  219, 242
Curzon, George Nathaniel, Lord,
  50
Curzon, Mary, Lady, 4

Daily Telegraph, 91, 247
Dale, Celia, 253, 280
Darjeeling, 19, 45–50, 79, 91,
  105, 109, 187, 201
Darrynane, Cornwall, 86, 97–8,
  100, 153, 190, 253
Das Gupta, Chidananda, 239
Das Gupta, Hari, 211
Davies, Nico, 74

Davies, Peter, 73, 74, 81, 89, 108, 160
de Sousa, Agnes, 61
Desert Island Discs, 309
Diamond, Father, 241, 251
Dickens, Charles, 252
Dickinson, Emily, 266
Dodds, Norman, 274
Dolphin Square flat, 235, 236, 252
Dongola (houseboat), 125–7, 134
Dove House, near Nishat, 146–60, 161–82, 293, 298–9
Drabble, Margaret, 287
du Maurier, Daphne, 90
Dyer, General Reginald, 36

Ears (manservant), 71, 75, 104, 116–17
East India Company, 45
Eastbourne, 27–32, 34
Elizabeth, Dame (Abbess of Stanbrook), 263, 266–7, 277
Enchantment (film), 201
Esher, 72–3
Evening Standard, 282, 287
Everitt, Raymond, 194

Farrar, David, 201
Fateh Singji, Prince, 224
Ferrer, Mel, 221
Financial Times, 282
Finlayson, Ian, 37
Fitzgerald, Geraldine, 197
Fleming, Ian, 268
Forster, E.M., 39–40, 154, 181, 202, 247
Foster, David (son), 72, 305
Foster, Dick (Ridgeby, brother-in-

law): marriage, 76–7; sons, 97, 147, 160, 237; life in Calcutta, 104, 198; Rumer's letters, 147; Kashmir visit, 158; opinion of Rumer's lifestyle, 163; career, 183, 198; friendships, 263; retirement in England, 264; death, 284
Foster (*later* Murray Flutter), Jane (daughter): birth, 72, 73; childhood in England, 74, 75; childhood in India, 75, 85, 86, 95, 99, 104, 105, 109, 118–19, 122, 124, 125; relationship with father, 75, 95, 122, 154–5, 190, 192, 196, 244, 285; education, 98, 128–30, 133, 138, 145, 154, 155, 192, 196, 200, 240; voyage to India, 100–1, 102–3; health, 116, 126, 138, 167, 256, 268; appearance, 118, 243; painting, 118, 130; character, 133, 154–5, 166, 192, 234, 243, 251; relationship with mother, 154–5, 166, 196, 240, 244, 251, 268, 288–9, 308; Sonamarg trek, 158–9; tobogganing, 162; poisoning mystery, 167, 169; return to Calcutta, 176, 183; journey to England, 189–90; life in England, 196; meeting Renoir, 213; school holidays, 214, 220, 223; relationship with stepfather, 234, 235, 244, 259; career, 244, 250, 251–2; marriage and children, 254–5, 256, 268; in Cyprus, 264, 268;

grandmother's death, 264; in Scotland, 268, 273, 280, 288–9; finances, 271; relationship with sister, 273; father's death, 285; management of mother's affairs, 288; mother's eightieth birthday, 290; filming of *Bookmark* documentary, 292–3, 296–307; mother's ninetieth birthday, 310

Foster, Laurence Sinclair (first husband): family background, 66; career, 66, 71, 109–11, 121; sporting interests, 66, 72, 73, 80, 305; appearance, 66; character, 66, 70; marriage to Rumer, 66–7; honeymoon, 69–70; relationship with wife, 70, 77, 80–1, 94–5, 98–9, 104–5, 121–4, 131–2, 136–7, 139, 142, 148–50, 156–7, 161–2, 170–1, 172, 189–90; finances, 71–2, 86, 89–90, 95, 103–5, 121, 129, 148, 161; death of son, 72; birth of daughter, 72; fatherhood, 75, 95, 96, 122, 126, 136; love of animals, 76; social life in Calcutta, 78, 79–81; birth of second daughter, 86, 88; in England, 94–6; return to Calcutta, 96, 98–9; family's return to India, 103; financial disaster, 108–11, 121; wartime career, 121–4, 131–2, 142, 156, 190; in Kashmir, 125–6; study of Urdu, 132, 136, 143; leave with wife, 135–7; divorce

plans, 144–5, 162, 171, 172; at Dove House, 149–50, 156–7, 160, 170–1; family's return to England, 189–90; in England with parents, 196; divorce, 206; re-marriage, 206, 285; death, 285; in Rumer's autobiography, 285–6

Foster, Nancy (sister), *see* Godden

Foster (*later* Kenilworth), Paula (daughter): birth, 88–90; health, 88, 89, 98, 103, 126, 128, 138, 139, 151, 166, 167, 189, 191, 219; relationship with father, 95, 122, 192, 244; relationship with mother, 98, 99, 103, 107, 128, 133, 151, 240, 244, 250–1, 273; character, 98, 103, 118, 133, 151, 166, 234, 243, 251; voyage to India, 100–1, 103; childhood in India, 104, 105, 118–19, 124, 125; appearance, 118, 126, 243; education, 128–9, 133, 192, 200, 240, 243, 250; Sonamarg trek, 158–9; tobogganing, 162; sixth birthday party, 176; return to Calcutta, 176, 183; journey to England, 189–90; meeting Renoir, 213; school holidays, 214, 220, 223; relationship with stepfather, 234, 235, 244, 259, 273; pony, 243; European travels, 250; career, 250, 258, 264, 271; religion, 251; Little Douce Grove fire, 260; marriage, 272–3, 286; *Bookmark* documentary, 293

Foster, Richard (nephew), 160, 226, 231, 237, 284

Foster, Simon (nephew): birth, 97; childhood in Calcutta, 104; childhood with Rumer, 121, 134, 135, 136, 144, 147, 152, 155; health, 139, 152; education, 202; career, 284; relationship with Rumer, 290

Foster family (Laurence's parents): birth of granddaughter, 72–3; financial help, 153; son's marriage, 161, 196; relationship with granddaughter, 192, 196, 244

Foyle's bookshop, 253

Frankau, Pamela, 253

Fraser, Antonia, 274

Gabrielle (Renoir's nurse), 217

Gandhi, Mahatma, 36, 60, 139

Garbo, Greta, 216

Garden School, Srinagar, 128, 129, 145, 154, 155

Garnett, Constance, 39

Ghulam Rasool, 130–1, 133–4, 136

Gilbert, Lewis, 255

Giuliana (nanny): arrival at Darrynane, 100; voyage to India, 103; playgroup in Calcutta, 104; in Darjeeling, 109; in Jinglam, 116; leaves Rumer, 120; returns to Rumer, 123; in Kashmir, 125, 129, 135–6, 137, 138, 144, 147; leaves Rumer, 148; visits to Dove Cottage, 158; returns to

Rumer, 173; marriage, 214; filming of *The River*, 293

Goddard, Paulette, 216

Godden, Arthur Leigh (father): appearance, 2, 4; career, 2–3, 8, 9, 17–18, 42, 50; family background, 3; marriage, 4; character, 4, 244–5; interests, 4, 16, 20; social status, 5–6; dogs, 6–7, 22–3; fatherhood, 15–16, 19, 34, 42, 57; politics, 36, 191; knowledge of India, 41; leave, 42; return to Assam, 50; opinion of son-in-law, 70; retirement in England, 75, 86, 97–8, 190; opinion of daughter's writing, 86; management of daughter's affairs, 153; old age, 190, 191, 244–5; opinion of daughter's lifestyle, 194; opinion of *Black Narcissus* film, 201; opinion of James Haynes-Dixon, 205–6; Rumer's second marriage, 223; move to Buckinghamshire, 240, 244–5; death, 264; daughter's financial help, 271

Godden, Betty (cousin's wife), 77, 111

Godden (*later* Oakley), Jon (sister): childhood in India, 1, 8–26; relationship with Rumer, 2, 15, 19, 25–6, 37, 74, 86, 98–9, 149, 158, 163, 172, 193, 194–6, 203–4, 205, 206, 219, 237, 242–3, 245, 251, 261, 271, 282–3; interests, 5, 38; health, 7, 44, 219; childhood in England, 7–8, 27–35;

character, 13, 15, 29, 283; appearance, 15, 33; art, 15, 25, 30–1, 39, 44; education, 16, 19, 25, 28–9, 31; writing, 16–17, 97, 158, 160, 194–5, 203–4, 243, 263, 272; pets, 22, 158–9, 160, 172; journey to France, 33–4; return to India, 35; commonplace book, 38–9, 84; engagement, 39, 44; death of husband, 72, 74; second marriage, 75, 76, 243; Calcutta house, 86, 104, 183; correspondence with Rumer, 89–90, 93–5, 96–7, 109, 119, 120, 128–9, 131–2, 135, 138–43, 151, 154, 156, 165, 167–8, 170–2, 176, 190–1, 195–6, 219, 297; wartime in Calcutta, 121, 125, 154; Dove House visit, 157–9; *The Bird Escaped*, 160; name question, 172; Rumer's stay in Calcutta, 174–5, 183; life in Calcutta, 183, 224, 243, 245, 254; stay in England, 190, 214; *The House by the Sea*, 203; writing career, 203–4; opinion of James Haynes-Dixon, 206; opinion of *The River*, 237; Rumer's religious conversion, 251; divorce, 254; life in Kent, 254; *Two Under the Indian Sun*, 263, 272; death of parents, 264; Rumer's financial help, 271; *Shiva's Pigeons*, 272; death, 283–4; *Indian Dust*, 286–7

Godden, Katherine Norah (*née* Hingley, mother): family background, 3; appearance, 3; marriage, 4; character, 4; interests, 4, 16; children, 6–7; household management, 14; motherhood, 15–16, 19; stay in England, 27–8, 34; journey to France, 33–4; illness, 33, 34; return to India, 34, 35; voyage to Calcutta, 44–5; Majumdar friendship, 46–7; return to Assam, 50; retirement in England, 75, 86, 190; health, 97, 190; anxiety about daughter, 153, 194; daughter's return to England, 174; *Black Narcissus* premiere, 201; opinion of James Haynes-Dixon, 205–6, 243; Rumer's second marriage, 223, 243; move to Buckinghamshire, 240, 244–5; in Kent, 254; death, 264–5; daughter's financial help, 271

Godden, Margaret Rumer (Peggie) – LIFE: birth, 1; childhood in India, 1–2, 8–26; family background, 2–6; childhood in England, 7–8, 27–35; education, 16, 19, 25, 28–9, 31–3, 34–5, 42–3; childhood writings, 16–17, 30–1, 35; poetry, 30, 164, 261; journey to France, 33–4; return to India, 35; engagement, 37; dancing teacher training, 42–3; career plans, 42–3; voyage to Calcutta, 44–5; dancing teacher in Darjeeling, 45, 49–50; dancing teacher in

Calcutta, 57–65, 279; love affair, 65–6; pregnancy, 66; marriage to Laurence Foster, 66–7, 70; honeymoon, 67, 68–70; birth and death of son, 72; birth of daughter, 72; in Esher, 72–4; first book published, 72–4; London literary life, 74, 201–2, 253; return to Calcutta, 75–6; birth of second daughter, 85, 86, 88–9; in Cornwall, 86–100; literary success, 90–5; motherhood, 98–9, 103, 117–19, 138; return to Calcutta, 98–101; voyage to India, 102–3; wartime life in Calcutta, 104–8; hospital work, 106–7; husband's debts, 108–11; at Jinglam, 111–24; career plans, 120; dance and music teaching, 129, 132, 145; social life in Srinagar, 132–4, 143; pregnancy and miscarriage, 138–41; houseboat life, 144, 145; divorce plans, 144–5, 162, 172, 192, 193; Dove House, 146–60; herb farm, 157, 158, 159, 161, 165, 274; name change from Peggie to Rumer, 163; poisoning mystery, 167–76, 181–2; return to Calcutta, 176, 183; voyage to England, 189–90; at Darrynane, 190–2, 194; in London, 192–4, 195; film of *Black Narcissus*, 194, 197, 201, 225; house in Belgravia, 195, 197; London literary life, 201–2, 253; house in Sussex, 203; divorce, 206, 251; house in Buckinghamshire, 206, 220; film of *The River*, 206, 207, 212–33, 236–40; in New York, 214–15, 219, 308–9; in Hollywood, 215–18; in New Hampshire, 219; return to England, 220; marriage to James Haynes-Dixon, 222–3, 233, 234–6; return to Calcutta, 223–5; return to England, 233, 234; married life, 234–6, 240; religious conversion, 241, 251; White House Farm, 241–2; life at Pollards, 242–5, 251–2; change of agent and publisher, 246–7; European travels, 250; Highgate house, 251–3; poetry readings, 253, 258; Jane's marriage, 254–5; Little Douce Grove, 255, 258, 260, 276, 285; Lamb House, Rye, 260–1, 265, 271, 275, 276–7; critical reputation, 261; death of parents, 264; lecture tours, 265–6, 268–9; Paula's marriage, 272–3; Whitbread Prize, 273; death of husband, 275–7, 281; houses in Rye, 276; film of *This House of Brede*, 277–9; move to Scotland, 280–1; in Paris, 281–2; life in Scotland, 288–9; eightieth birthday, 290; OBE, 291; BBC *Bookmark* filming in India, 292–307; *Desert Island Discs*, 309; broken hip, 309;

ninetieth birthday celebrations, 310
- PERSON: appearance, 15, 19, 64, 87–8, 192, 193, 282, 288; character, 13, 29, 32, 257; commonplace book, 38–9, 84; finances, 57, 70–2, 89–90, 94, 95, 102, 108–11, 119–20, 129, 136, 161, 202, 213, 242, 245, 246, 267–8, 271, 281, 309; health, 6, 21, 43, 90, 138–41, 147, 156, 162, 163, 166, 202, 246, 289, 293, 304–5, 309; punctuation, 259; religion, 70, 240–1, 251, 256–7, 265
- RELATIONSHIPS: admirers, 64–5, 192–3, 202, 205–6; daughters, *see* Foster (Jane and Paula); friendships, *see* Corrigan (Dame Felicitas), Hopman (Clara and Tontyn), Shelagh, Simon (Jay and Jimmie); husbands, *see* Foster (Laurence), Haynes-Dixon (James); motherhood, 98–9, 103, 117–19, 138; parents, 15–16, 22–3, 42, 70, 97–8, 100, 113, 153, 190, 191, 194, 234, 240, 244–5, 271; pets, 22–3, 30, 35, 73–4, 75–6, 81, 86, 104, 114, 138, 159–60, 161, 164, 235–6, 280, 289; sisters, *see* Godden (Jon, Nancy and Rose)
- WORKS: autobiography, 2, 28, 70, 176–7, 245, 284–6; *The Battle of the Villa Fiorita*, 258–60, 261; *Bengal Journey*, 184–9, 195; *Black Narcissus*, 86, 89, 90–8, 109, 120, 143, 146, 147, 153, 191, 194, 195, 197, 201, 202, 207, 216, 225, 260, 309; *Breakfast with the Nikolides*, 107–8, 120, 124, 146; *A Breath of Air*, 204, 219, 234, 242; *The Butterfly Lions*, 280, 282; *A Candle for St Jude*, 203, 204, 205, 219, 220, 234, 241–2, 246; *China Court*, 84, 254, 257; *Chinese Puzzle*, 73; *Cockcrow to Starlight*, 308; *Coromandel Sea Change*, 69–70, 287, 306, 308; *Cromartie v. the God Shiva*, 308–10; *The Dark Horse*, 283, 309; *The Diddakoi*, 273–5; *The Dolls' House*, 196–7, 204; *An Episode of Sparrows*, 248; *Fairy Doll*, 249; *Five for Sorrow, Ten for Joy*, 281–2; *Fugue in Time*, 155, 158, 160, 161, 162–3, 191, 194, 201, 254; *Gok*, 73; *Gulbadan, Portrait of a Rose Princess at the Mughal Court*, 282–3; *Gypsy Gypsy*, 97, 98, 99–100, 107; *The Greengage Summer*, 33–4, 250, 251, 253, 255; *Hans Christian Andersen*, 248–9; *Impunity Jane*, 249; *In This House of Brede*, 262–3, 266–70, 271, 277–9, 309; *Indian Dust*, 286–7; *Kingfishers Catch Fire*, 177–81, 245–8; *The Lady and the Unicorn*, 77–8, 81–4, 89, 305; *The Little Chair*, 308; 'The Little Fishes' 28; *Miss Happiness and Miss Flower*, 249; *Mouse House*, 253; *The Mousewife*, 204; *The*

Peacock Spring, 25, 279–80,
309; *Pippa Passes*, 290; *A Pocket
Book of Spiritual Poems*, 308;
Prayer from the Ark, 261;
*Premlata and the Festival of
Lights*, 308; *The Raphael Bible*,
271; *The River*, 2, 26, 188, 191,
195, 197–201, 206, 207–33,
234, 250, 305, 309; *Rungli-
Rungliot*, 112–13, 160, 161;
Shiva's Pigeons, 272; *The Story
of Holly and Ivy*, 249, 253–4;
Strange Cygnet, 87, 89, 93; *Tale
of the Tales*, 271–2; *Thursday's
Children*, 284; *Two Under the
Indian Sun*, 2, 263, 272;
reviews of work, 84, 91–2, 96,
200, 247, 266, 282, 287,
309–10
Godden (*later* Foster), Nancy
(sister): birth, 6–7; childhood
in India, 1, 15, 19, 199;
appearance, 16, 45, 76; pets,
22; education, 31, 34; return to
India, 44, 45; horse-mad, 45,
48, 76; teenage crush, 48–9;
teaching dancing in Calcutta,
65, 76; Rumer's wedding, 67;
marriage, 76–7; character, 77;
birth of son, 97; life in
Calcutta, 104, 183, 224, 245,
263; wartime in Calcutta, 121,
134, 144, 156; in Srinagar,
135, 136; in Sonamarg, 140,
142; Rumer's letters 147, 149,
150, 152, 156; pregnancy, 158;
Dove House visit, 158; birth of
second son, 160; opinion of
Rumer's lifestyle, 163, 181; stay

in England, 190, 191; opinion
of James Haynes-Dixon, 206;
work on *The River*, 209–10,
237; Rumer's visit (1964),
263–4; return to England, 264;
death of parents, 264; work on
The Dark Horse, 283; death of
husband, 284; Rumer's
autobiography, 286; Rumer's
visits, 290, 308
Godden (*later* Smith), Rose
(sister): birth, 10; childhood in
India, 1, 15; appearance, 15;
education, 31, 34, 44; Rumer's
wedding, 67; marriage, 76, 100;
return to England, 100; death
of lover, 153; opinion of James
Haynes-Dixon, 206; life in
England, 234; return to
Calcutta, 245; return to
England, 264; death of parents,
264; Rumer's financial help,
271; move to Scotland, 284;
Rumer's autobiography, 286;
Glyndebourne visits, 290, 308
Godden, Will (cousin), 77
Godden aunts, 7–8
Godden grandmother, 7
Gondal, Maharajah of, 222
Govind (head gardener), 14
Great Eastern Hotel, Calcutta,
225
Griffiths, Percival, 60
Groves, Mary, 128
Guinzberg, Tom, 267
Guru (gatekeeper), 13, 23–4

Haggard, Edith, 214
Hannah (nanny), 13, 19, 23

Harper's magazine, 100
Hartshorn House, Rye, 260
Harvey, Lilian, 56
Hassall, Christopher, 253
Hastings, Warren, 5, 77
Haynes-Dixon, James (second
    husband): relationship with
    Rumer, 192–3, 197, 202,
    205–6, 219–20, 234–6,
    242–3, 246–7, 249–50,
    252–3, 262, 275–6;
    appearance, 193; background,
    205; relationship with Godden
    family, 205–6; Renoir dinner,
    213; marriage, 222–3, 233,
    234–6, 240; White House
    Farm, 241–2; management of
    Rumer's financial affairs,
    246–7, 249–50, 252–3,
    267–8, 271, 276; character,
    253; retirement, 255, 271;
    Little Douce Grove, 255,
    258–60; Lamb House, 265;
    Rumer's lecture tours, 265–6;
    death, 275–6
Heflin, Van, 221
Heifetz, Jascha, 29
Hely-Hutchinson family, 24–5
Hensher, Philip, 310
Heyward, Dorothy, 219, 220
Hindustan Standard, 84
Hingley, Alfred (uncle), 3, 27, 29
Hingley, Ethel (aunt), 3
Hingley, Harriet (grandmother), 3
Hingley, Mary (aunt), 3, 8, 10,
    16, 20, 27, 37
Hingley, Samuel (grandfather), 3
Hingley family, 3
Hitler, Adolf, 96, 101

Hodgkin, Marni, 249–50
Home Chat, 120
Home Farm House, Sussex, 203
Hopman, Clara: sculptor, 133;
    friendship with Rumer, 133,
    149; herb farm, 157, 158, 159,
    165; family, 161; relaxation
    techniques, 162; Godden
    family's view of, 163; poisoning
    mystery, 168, 175;
    temperament, 298
Hopman, Granny, 161, 164, 165
Hopman, Tontyn: painting, 133,
    142–3; friendship with Rumer,
    133, 149, 154; collaboration
    with Rumer, 142–3. 156; herb
    farm, 157, 158, 159, 165;
    family, 161; Godden family's
    view of, 163; poisoning
    mystery, 167, 168, 175
Huebsch, Alvilde, 214, 219
Huebsch, Ben, 214–15, 242, 257,
    261–2, 266
Hughes-Hallett, Lucy, 287
Hunt, Frank, 58
Hunt, Jimmie, *see* Simon
Husain, Shahrukh, 282–3, 290
Huxley, Julian, 56
Hyde, Montgomery, 260

Imelda, Sister, 281–2
Independent on Sunday, 287
Indian Civil Service (ICS), 3, 5,
    40, 78–9, 224

Jameel, Yusuf, 293
James, Henry, 260
Jean-Dominique, Sister, 282
Jefferson, Thomas, 5

Jenkins, Owain: career, 44–5; friendship with Goddens, 45; social life in Calcutta, 52–4, 60, 64–5, 224; wartime experiences, 105; retirement, 283; *The Dark Horse*, 283

Jetta (bearer), 13

Jinglam, near Darjeeling, 111–24, 131, 187

Jobara (bearer): Sonamarg treks, 137, 142, 159, 170, 172, 300; Rumer's illness, 142; Dove House, 150

John O'London's, 247

Johnstone, Johnny, 80

Johnstone, Lenore, 79–81, 111

Jones, Jennifer, 247

Joyce, James, 214

Judd, Forrest, 209

Kashmir, 19–21, 123–4, 125–82, 247–8, 292–302

Kaye, Mollie, 133, 169, 285–6

Kenilworth, Barry (son-in-law), 272–3, 286

Kenilworth, Paula (daughter), *see* Foster

Kennedy, Margaret, 96

Kenwood House poetry readings, 253, 290

Kerr, Deborah, 201

Key, Thomas Hewitt (great-grandfather), 4–5

Khokil (sweeper), 104

Kipling, Rudyard, 27, 40, 51

Knight, Esmond, 225

Koestler, Arthur, 92

Konarak temple, 68–9, 306

Kubelik, Jan, 29

Ladies' Home Journal, 191

Lamb House, Rye, 260–1, 265, 271, 272, 275–7

Lanchester, Elsie, 56

Laughton, Charles, 56, 215

Lawrence, D.H., 39, 214

Lehmann, John, 89

Linlithgow, Doreen Maud, Lady, 106

Linlithgow, Victor Hope, Lord, 105–6

Lissanevich, Boris, 65

Little, Brown, 95, 96, 160, 161, 194, 200

Little Douce Grove, East Sussex, 255, 258, 260, 276, 285

Lourié, Gene, 229, 232

Lovat Dickson, Rache, 247

Lydd House, Aldington, 254, 264

Macaulay, Rose, 201

McDairmant, Brian, 294

Macdowell Colony, New Hampshire, 219

McEldowney, Kenneth: *The River*, 208–9, 218, 222–4, 228–9; in Hollywood, 208, 215; finance problems, 213, 220, 236–8

McKeever, Peggy, 290

Mackinnon Mackenzie, 59

McLachlan, Dame Laurentia, 257

Maclean, Alan, 247, 261, 285, 290, 308

Maclean, Robin, 290, 308

Macmillan: Rumer's move to, 247; Rumer's sales, 261; James' work, 265; *In This House of Brede*, 267; Rumer's seventieth birthday party, 280; *The Dark*

Horse, 283; 150th anniversary
    party, 291; Rumer's ninetieth
    birthday party, 310
Macmillan, Harold, 274, 281
Maguire, Sharon, 292, 294,
    296–7, 300, 303–4
Mail on Sunday, 310
Majumdar, Agnes (*née* Bonnerjee):
    friendship with Goddens,
    46–8, 116, 143, 165; family,
    47–8, 79, 244; godmother to
    Paula, 88
Majumdar, Jai, 47, 49
Majumdar, Joya, 244, 250, 290
Majumdar, Karun, 47
Majumdar, Sita, 244
Majumdar, Tara, 47, 48, 116, 244
Majumdar family, 48–9, 60, 79,
    244
Manders, Mrs (cook), 258
Mansfield, Katherine, 39, 97
Marlow, Marilyn, 290
Martyn, Margaret, 78–9, 105–6,
    108
Martyn, P.D., 105–6
Marx, Erica, 253
Mason, James, 215, 221
Mason, Pamela, 215
Matthews, Billy, 116
Matthews, Marjorie, 116
Mehta, Mr (landlord and student),
    71
Michael Joseph: Rumer's move to,
    161, 173; *Kingfishers Catch Fire*,
    176; *The River*, 191, 195; Jon's
    work, 203; Rumer's move from,
    247
Milne, A.A., 96
Mitchell, Margaret, 90

Moira House, Eastbourne, 31–3,
    35, 240
More, Dame Gertrude, 256
Morris, Jan, 55
Mrs Manders' Cookbook, 263
Mukerjee, Suprova, 226
Murray Flutter, Anthony (son-in-
    law): marriage, 254; in Cyprus,
    264; in Scotland, 268, 273,
    280; finances, 271; relationship
    with mother-in-law, 273,
    288–9, 310
Murray Flutter, Charlotte
    (granddaughter), 268
Murray Flutter, Elizabeth Rumer
    (granddaughter), 256, 268, 290
Murray Flutter, Emma
    (granddaughter), 268
Murray Flutter, Jane (daughter),
    see Foster
Murray Flutter, Mark (grandson),
    254, 268, 290
Mustapha (khitmagar), 13

Nana (nanny), 12–13, 21
Narayanganj, 8–18, 22–6, 35–6,
    38–9, 50, 70, 188, 198, 209,
    213, 293, 294, 303–4
Nehru, Jawaharlal, 141, 237
New Empire Cinema, Calcutta,
    237
New Writing, 89
New York Times, 96, 237, 266
New Yorker, 96, 200
News Chronicle, 91
Newsweek, 237
Nichols, Dudley, 217
Nitai (sweeper), 13, 23–4

Oakley, Jon (sister), *see* Godden
Oakley, Roland (brother-in-law):
    marriage, 75, 76; Rumer's visits,
    86, 174–5, 183; life in
    Calcutta, 104, 183, 198; career,
    111, 183, 198; present to
    Rumer, 160; opinion of
    Rumer's writing, 163, 193;
    divorce, 254
Oberon, Merle (Queenie
    Thomas), 56, 61
Observer, 91
O'Hara, Maureen, 261
Old Hall, Highgate, 251–3
Ordish, John, 24
Oriental International Films, 208

Parents' National Educational
    Union (PNEU), 138, 154
Paris, 281–2
Pasteur Institute, 6
Peggie Godden School of Dance,
    61–5, 76–7
PEN, 253
Philipps, Bob, 168, 193, 241
Philipps, Monica, 193, 241
Place Siddons, 66, 71, 110
Plomer, William, 258
Plomley, Roy, 309
Pollards, Buckinghamshire,
    242–5, 251–2
Pope-Hennessy, Dame Una, 201
Potter, Beatrix, 272
Powell, Michael, 197, 201
Prescott, Lilias, 266, 290, 308–9
Prescott, Orville, 266, 290, 308–9
Pressburger, Emeric, 194, 197,
    201
Primrose, Jean, 253, 261

Pumphrey, Melvina, 208, 238
Puri, Bay of Bengal, 67, 68–70,
    76, 294, 306

Ray, Satyajit, 211–12, 232, 239
Reader's Digest, 261, 267
Renoir, Auguste, 207, 215, 217
Renoir, Claude, 208, 229
Renoir, Dido: marriage, 208;
    relationship with Rumer, 210,
    213, 217, 231, 236; life in
    California, 215
Renoir, Jean: response to *The
    River*, 200, 206, 207; career,
    207–8; marriage, 208; filming
    plans for *The River*, 208–9;
    relationship with Rumer, 209,
    213; visit to India, 209–12;
    casting *The River*, 210, 220–2,
    225–8; Rumer's California
    visit, 215–19; filming in India,
    223–33; finishing work on *The
    River*, 236–7; success of *The
    River*, 237–40, 303;
    Amphitryon, 242; *Kingfishers
    Catch Fire*, 247; correspondence
    with Rumer, 279; death, 279;
    documentary on, 309
Rigg, Diana, 279
Roberts, Archbishop, 251
Rossellini, Roberto, 218
Royal Ballet, 203
Royal Calcutta Golf Club, 53–4,
    66
Rubbra, Dominic, 243
Rubbra, Edmund, 243
Rubinstein, Artur, 29
Rumer Productions Ltd, 268
Rutherford, Margaret, 252

St Faith's mission, 145, 147, 148, 157
St Paul's Cathedral, Calcutta, 67, 76
Sassoon, Siegfried, 257
Saturday Club, 53, 62, 63, 64–5
Saturday Evening Post, 261
Saunders, Kate, 287
Savitri Cottage, Srinagar, 135–6, 142–4
Schaefer, George, 278
Scott, Paul, 181
Selznick, David, 247
Sen, Monisha (*later* Chaudhuri), 62–3, 77, 78, 305
Shah, Mr (lawyer), 298–300
Shaw, George Bernard, 257
Shelagh (schoolfriend), 35
Shields, Arthur, 226
Siddika (cook), 164, 167–8, 170–7, 179, 181, 299
Simmons, Jean, 201
Simnells, Kent, 264, 284
Simon, Jay (Gilbert): marriage, 58; background, 59; life in London, 192, 197, 202, 206; Goddens' opinion of, 194; cottage in Chilterns, 202; Rumer's wedding, 223
Simon, Jimmie (*née* Hunt): family background, 58–9; friendship with Rumer, 58–60, 192–3, 202, 206; dancing, 58–61; on Rumer's marriage, 66; life in London, 192–3, 197, 202; Goddens' opinion of, 194; cottage in Chilterns, 202; Rumer's wedding, 223
Simon, Sir John, 59

Simon family, 79
Sisters of Bethany, 281–2
Sketch, 17
Skinner, Cornelia Otis, 143
Smallwood, Nora, 272
Smith, Clive (C.D., brother-in-law), 76, 100
Smith, Rose (sister), *see* Godden
Smith, Stevie, 258
Snead, Stella, 272
Solley, Adrienne, 294
Sonachora (launch), 18
Sonamarg, 137–9, 158, 159, 174–6, 300–1
Spark, Muriel, 253, 291
Sri Ram, Radha, 226–8, 231, 236, 238
Srinagar, 125–55, 293, 294–300
Stanbrook Abbey, 256–8, 260, 262, 265, 268–9, 278–9
Statesman, 17, 55, 67
Stein, Gertrude, 87
Stern, G.B., 73, 151
Stewart, James, 221
Strathallan, SS, 100
Stravinsky, Igor, 215
Subhana, 167
Sunday Express, 268
Swann, Mona, 31–2, 35, 240, 265
Swinburne, Nora, 225

Tagore, Rabindranath, 36, 41, 211
Tatler, 17
Taylor, Elizabeth, 216
Teresa, Mother, 263
Theatre Royal, Calcutta, 54, 56
Theosophical Society, 227, 228, 238

Thomas, Queenie, *see* Oberon
Thompson, David, 239–40
Thomson, George Malcolm, 274
300 club, 64–5
Time and Tide, 194
Time magazine, 237
Times Literary Supplement, 84
Tollygunge Club, Calcutta, 54,
    80, 111, 229, 305
Travers, Ben, 56
Trevelyan, Raleigh, 27
Troward, Richard Ironmonger
    (great-great-grandfather), 5

United Artists, 237
United Services Club, 53

Valois, Ninette de, 95
Vandyke School, Finchley Road,
    43
Venice Film Festival, 237
Viking, 214, 261, 267–8, 274,
    286
Vogue, 191, 194, 237

W. Colston Leigh Inc, 266
Walpole, Hugh, 91–2
Walters, Patricia, 226, 228, 236
Watson, Dorothy, 276, 281
Watson, Graham, 247, 267, 271,
    276–7
Waugh, Auberon, 282
West, Benjamin, 5
Whitbread Prize, 273
White, Evelyn Denham, 48
White, Joan, 169
White, Patrick, 238
White House Farm,
    Buckinghamshire, 241–2
Wilder, Billy, 237
Williams, Alan, 267
Williamson, A.N. and C.N., 17
Wilson, Angus, 287
Women's Voluntary Service
    (WVS), 184
Woolf, Virginia, 39
Woollcott, Alexander, 96
Wright, Bob, 305

York, Susannah, 255